Out of Bullets*!*
More Tales of Adventure

Out of Bullets!
More Tales of Adventure

by
Johnny Chilton

Foreword by Larry Weishuhn

SAFARI PRESS

The trademark Safari Press ® is registered with the U.S. Patent and Trademark Office and with government patent and trademark offices in other countries.

Chilton, Johnny

Second edition

Safari Press Inc.
2011, Long Beach, California

ISBN 978-1-57157-378-0

Library of Congress Catalog Card Number: 2010926319

10 9 8 7 6 5 4 3 2 1

Printed in China

Readers wishing to receive the Safari Press catalog, featuring many fine books on big-game hunting, wingshooting, and sporting firearms, should write to Safari Press Inc., P.O. Box 3095, Long Beach, CA 90803, USA. Tel: (714) 894-9080 or visit our Web site at www.safaripress.com.

This book is for Mom and Dad,

who have made all the difference.

Table of Contents

Foreword

As a hunter, wildlife biologist, outdoor writer, and a guest on outdoor television shows, I have been able, and also very fortunate, to travel to many parts of the world in search of adventure. No matter where I roam, I always seek out hunting tales and good "reading." I have long been a collector of hunting literature, primarily books about hunting big-game species and tales of adventure in the pursuit of such animals. It follows I am a "reader."

I grew up in southern Texas in a family of hunters to whom the outdoors was not only a way of life—it was the essence of life. As a youngster I could hardly wait for copies of *Outdoor Life* and *Sports Afield* to appear in our rural roadside mailbox each month. The articles and stories found in those publications of the 1950s and 1960s were quite often masterpieces of hunting literature, whether told in absolute truth or in a manner where the truth was not allowed to stand in the way of a good story. They were fun to read and allowed the reader to be "transported" alongside the writer. In the process of reading those hunting tales, the reader learned while being entertained.

Alas, as we passed into the last third of the twentieth century, it seemed editors changed what they were looking for. Sadly, most started to believe that hunting stories should be little more than "dull recipes." Editors asked for literature that was readable, but no longer fun. Gone was the adventure and excitement these tales once generated. Outside a few writers in the last twenty years, such learning while entertaining writing seems to have become a lost art.

It was about 1990 while perusing an issue of *Sporting Classics* that I ran across an article by a fellow Texan, Johnny Chilton. That caught my attention. As a wildlife biologist who had long worked in the brush country of South Texas, I knew the Chilton name but had always associated it with the fabulous San Roman Ranch. As a member of the Dallas Safari Club, I kept hearing the Chilton name, but now associated with African adventures. I could not get out of my mind the excellently written, entertaining, and surprise ending of the article Johnny Chilton had written for *Sporting Classics*. As a writer I dearly love surprise endings.

I would occasionally read a hunting tale expertly written by Johnny Chilton and wonder when he would take the time to write a book. He did not disappoint. His book, *A Bullet Well Placed,* published by Safari Press, proved what others and I already knew: Johnny Chilton is an excellent writer who makes reading fun once again. Upon finishing Chilton's book, I put it aside in a place of honor. Then three months later I read it again. While I enjoyed my first read of Chilton's book, by the time I finished reading it a second time, I longed for him to write another. It was my hope that this time he would include at least a couple of his "short stories" I had so dearly enjoyed and appreciated.

Again, Señor Chilton did not disappoint! When Johnny Chilton sent me several advance chapters of *Out of Bullets!,* I sat down and read them all in one sitting. I suspect you'll want to do the same, too. Chilton's writing is fun to read. It's got lots of good information, so it's also educational. But, best of all, it's full of good writing and surprise endings. For me, it's hunting literature at its finest!

Johnny Chilton is certainly someone with whom I would like to "ride the river"!

Larry Weishuhn
May 2010

Acknowledgments

I wish to express my deepest gratitude to PH Gerard Miller, who invited my younger self to join him for an entire safari season in Tanzania. This "behind-the-scenes look" at the safari industry was a gift greater than gold.

Thanks to my friend Jim Speece for allowing me to accompany him on his Botswana safari.

Last but not least, a big round of thanks to all of the guides and outfitters out there who make this hunting life possible to the rest of us.

Part I

Tanzania
1984
Apprentice Professional Hunter

A Deadly Lesson

Chapter 1

In a flash, we were in mortal danger, and none of us had seen it coming. What had seemed a harmless task of photographing a roaming herd of elephant had turned in a heartbeat into a potentially deadly affair. PH Roy Carr-Hartley had maneuvered the Toyota up close, while Enrique Guerra, our client, clicked photos of the departing herd. Our mistake was in getting too close to a straggling calf. When the calf bawled in alarm, our destiny was set in motion. Instantly mama whirled, trumpeted, and came charging at us—ears spread wide.

It goes without saying that a number of thoughts explode inside your head when you are faced, unexpectedly, with a charging elephant. It plays out something like this: Your first thought, no matter who you are or how much experience you might have, is undoubtedly unprintable. Your second thought is when to shoot. Your third and final thought is where exactly to shoot. There really isn't time for a fourth thought because a charging elephant, despite its size, covers a surprising amount of ground in a short period of time. Wait a second too long, or miscalculate the trajectory to the brain, and you will find yourself doubling as a human pizza.

Those are the thoughts that enter your mind if you have a rifle in hand.

If you do not have a rifle in hand—as in this case—the exploding thoughts are of a different sort. Chiefly, I was concerned with my immediate life expectancy. I figured I had a good ten seconds left on planet Earth, so there really wasn't time for regrets, apologies, or pining for whatever had yet to pass in my young life. The whole event was simply happening much too fast.

My selfish concerns aside, those most in danger were Roy and Enrique, who were sitting exposed in the front seat of the Land Cruiser. In typical safari fashion, the cab and doors had been removed and the windshield lowered and fastened against the hood. There was nothing between these two men and the angry cow now bearing down on us, ears out, trunk coiled, not thirty yards away. I was standing in the bed of the truck with Roy's tracker Nyamaiya and a government game scout named Daniel.

Game scout Daniel tends a busted lip, while I point out where the elephant's tusk gouged the truck.

The cow elephant on the left of this departing herd nearly did us in.

Complicating matters, we had found ourselves suddenly hemmed in by an unfortunate placement of *miombo* trees on either side of the truck. The trees formed an alley of sorts, with mama elephant trumpeting and charging at us from the opposite end, and leaving us in the regrettable position of being unable to turn left or right. Further, there wasn't time to stop and reverse out of the situation—the elephant was simply approaching too fast. Quickly running out of options, it was at this point that Roy did something completely unexpected. He stomped on the accelerator and hurled us directly toward the charging elephant! My first thought was that Roy had lost his mind and had opted for suicide. We were now racing toward certain collision with the raging behemoth. I figured the elephant's front legs would buckle under impact and the combined momentum would cast her headfirst onto Roy and Enrique—an avalanche of elephant in their laps—crushing them instantly.

Even if by some miracle the elephant managed to keep her footing and did not collapse on top of my comrades, with no cab or doors to interfere, she could easily pluck them out with her trunk and crush them

at her leisure. Fact is, they were dead men under either scenario. Yes, our outlook was grim.

As it turned out, Roy did have a plan, outlandish as it first appeared. Just as we cleared the last of the confining trees, Roy swung the wheel hard left—an instant before frontal impact—at which point the elephant slammed into us broadside. Her forehead plowed into the roll cage no more than an arm's length from me, and with the great clarity that comes from gallons of adrenaline pumping through your system I was able to observe every detail. The deep wrinkles in her brow. The sparse, wiry hairs covering her creased hide. The gray clots of dried mud stuck here and there. The fury with which she now gouged the side of the vehicle with her tusks and tried to do us in.

The impact was substantial, as if we had collided with a school bus. The vibrations drummed my hands, arms, and back. The angry elephant lifted the truck onto its side, driver-side wheels suspended in the air. We were going to roll for sure. I was trying to decide whether to remain in the vehicle or make a run for it and try to hide behind a tree. Gerard had told me about a rogue elephant the year before that had plucked a tracker from the vehicle of another hunting company, killing the man instantly. So staying in the truck didn't sound like such a great idea. But neither did running away on foot!

A last-ditch effort would have been to grab a rifle from the rack in front of me and shoot the beast. But as tempting as that idea sounded in theory, it was no good in practice. Though such a maneuver might provide the satisfaction of taking action, none of the rifles had solid bullets and I knew that shooting the elephant with "softs" would only fuel her anger. It would be the equivalent of waving a red cape in front of the bull; it would only serve to draw attack. It was a strategy to be employed solely to distract her from ravaging whichever victim she had happened to claim.

Thankfully, a split second after the collision, the racing engine brought momentum to the passenger-side tires. The accelerating truck promptly settled down onto all four wheels and we sped away, leaving the furious elephant charging into our dust.

A mile or so away, we stopped to take stock of the damage to vehicle and crew. An unseen branch had whacked the game scout in the face and busted his lower lip. Blood dribbled over his fingers as he tried to clasp it together. The same branch had knocked a chunk of flesh from my knuckle. As we examined the tusk gouge in the side of Gerard's vehicle and Roy wondered aloud how he was going to explain the incident to his boss Gerard, there came a tremendous "CRASH!" behind us. The five of us just about jumped out of our skins, figuring another elephant was barreling down on us for sure. But it was just a dead tree that had picked that particular moment to come crashing to the ground.

The bottom line is that we were exceptionally lucky to have escaped with the little damage that we did. It was the kind of incident—hinged on a nanosecond either way—that easily could have turned deadly. There wasn't one among us who wasn't breathlessly humbled by the event.

It was a stark reminder to the hunter that Mother Nature has a way of imparting her deadliest lessons when you least expect them.

How It Began

Chapter 2

In January 1984 I received an astonishing offer. To put this offer in perspective, I felt like I had won the lottery—but not just any lottery. For a young man obsessed with hunting, and hunting in Africa in particular, it was like winning the lottery of all lotteries.

At a Dallas party I ran into Gerard Miller, the PH with whom I had enjoyed a great safari in Tanzania two years previously. Gerard was in a jovial mood and was happy to see me. I was glad to have a beer in my hand and even gladder to be out of my client's office, which had become my home for the last few weeks of the audit season.

"How are you, kid?" said Gerard, clasping the back of my neck with his hand.

"Fine, fine. Just busy. They've got me working eighty-plus hours a week!"

"Rotting away in an office, are you?"

Then I saw that familiar twinkle light up his dark eyes.

"I was just thinking, why don't you come spend this hunting season with me?"

I chuckled, then sighed.

"I wish!"

"No, I mean it," he said. "Come spend the whole season with me. Six months. You can help set up camp, scout game, be my assistant."

Gerard flashed those straight white teeth of his, a surprising attribute for someone raised in Africa and often far from the services of a dentist.

"Gerard, don't ask me unless you mean it, because I will say yes."

He tried to persist with the invitation, but I held up my hand.

"I'm telling you, Gerard, don't ask me again unless you really mean it. Unless you really, really mean it. Because I will say yes, and I will start packing my bags tonight. You can't believe how ready I am to quit this job. I can't even see straight from lack of sleep."

He grinned at what I said.

"I really mean it," he reiterated, and we shook hands.

No more was said about it that night, and by the next day, it seemed no more than the vague remembrance of a wonderful night's dream.

A couple of days later, I ran into Gerard at my parents' house.

"So, when are you coming?" he asked me, first thing.

A candelabra tree (Euphorbia cooperi) *outlasts a neglected colonial barn.*

"When do you want me?"

"End of May," he said. "Take us a month to get the supplies, boys, and vehicles ready, another couple of weeks or so to make the journey. That would allow us to get camp set up by 1 July, the start of the season. We are hunting in the Selous this year."

No, not the Selous Game Reserve! I thought to myself. The remote wildlife sanctuary named after explorer Frederick Courteney Selous was famous for giant elephant and limitless herds of wild game. I had heard and read about the Selous but had yet to experience it. What an amazing opportunity!

"We will be traveling to an area that hasn't been hunted in years," he added. "Building a camp from scratch."

That is how it started.

The Professional Hunter's Checklist

A smiling Gerard was there to collect me at the Nairobi airport. I was a little groggy from jet lag, but not too tired to give him a playful poke in the belly—something he did not have the last time I had seen him.

Gerard had enjoyed the "off" season and had put on a bit of weight, like a buck building its fat reserves before the onset of winter and the rut.

As a professional hunter, his is not a nine-to-five job. It is six months on and six months off. By the end of the season, he would be lean and fit again.

Before long, the Range Rover was past town and was hurtling along a narrow blacktop road with the sloping Kenya plains on either side. An occasional flat-topped acacia granted shade. On the drive Gerard brought me up to speed on our state of readiness for the upcoming safari season and described what was left for us to complete.

Gerard, his wife, Cally, and their three-year-old son, Shawn, lived on a farm fifty miles southeast of Nairobi, in an area referred to as Ulu, after the abandoned railway station *(ulu* means railroad) nearby. Though Gerard's place was called a farm, there were no plowed fields or visible cultivation in sight. The terrain consisted of rolling hills above a vast yellow plain. Like his neighbors, Gerard's house had been built in the 1920s, and it was quite large, with many rooms and bedrooms and an expansive veranda that offered a spectacular view down into the open lowlands. The walls were constructed of thick concrete, a material that works like adobe to keep the inhabitants warm in winter and cool in the summer. Of course, the equator lacks those specific seasons, but the massive walls serve the same purpose on cool nights and warm days. Once owned by wealthy colonialists, the farms and adjacent houses had been confiscated by black Africans after independence. Later abandoned, they had fallen into disrepair and were now rented to white Africans like Gerard for sixty dollars a month.

East Africa was nearing the end of what was supposed to be the rainy season, but it had been abnormally dry. The grass was scorched brown; the leaves of the trees were wilted. It looked to be a brutal dry season ahead.

PH George Angelides, his wife, Jillian, and their son, Nicholas, were living temporarily with Gerard. George was his usual grinning, quiet self. He is one of those professional hunters who, to his credit, never brags about his close scrapes and adventures with dangerous game. He's the kind of person who wouldn't think to tell you about the angry buffalo that had pinned his Greek ass to the ground that morning and nearly ended his mischievous career. If it came up in conversation, it would be because you asked, and his answer would be casual: "I had bit of a scrape with *mbogo.*" Having spent four weeks on safari with him when he guided my dad two years before, I knew him quite well. Despite his calm demeanor, a sly grin betrayed the rascal underneath.

We spent the entire next day in town, purchasing supplies and checking the status of orders and repairs to equipment in alley shops across the

Gerard preps the mighty Volvo for the demands of the upcoming season.

urban sprawl of Nairobi. As you can imagine, it is no small task to organize supplies for a six-month safari. There is a lot to buy and a lot to arrange before heading into the bush. For starters, there are canned goods, condiments, utensils, soap, fuel, batteries, toilet paper, towels, sheets, blankets, flashlights, tanning salt, rope in assorted sizes, canvas, knives, machetes, spare inner tubes, tires, patch kits, carburetors, springs, radiators, automotive oil, and assorted fluids. There are first-aid kits; medicines for every conceivable toxin, virulence, and venom (of which there is a vast and lethal variety); devices for medical emergencies; ammunition; bunks; tents; radios; wash basins; mirrors, tables, and chairs; and pots and pans. Just to be sure you had better throw in a kitchen sink because the cook will need that, too. If you arrive in the bush and you didn't bring something with you, it is too late. There are no parts stores, no automotive service stations, no grocery stores in which to get something as simple as a box of toothpicks. You are responsible for bringing everything yourself. Santa may check his list twice, but a professional hunter must check his list a hundred times. You can't tell a client dying of malaria that you forgot to pack the Fansidar. You simply have to plan for that contingency before you leave for the bush.

It didn't help that the East African economy was in shambles. A number of people were starving, or close to it, and crime was a way of life for many. That day a pickpocket went for Gerard's wallet. Gerard punched the would-be robber twice in the ribs before the fellow ran off empty-handed. Before the day was over, though, an African pushed an arm through the open window of Cally's car and wrenched four hundred shillings from her hand. But these incidents of crimes committed in the light of day and on busy streets paled in comparison to tales of what could happen in the city at night. Roving gangs, armed with machine guns, would break into white people's homes to rob and slaughter everyone inside. The only citizens with access to machine guns were the army and the police. So, guess who were the culprits? It was also no wonder that the perpetrators of these horrendous crimes were never caught or brought to justice.

While doing more errands in town one day, we stopped for lunch at the Burger Chef. There we met Cally's uncle Bob Brown, a retired PH. Bob was a short, burly bear of a fellow with a thick beard and a set of bulging forearms to match Popeye's. He seemed an amiable fellow, and we had a good chat.

Unfortunately, not long after that trip, Bob was killed by something that was to become more deadly than any dangerous game animal or poisonous snake on the continent. Something we knew nothing about at the time. While Bob was out buffalo hunting, a bull gored him badly, nearly killing him on the spot. He made it to the hospital, where a blood transfusion saved his life. But this saving grace turned out to be short-lived. Not long afterward it was discovered that the blood he had received was contaminated with the AIDS virus. Africa never lacks for ways to apply its deadly grip.

The next day was filled with more errands still. A professional hunter's "to do" list before safari is practically endless: Check on parts and equipment ordered or under repair, search for hard-to-find supplies, plead with the game department for this or that permit, file endless government forms and paperwork, meet with this fellow or that, check your mail and messages, and fire off communications to upcoming clients.

We dropped in at the house of Reggie Destro, a well-known and recently retired PH who had a lorry Gerard was interested in purchasing. It was a great big military vehicle, the kind you might expect to see carting a dozen soldiers under the tarp top in back. It obviously was capable of carrying a substantial load, and the high clearance and four-wheel drive would come in handy on the rough roads in the bush. While Reggie and Gerard negotiated, I noticed a deep but healed wound in Reggie's forearm, like a divot in the turf left by a golf club. "The result of a buffalo goring," he later informed me.

At sixty-five, the learned hunter was patient with the relentless questions of a novice, and I dearly wished we had had more time together. He was one of a select and disappearing breed. You could tell the man was a wealth of hunting knowledge, especially with regard to safaris from a bygone era. He knew things about hunting that I would never know. Ever.

Over lunch he shared several stories from his hunting career, including the story of an elephant hunt with a surprise ending. He and a client had been hiking in the hills all day in a fairly remote area of the country. While mounting one of these hills, they spotted below them a magnificent bull with tusks that would easily go one hundred pounds apiece. The hunters were absolutely beside themselves. They were anxiously deciding the best approach for a stalk—and were still looking at the old boy in their binoculars—when the elephant unexpectedly collapsed. A second later came the report of the rifle that had caused it. Another PH and his client, unseen in the bush below, had just shot their prized bull! What are the odds of that happening?

Diversions

Chapter 3

Off-Road Rally

There was still a lot to do before safari, but Gerard was involved in one of his off-season hobbies. The next two days were spent getting his Range Rover ready for the Firestone 600 rally. The past year he had competed in the famous Paris to Dakar Rally, a grueling off-road race of some three thousand miles. Sponsored by a wealthy Spanish client whose only request was to serve as navigator, Gerard placed fifteenth, a feat that was even more amazing in light of the fact they were competing against professional European drivers with helicopter pit crews and princely budgets.

The rally started just before dark from Safariland Lodge. Young Rick Mathews, son of PH Terry Mathews, served as navigator. Brothers Phil and Michael Strong and I used Angelides's Land Cruiser to service our team at midnight and again at four in the morning. Using a hose, we fueled Gerard's

A view of the plains from the Rift Escarpment.

car from big drums in the bed of the truck, and we checked the tires and springs. There was no sleep for the racers that night, and none for the roving pit crews who had to reach the next service stops ahead of our racers, despite the pit crews' shorter routes.

As we drove across the steep face of the Rift Escarpment in the dark of the African night, we passed above the towns of Nakuru and Limuru, fast asleep in the valley below. There was no light pollution here. There was nothing but a solid expanse of blackness below us.

The race ended at 10 A.M. Gerard finished sixth. The man was a hell of a driver. While on safari, he would scare the pants off you as he dashed in and around trees, often swerving and sliding about the dirt roads in the bush. Whenever I warned him that he was going to hit a tree someday, he just smiled, shook his head, and said, "Me? Never! No way, boy!" and stomped on the gas to spite me.

A Trip to the Coast

One night Rick Mathews and his friend Sue Belcher dropped in at Gerard's house. They were on their way to Malindi to fetch Gerard's boat, and they invited me along. We left that evening in an ancient white Land Cruiser for the famous Kenyan coast.

After passing through the popular port city of Mombasa, we arrived in Malindi after midnight. Two flat tires had slowed our progress, but the real culprit was Rick's fascination with snakes. On the drive we glimpsed several lions, giraffes, hyenas, and snakes, but it was the snakes that brought an instant screeching of tires. Each time we spotted a snake, either slithering across the road or coiled beside it, Rick would slam on the brakes and jump out to inspect the reptile, giddy as a prospector who has just struck gold.

He used a hooked tool to handle the bigger snakes and the poisonous ones. He used his hands on smaller specimens, like the one he had just chased down. It was tan, with a patchwork of darker markings similar to those of a giraffe.

"It's a sand boa," he stated, ecstatic to have found it.

He declared the writhing serpent nonpoisonous, though I wouldn't have bet on it. Then he cheerfully picked it up and stuffed it into a shirt pocket, ignoring the bite it gave him on the hand. Granted, the snake was only a foot and a half long, but that was still plenty of snake to deal a lethal dose if it were poisonous. We also passed a road-kill cobra and a large, unidentified serpent with a bulge in its tummy, evidence of a late-night snack. Rick fully inspected them both.

We spent a short night at the cottage of Rick's parents. Each bed was furnished with a drop-down mosquito net, which was a real lifesaver because the wicked insects were out in full force.

Up early, we left for Kilifi, the small village where Gerard's boat was stored. But we didn't get far before the car's engine suddenly called it quits, and we spent the whole of that day trying to get it started. Not even a mechanic from town could get the engine to rev. A tow at thirty miles per hour finally did the trick.

By this time, the rain was really pouring down, and it was quite late. We had no choice but to return to Malindi. As Rick put it, "At least you can say you've been to Malindi three times!"

The next morning, despite prior grievances, the old Rover started right up. The boat and trailer placed a tremendous strain on the old car. Rick persevered and managed to stay above eighty miles per hour. The roads back to Ulu were poor and narrow, so it was hazardous to pass slower traffic, especially towing a boat. But we did. Young Rick drove like a madman.

He may have a future as a rally driver yet, I thought.

Rick Mathews strikes a mad pose with his snake-catcher in hand.

Towing a boat, safari style.

Fishing in Lake Victoria

Gerard and I left early for Kisumu, a fishing village on the eastern banks of Lake Victoria, the third-largest lake in the world and one of the deepest. Gerard's friend Robin Elliot arrived at the lake around the same time we did.

After launching the skiff, the three of us climbed aboard, cranked the small outboard, and set out for deep water. I found the lake surprisingly calm for such a large body of water. The depths were dark blue, and across the horizon the surface seemed endless. Crocodiles inhabit the lake, though I never saw one. My guess is they spend most of their time cruising the shores. Very quickly we were out in open water, where the best fishing was.

With a late start, we were able to fish for only an hour and a half before it got too dark to see. But within that short time I was in for a real surprise. Unfamiliar with Nile perch, I had expected them to weigh five to ten pounds. What we caught were enormous, two of which weighed more than seventy pounds each! Gigantic proportions aside, these silver-scaled fish bear a resemblance to our largemouth bass.

One morning, we had been out only ten minutes when my line went crazy. Gerard was certain it had snagged bottom. But then the rod tip

My 81-pound Nile perch, caught in Lake Victoria.

twitched, and, sure enough, it was a fish. But it was not just any fish. It was a hell of a big one! It fought hard at first, making me struggle to keep control and gain line. The process was somewhat compromised by the small confines of the boat; there was no easy way to set your body against the pull of the large fish. Once alongside the boat, however, the big fish submitted with surprisingly little struggle.

"The lake perch don't have near the fight in them that the smaller river perch do," Gerard informed me. "They grow big and lazy in the lake, while in the river they must constantly fight the current."

With the help of a gaff, we wrestled the massive fish into the boat. Because the fish was played out, it was purely a matter of hoisting the dead weight. Even so, it was no easy task in the small craft with three men moving about, trying not to tip it over.

Of the twenty-four fish landed from the big lake the day before, the largest was about forty-five pounds. As it turned out, mine was the biggest fish caught on the trip. Of course, I had to inform Gerard that such an outcome was purely a matter of skill on the part of the angler at hand. My fish measured five feet long and weighed eighty-one pounds, according to the scale on the bank by the yacht club.

Kisumu Yacht Club, that is.

Professional Hunters' Reunion

Chapter 4

Gerard was trying to soak up as much family time as he could, and sitting around watching movies was a good way to do it. There was no television reception at the farm, so, for the next several nights, we gathered around the television with whatever family and friends and hunters happened in or out and watched rented bootleg tapes. The beer flowed, and everyone commented on the characters, the script, the setting. It was like hecklers' night at the movies, where the viewers have more dialogue than the actors. Gerard bounced Shawn on his knee and called him his "big boy," and I realized for the first time how tough it must be on the men of the hunting profession to leave their families for seven months at a time.

One day Nicky Blunt, a most respected and truly legendary professional hunter, arrived from England. To say that Nicky's reputation preceded him would have been an understatement. Every PH I met seemed to have a story or two about him. It was Nicky Blunt this, Nicky Blunt that. How he lived by the old school, boy! None of this shooting from near the vehicle. That would never do. No, he made his clients crawl on hands and knees through the brush on every stalk, and if they didn't rub their knees raw and rip most of their flesh in the wait-a-bit thorn, then the hunt had not been worthy of them as hunters; they had been cheated of the complete experience.

I was excited finally to get to meet this living legend. But Nicky Blunt in person was nothing like the Nicky Blunt I had pictured. Despite a name that practically rang with the essence of ruggedness, Nicky Blunt, the hero of all those hair-raising escapades, was a smallish, slight fellow with a soft, almost comical voice.

Fortunately for Nicky (and others of us as well), it is a fact that a great hunter is not measured by physical size. If anything, a smaller frame and stature are superior in making a successful stalk. They are also an advantage in the mountains or when covering any distance on flat land—the more you weigh, the more weight you have to "carry." A nimble fellow like Nicky could easily out-hike, out-crawl, out-climb a heavier man. At forty-five, Nicky had been involved in the hunting

A herd of bachelor bulls in the Ngorongoro Crater.

business since he was eighteen. He now lived in the U.K. during the off-season. I wished he were hunting out of Gerard's camp. He seemed a super fellow, and I knew he would be great company.

Young PH Simon Evans dropped in as well. Built like a football player—tall, broad-shouldered, and all muscle—Simon was happy as a dog with a bone in his new profession.

"Never seen anyone try so hard," Gerard told me later. "Simon wants to do his best, trying hard to get his clients the biggest trophies possible. If crawling on his belly to Egypt would produce a record-book buffalo, I believe he'd do it!"

When Simon voiced his concern over the Americans' fascination with taking long shots at game, Gerard recommended saying to such people: "I consider myself a fair shot at two hundred yards, but I'm really good at two yards—where it counts!"

Late that afternoon, Nicky, George, and I wandered down the hill to Nick Swan's house. Nick, a retired PH, managed the neighboring cattle farms. At sixty-four, he was a strong, stoutly built, no-nonsense fellow who could have wrestled bulls in his younger days. His obliging wife, Moira, kept our group in a steady supply of cold beer, and as a result the stories really began to flow.

Nicky Blunt had one of the best. He had once heard a lion's mating growl in the bush, and he walked without a gun to the spot it had come from, hoping to catch a glimpse of this rare occurrence.

The king at rest on the plains.

"When I saw nothing, I started back. Just then, however, there was an explosion of movement in the brush. A lioness broke into a run away from me. In the same instant, the male appeared and came directly at me! It was truly alarming, yet I knew what I had to do. I took a step forward, raised my arms high overhead, and shouted at the top of my lungs. But the lion didn't stop or falter, as I had expected. In fact, on he came at top speed! I knew I had no choice but to stand my ground and keep up the shouting and waving, for to run, without a doubt, would have meant *chop! chop!* Running from any predator triggers their instinct to chase you," he added, for my benefit.

"So I found myself in this sudden standoff. It was a little like two cars approaching each other in a game of chicken, where the first to back down is the loser. That was really my only strategy, as I had no weapon whatsoever on my person. The lion approached within several feet of me and stopped, growling and hissing the whole while, now sizing me up. He was a great big brute, and he was angry. I mean, really agitated. He began circling me no more than a couple of arms' lengths away."

I could only imagine what an incredible test of will it had been to stand face to face with an absolute killing machine, a brute of an animal that outweighed Nicky's slight frame four-to-one, an adversary with every advantage except a bigger brain. Nicky refused to back down an inch, so he kept up the ruckus. The shouting and the arms waving—essentially the bluff—continued until finally, finally, the angry lion slowly turned and disappeared into the brush. Nicky had done the unthinkable. He had won a hand-to-hand showdown against Africa's biggest and most fearsome predator.

With the arrival of a fresh round of beers, Nick Swan talked about the difficulties he'd had with various cattle killers on the farm. It was his job as manager to dispose of any lion or leopard that attacked the defenseless herds. Far from a simple task, this was mostly done in the dark of night when lions are most active and when they have every advantage over human pursuers. Incredibly, a single lion had killed 197 cattle before Nick could put a bullet into it! According to Nick, African lions in general are expertly quick and effective at killing cattle. The casualties can run up quickly, making his job that much more difficult.

"One night," he told us, "while I was waiting up for a pride of cattle killers to show, I heard a cow moan in the distance. In the few seconds it took for me to get there, a total of eight cows had been slaughtered. Two lions were the culprits."

The next time someone tells you that animals kill only to eat, tell him he doesn't know what he is talking about. Antihunters, of course, would like us to believe that man is the only animal that kills for pleasure. Such a statement is pure sentimental nonsense. These two lions obviously had killed much more than they could eat and were enjoying the easy catch and kill of the domestic game. This behavior is true of any predator. Just watch a cat with a mouse, and there is little doubt that a predator takes pleasure in the act of killing. A cat will gladly kill mice when it has no desire to eat them.

Probably the best example I have ever heard is the story of a single leopard that stole into Gerard's goat pen one night. The leopard killed all thirty-five goats, carrying off only one goat to eat. What animal would take the time to kill thirty-five goats, only to eat one, if not for the pleasure of the kill? Likewise, a lion will kill any leopard or hyena or jackal it can catch, often without eating a bite, because each of these predators is a competitor.

The Wives of
Professional Hunters
Chapter 5

O ne morning Cally and I ran errands in Nairobi, and on the drive she puffed nervously on cigarettes.

"Don't tell Gerard I smoke," she warned.

Cally was getting frustrated with the last-minute details left to her to iron out for Gerard. Her "to do" list kept growing. In his absence, which was more than half the year, she was responsible for dealing with African bureaucrats; charged with making things happen fast in a country where things are slow to happen; charged with making requests and asking favors in a black town where a white woman is at the bottom of the totem pole.

Town was a two-hour round trip; any errand there was a half-day affair at a minimum. Most trips ended with the news, "The part isn't in yet," "Mr. Bagabi is not available," "Come back tomorrow," "You have the wrong form," "The import duty is 200 percent," "That's not possible," "I can't help you." The problems were endless.

Performing the duties of a professional hunter's wife is quite an undertaking, especially when the hunter operates his own hunting company. The wife becomes his office manager, secretary, power of attorney, accountant, banker, radio operator, publicist, and chief gofer, all rolled into one. The PH could hire someone else to do these tasks, but that would cut into much of the year's profit, and it would be nearly impossible to find someone who would perform the job as earnestly and effectively as one's spouse, who has everything to lose or gain by her actions. I doubt there are any statistics available, but the divorce rate in the African professional hunter community must be sky high. Unfortunately, not long after this trip, Gerard and Cally divorced.

While I was writing letters one morning, Jillian Angelides joined me on the veranda. She was a sweet and pretty lady, petite in every respect except for her eyes, which were large and doelike. She delighted me with stories of how she and George met, eventually married, had their son Michael, and then divorced. George then married an American girl. She arranged his safaris from the States (including our 1982 safari) until they divorced and she ran off with all his hunting deposits. He still refers to her as Dracula. George and Jillian married a second time, and they had son Nicholas, who was then four. He was running around between us in green rubber frog-faced boots that made his feet smell. The story was difficult to hear, if not a little disjointed, with little Nicholas whacking this and that with a stick, yelling at his mother, and wrestling noisily with Shawn. Jillian was reluctant to discipline her son, but you could tell there was a fire inside her to match George's, which was a good thing, I thought, because she would need it to keep that rascal in line.

Another day I went to see Cally's sister Jeanette ride in a motocross race outside Nairobi. Jeanette's attractive figure was hidden under a leather jumpsuit, a helmet, and bulky body armor. Her boyfriend, Glenn Mathews, the older brother of snake enthusiast Rick, came by to see her race. Jeanette's professional hunter husband A had run off with B, the former wife of professional hunter C, who had recently divorced B because of her affair with his professional hunter partner D. Hollywood has never invented a soap opera with so much drama! Put it all in a book and no one would believe it.

Gerard felt partly responsible for Jeanette's divorce because he had introduced Jeanette to her husband. In addition, Gerard had taken the fellow under his wing, mentoring him in the world of professional hunting, introducing him to friends and contacts, and furnishing him the inside scoop.

In East Africa white people are in such short supply that it seems a shame for them to involve each other in such shenanigans, but perhaps it is because the population is so small that it is fraught with infidelities and love scandals. Everybody knows everybody, and there really isn't anyone else to date—except the natives, and it's taboo to date them, at least publicly. But romantic antics have been a part of East Africa for as long as Europeans have settled there.

If it is a hard life for a professional hunter, it is even harder on his wife and family. A PH will leave his family for six or seven months at a time. Professional hunters are occasionally hit on by the trophy wives of their rich clients or by the lonely wives of their PH friends who are out in the bush. That's not to say that PHs are entirely innocent, for they do their fair share of instigating the "hitting," too. Several are legendary for their lack of standards when it comes to pursuing the opposite sex (probably understandable after months of celibacy in the bush) and will hit on anything with a skirt. Add a few drinks to the equation, and I'm sure what some of these rascals wake up to in the morning is scarier than a charging rhino.

Setting Sail for the Selous

Chapter 6

A few days later, Cally took me to Reggie Destro's house to wait for Gerard. He had traveled solo to Tanzania, afraid my visa would not allow for multiple entries into the country. We got word that Gerard had caught a ride from Arusha, leaving the Volvo in Tanzania because he did not want to pass through Customs with it again. Relations between Kenya and Tanzania were tense, and the frustrations of both sides were often unleashed on the unlucky victims crossing the border. You were at the mercy and whim of whichever border guard you happened to encounter. There was a long list of prohibited items, and, besides that, the Kenyan guard could prevent you from taking fuel or food or even the vehicle itself into Tanzania, while the Tanzanian guard would tax you on whatever his Kenyan counterpart let through.

Getting certain supplies across the border was critical to the success of Gerard's safari operation. The Tanzanian economy was in the tank, and the fault was directly attributable to the policies of the communist government. You couldn't buy anything in Tanzania, and when I say anything, I mean anything. The place was a ghost town. Car dealers, grocery stores, and clothing shops all stood empty and rotting, a silent attestation to what once was a viable economy in colonial East Africa. Not a roll of toilet paper, not a battery, not a light bulb could be had—not in the stores, anyway. The economy was totally collapsed and broken—like a drug addict who had hit rock bottom. It was a textbook case on why communism does not work.

Gerard finally arrived, but we encountered another delay. Reggie was still waiting to get the papers in order on the lorry he had sold Gerard. Something that would take an hour in the States takes weeks in East Africa: The red tape on any transaction was endless. So we were stuck for the moment. We couldn't go on safari without the four-wheel-drive MAN lorry. It was needed to carry refrigerators, crates of supplies, tents, and the staff, for starters.

We were all set to leave on safari the following day, but the promised export papers for the lorry never arrived. By lunchtime, Gerard was ready to pull his hair out.

We went to Reggie's early the next morning, but the export permits did not come until late afternoon, around four o'clock. We would have left right then, but it was against the law to drive a lorry at night. The Kenyan government is always worried about coups and such. We went to the New Stanley Hotel to meet PH Roy Carr-Hartley, a close friend of Gerard's who would be joining us in the bush, to set him straight on the news and to inform him that we would pick him up at the Malay airstrip a week later, God willing. Based on current reports, the rain hadn't been heavy in the Selous, making us hopeful for a less-than-difficult journey. We drove back to Ulu in Gerard's Alfa Romeo sports car, flying at top speed across the open plains.

We left Ulu in the Land Cruiser in the early dark in order to meet the MAN lorry at the turnoff outside Nairobi at 7 A.M. We reached the Tanzanian border at 9:45 A.M. and had surprisingly little trouble with Customs. (On Gerard's last trip, the border guards had made him empty his spare fuel drums onto the ground!) We got to Arusha at noon and went straight to the Immigration office, where I was in for a disappointment. They would grant me only a week's stay in Tanzania, although I had purchased a six-month visa from their embassy in the States.

"Don't worry, Johnny," Gerard said, as we drove off. "We'll get that fixed. The scoundrels just want a payoff."

We were to stay the night with Gerard's friends Paul and Maria Cheriex, an elderly Dutch couple who lived on a farm outside Arusha. They were quite hospitable and took me in as if I were family. They treated Gerard like a son; they positively glowed when he showed up at their door.

We spent the rest of the day packing the MAN from Paul's "store," a warehouse not far from his house. All the supplies and equipment for the season had been stored there, including some from the prior season, such as refrigerators, generators, tents, tables and chairs, and automotive parts; then there were the items Gerard had brought from Ulu in the Volvo the week before and supplies Gerard had put together in Arusha on previous trips. Because foodstuffs could not be exported from Kenya, he had to buy cooking oil, salt, flour, and other items in Arusha. It was not easy—he had to pay top price for these things on the black market, if they could be found at all.

Maria served us Paul's favorite for dinner that night: warthog stew over rice. It was indeed excellent. Afterward, we chatted over beer in the den. Paul had gotten his hands on a case of Grolsch beer, which he was quite proud of and was anxious to share. Not wanting to take his treasure, I stuck with Safari Lager, the only beer made and available for purchase in Tanzania. It comes in a plain brown bottle—no label, with "Safari Lager" printed in red letters on the cap.

******

We finished loading the MAN in the morning, but it was quite a chore getting everything to fit and packing it in accordance with Gerard's strict instructions. Every inch of space had to be utilized, and everything had to be packed so it wouldn't jar and break or crush something else on the long trip. I say we loaded the lorry, but it was really Gerard's native hands, who numbered a dozen or more. All I did was watch and marvel. With my limited Swahili, I was more of a hindrance than a help, and I got a kick out of watching Gerard in action. He was in fine form, strutting about like the captain of a ship. Shouting. Pointing. Waving his arms. He was barking orders in a loud voice, and the men were scrambling about the bed of the truck. He shouted, "Left" or "Right," he jumped in and out of the truck, he tested a load here, moved a load there.

He hollered, "Dewey, you idiot! What are you crushing our eggs for, huh? I should dock your pay!"

He said it in Swahili and in English so everyone would understand, and the men smiled; a couple of them laughed. Gerard took a playful swing at the young native, and Dewie ducked his head, embarrassed.

Gerard wanted it done right, but, most important, he was setting the tone for the rest of the safari. He was putting them on notice. He wanted it known that he demanded perfection and would tolerate nothing less, that he expected their best with his supervision or without, and that everyone must pull his own weight. When no one jumped to right the egg problem, Gerard flew into a tirade and began cursing like a one-eyed pirate.

"Get these blankety-blank crates unloaded and start the blank over! What the bloody hell am I paying you for, huh? Lazy rascals! Why, in all my years on safari I've never seen such a miserable, motherless, pitiful-looking group such as yourselves—and Christ, Kipper, don't put that lantern there! Use your head, man! Think! Has every one of you forgotten every blankety-blank thing you knew since last season?"

And so it went. But his scolding had broken the ice. This was not unlike men readying to set sail at sea; these men would not see their homes or families for six months. Children would be born in their absence, and children would die.

Gerard was their captain, and he alone would hold this crew together for the next half-year. No matter what crises appeared, and there would be many—sickness, superstition, tribal conflict, to name a few—it was he alone who would prevent unrest among the troops, he alone who would quash mutiny before it reared its ugly head.

I would write in my diary:

His is not a democracy. He is a dictator, pure and simple. He is king while on safari, and the sooner everyone recognizes that fact, the better. But everyone recognizes it. These are all old hands, except for two or three new ones. They know the drill. He is the master. He is the chief. He is the bwana.

It is a position of great power that he holds. While presiding over this small society for the next few months, Gerard will be more than just employer to these men. He will be friend, counselor, doctor, priest, policeman, judge, and jury. It is because of this that a client can leave his wallet in the tent and never worry that a dollar will go missing. You will never return to camp to find that there is nothing for dinner, that your clothes have not been washed, or that the shower water has not been heated, for if any of those things happen, there will be hell to pay. Gerard runs a tight ship.

A Leyland lorry with an Indian driver had been hired and was all set to go; it contained forty-two drums of fuel, both diesel and petrol. Paul had organized that project the week before, though the drums of fuel had been purchased over a period of many weeks as it became available.

The official start of the safari had arrived! At eleven that morning, the caravan—comprised of three lorries and two hunting cars—pulled out, making quite a racket and raising large plumes of dust on the dirt roads. They looked every bit like the circus coming to town. The third lorry was a Bedford truck, borrowed at the last minute from Paul to carry the leftover supplies and equipment that would not fit into the other two lorries. The MAN was the only four-wheel drive of the three. It would have its work cut out for it when we reached boggy terrain, having to pull not only itself across but the others as well.

Farouk Qreshi, an apprentice hunter to Gerard, had arrived that day to join us for the season, and the three of us would follow the caravan later. If you read my first book, *A Bullet Well Placed,* then you know Farouk. He was a short, handsome, and friendly fellow, a third-generation East African who carried the thick Pakistani accent of his heritage. Farouk also was a mechanic—indispensable in the bush—and an overall handyman who would assist Gerard in the one hundred and one tasks that come up on safari. Gerard could not attend to them all while hunting twelve, fourteen hours a day with his clients. So it was that after a fine plate of

Our caravan begins the week-long trek to the Selous Game Reserve.

Maria's warthog stew, Farouk and I followed the caravan in the Land Cruiser. Gerard, however, stayed to finish some permit business, which included trying to extend my visa.

Farouk and I caught up to the lorries in early evening. A couple of hours later, the whole caravan pulled off to the side of the dirt road, where we would camp for the night. With so much packing and other work at Paul's shop, there had been little time for greetings. This was my first real chance to greet the new staff and reacquaint myself with the old, the ones who had been on my 1982 safari. We all shook hands—which in Africa is more like a loose, unmoving clasp—and they asked how I was and how my mom and dad were doing, and I asked how they were. Kipper, the head tracker, who had led me to many fine trophies on my previous safari, was there.

New to me, but the most senior hand by far, was old Abdi, Gerard's headman and skinner, who now held my hands and patted my arms and gave me a sincere welcome. As headman, Abdi was in charge of the camp and staff in Gerard's absence. Incredibly, Abdi had worked for Gerard's parents, both professional hunters, when Gerard was but an infant. Abdi was outfitted in a blue jacket and matching blue shorts, with well-used sandals and a white knitted fez on his head. He had slowed with age but was steady and soft-spoken, typical for someone with his vast experience and know-how.

The men made a small fire and placed ears of corn in it, squatting in a circle and warming their hands against the night chill. I hunkered with them but was not limber enough to achieve their unique butt-to-heel squat, knees tucked under their chins, a position they could maintain for hours. I tried an ear of corn, dry and burned black in spots but not bad if you were hungry. They cooked some meat, too, but I passed, since I had no idea how "aged" it might be. The butcher shop in Nairobi had reeked of spoiled meat, perhaps because the refrigerators weren't cooling properly. Whatever the case, both times we ate steak at Ulu I ended up with diarrhea the next day. So I decided to abstain from meat until we got into the bush and could secure fresh game.

In the past I had resisted the temptation to medicate the condition. In 1982, when my whole family came down with a brutal attack of the lower intestine, we passed the Lomotil around like candy. It cured the runs, but only temporarily. A day or two later, the condition would return in full force. We repeated the cycle again and again for five weeks! This time I decided to let nature run its course, let the body rid itself for good of whatever bug was causing it to act up. Only as a last resort would I reach for the medicine.

We squatted around the fire and crunched corn. Kipper spoke little English and I spoke little Swahili, but we got by. I gave him a hard time about his smoking. All the blacks smoke when they can get their hands on tobacco. And they smoke the most God-awful stuff you can imagine. Ragged tobacco rolled in torn scraps of newspaper. It smells more like burning trash than burning tobacco. Kipper's teeth were stained dark yellow from the filth.

"*Mingi sana*" (too much), I told him, pointing at the stub of cigarette that would have burned his fingers were they not toughened to leather. I meant, "You smoke too much."

"*Hapana*" (no), he said, laughing hoarsely. "*Mzuri. Gude,*" he reiterated.

"No good!" I told him.

The men squatting around the fire laughed, cutting chunks of cooked meat and peeling ears of corn. Maybe by the end of the trip I would limber up enough to assume the squat. The squat makes sense in a place where so many things on the ground can bite you, where any number of roaming threats might require an instant dash to the nearest tree. It is Darwin in action. In Africa you can never let your guard down.

The lorries left around four the next morning, and Farouk and I followed at half past seven. We passed through the Masai town of Kibaya, the one Hemingway wrote about in *The Green Hills of Africa*. Farouk pulled up to a ramshackle, one-story hotel and disappeared inside with a Thermos to fetch hot tea. While I waited in the car, a fight broke out between two Masai warriors. I could see a scuffle in the dark of the open doorway, and I heard punches landing hard against flesh before some men broke it up. The culprits, both drunk, came staggering out into the sun and wandered off their separate ways.

We stopped in another village, where Farouk ran an errand. While I waited in the car, two Masai men appeared at my door. They were quite friendly and wanted to chat. The younger, named Richard, was twenty-four, and I would not have guessed he was a Masai. He was dressed in modern yet tattered slacks and a shirt and spoke respectable English. The older Masai, who was thirty, wore traditional Masai garb: a red robe, beads, and sandals. His hair was dyed red ocher, and he wielded the obligatory spear. He recognized our vehicle and apparently knew Gerard. With Richard translating, he went on to tell me he had six wives and twenty children! In addition, he owned some two thousand goats—a rich man by Masai standards (by most standards in the world, actually). Richard had just one wife but aspired to acquire more. He was clearly in awe of the wealth and status of his older friend.

"What does a wife cost?" I asked.

"Sixty cattle," he said. "But you can buy two wives for one hundred."

I wondered who was getting the better deal on that transaction—the groom or the bride's father!

"Our custom," he explained, "is to keep each wife in a different house, which is, of course, constructed by the woman."

"Do the wives get jealous of one another?" I asked the older Masai.

"Every now and then," Richard translated. "The older wives get jealous of the younger, prettier ones."

When Farouk returned, we followed in the lorries' tracks. Soon we came across an unusually large flock of guinea fowl milling in the road and actually hit two of them with the truck. Farouk stopped, and I jumped out to collect the flapping birds, which were the size of young turkeys.

"That weell make a nice soopper," Farouk declared in his thick accent. He was nodding his head and grinning out of the side of his mouth, a mannerism that would become quite familiar.

We later caught up to and passed the lorries, which allowed us to move outside their choking, dusty wake. Then we turned onto one of the few paved roads we would see on this journey and headed for the town of Morogoro. There, Farouk and I stopped to get the men something to eat—the two guinea fowl would not feed the whole crew.

Counting lorry drivers and a couple of caravan assistants, our party numbered nearly twenty in all. Understandably, it was no small task to keep this sizable group fed. Further, the physical demands on the staff would only grow as we encountered more remote and difficult terrain, increasing appetites all around from the long days and short nights. Game meat would not appear on the menu until we reached the Selous. But that was OK. Most of the staff, who ranged in age from seventeen to seventy, were veterans of these cross-country voyages.

We made camp at dusk on a dirt road twenty-five miles outside of town. Gerard met up with us in the Volvo that night and handed me a package from home. He was hovering, quite anxious for me to open it. Candy and sweets were a novelty in the East African economy. Tucking the package protectively under one arm, I said, "I'll open it later."

At that point I was forced to fend off his groping hands. Finally, Gerard pulled out a knife in jest and demanded, "Open it!"

Two days earlier I had received the best birthday present ever—two letters from Alexandra and one from Mom. Now there were more letters and pictures from home and lots of goodies. The shoebox was filled to the brim with Oreo cookies, Hershey bars, and assorted treats. You don't realize how good chocolate tastes until you go without it for a month. It was hard to believe I had just turned twenty-four. It was great to hear from home. Everyone was well.

Gerard and I feasted, while Farouk preferred his endless cigarettes. We fell quickly to sleep in bedrolls on the ground.

Breakdowns and
Other Obstacles
Chapter 7

The Bedford broke down first thing the next morning and brought the whole caravan to a halt. After wasting an hour or two trying to fix it, then getting it going several times, only to have it break down shortly thereafter, Gerard discovered the real culprit was a worn drive-shaft bearing, and he declared the Bedford could not continue. Farouk would remain behind to get it fixed. I accompanied Gerard in the Volvo—his new toy. A hulking Swedish military vehicle, it was three times the size of a Jeep with giant tires and four-wheel drive at the push of a button. Gerard was eager to test it out on the trip.

Early in the day we came to a couple of log bridges that were too narrow to accommodate the wheelbases of the larger lorries. A slip off the edge and the lorry would roll for sure, and with soggy marsh on either side, it would be impossible to right or retrieve one if it did roll. Then there was the question whether the bridges could even support the weight of the great trucks. The men piled out with shovels and picks and built up the sides of the bridges with dry dirt and logs. When they were done, Gerard made a quick calculation of the combined weight of the fuel drums and shook his head, then crossed his fingers. There was some creaking and crunching as each lorry rolled across the wooden structures. Fortunately, all vehicles made it across.

Our next obstacle came in the form of several large pools of water that had formed in the road after the last night's rain. These pools were three feet deep in places and stretched one hundred yards or more in length. The good news was that the pools featured sandy bottoms, which had better traction than clay. Had the bottoms been made of clay, we never would have made it.

Stranded in the middle of one pool was a Land Rover. A lone European gentleman, standing thigh-deep in water and trying to figure out what to do next, was very glad to see us. The beastly Volvo winched him out in a snap. Both lorries made it through with little difficulty. The heavy trucks plowed through the water, throwing great wakes like deep-drafted tugboats plowing a bay do. Farouk would be on his own to get through when he followed in the Bedford. We hoped the rain would hold until he had passed.

After a tow and a jump-start, this marooned missionary was happily on his way.

We stopped in the town of Kilombero to pick up the government game scout, who worked for the government-owned Tanzania Wildlife Corporation (TAWICO). He was not ready, so Gerard was forced to return for him later that afternoon.

It's hard to imagine how anyone could have a traffic accident out there in the middle of nowhere, but we did. Going up a steep a hill, around a bend, the MAN lost traction, slipped in the mud, and sideswiped another lorry already stuck up to its axles in the brown muck. After an intense argument, Gerard agreed to pay the owner five thousand shillings.

While passing through Mikumi National Game Park, we saw several elephants with respectable tusks. They stood wisely in the shade of tall trees and reached up with trunks to pluck leafy branches, which they stuffed into their mouths. They paid no attention to us, a sure sign that poaching activity had been minimal.

Now in the lowlands, we came to a squishy spot, where the Leyland bogged down and got stuck. The MAN had to winch it to drier ground. In early afternoon we hit the worst stretch so far: a muddy swamp nearly a quarter-mile across. Here the men bailed out with pangas and axes, and they set to work chopping limbs and logs to fill the mucky, water-filled ruts. The four-wheel-drive MAN eventually got through, but it took every bit of help the Volvo and a winch could offer. Because the tires of the heavy truck had carved so deeply into the bottomless mush, however, there was now no chance that the Leyland could make it across. We spent the rest of the afternoon chopping more logs and branches from nearby trees and placing them in the soupy ruts.

Farouk arrived later that evening with the Bedford right behind him. I think Gerard was surprised to see him so soon. Getting the Bedford fixed so quickly was quite a feat, a task I had expected to take two or three days at least, and then only if the parts were available—a highly unlikely event in itself. Then there were the pools of water to cross. The Bedford had, in fact, conked out in one of the deeper pools, Farouk reported, and he had to dismantle the distributor to get it started. Even then, he confessed, he would not have made it across the deep pools without the assistance of the four-wheel-drive Land Cruiser, which towed it.

Gerard went through the steps of setting up the radio to call home, which was a bit of a process. The radio, powered by wires attached to the vehicle's battery, was about the size of a bread box. Gerard uncoiled the lengthy antenna wire and strung it high in the treetops in the direction he determined would fetch the best reception. To do this, he tethered blocks of wood to each end of the antenna with rope and then pitched them over suitable limbs. The ropes hanging down from the trees were pulled taut, stretching the antenna overhead in the shape of a T. We were supposed to call Cally at 7 P.M., but another PH and his girlfriend remained on the

The swamps proved more challenging. We had to cut logs and branches to fill the ruts.

Now it was our turn. We plowed through the sandy pools with little difficulty.

channel for another half-hour. As it was with the telephone party lines of old, you had to wait your turn unless it was an emergency.

We spent the night in this swampy, boggy bottom, but I hardly slept a wink. The surrounding swamps were home to thousands of croaking frogs and millions of starving mosquitoes. I sat scrunched in the front seat of the windowless Volvo, tortured by the constant buzzing in my ears. The little monsters stung me from head to toe, and sleep was impossible under their attack. Despite the stifling heat, I finally wriggled into my sleeping bag and pulled a sweater around my head. The sweat poured off me as in a sauna, but it was the only way to keep the buzzing little devils away. Even so, sleep came no easier. It was a long and miserable night. At one point I got out of the Volvo to sleep in the Land Cruiser because I could roll up the windows. When I opened the passenger door, a cloud of smoke wafted out. Farouk was lying across the seat in a fetal position, a burning cigarette in his hand.

"Mohsqueeto reepellahnt," he said, dropping his sleepy head back onto the pillow of his arm.

Swamps and Quicksand

Chapter 8

The men spent all the next morning chopping logs with pangas and filling the long stretch of ruts, but it was quite a job, and Gerard ended up hiring five or six locals to help. The natives live in tiny grass huts built atop termite mounds—everything else is under water in the rainy season. The men, smiling, came out to greet us. The women came, too, carrying babies in swaddling clothes tied to their backs. Kids came to stare and giggle, and they ran when I tried to take their picture. For some, we were the first white men they had ever seen. All the kids were barefoot and grinning, their distended bellies in sharp contrast to their bony arms and legs. The clothes they wore—adults and kids alike—were rags, patched and re-patched, with enough holes to make a punk rocker jealous. The soiled rags literally hung from their black bodies, in some cases more holes than material, making you wonder why they even bothered.

Gerard tests the men's handiwork in the Volvo before allowing the lorries to proceed

Quicksand!

We finally got all the vehicles across the muddy ruts in early afternoon. But we had driven no more than a few miles when the Leyland sank in mud up to the axles. It was stuck like a ship run ashore—there was absolutely no budging it. Frustrated, Gerard decided we would never make it to camp at the pace we were going, so we left the lorry there with a couple of boys to guard it and its precious cargo of fuel.

Later that afternoon, we were in for a real surprise. The behemoth MAN was swallowed by a pit of quicksand. One minute the giant truck was trundling along the dirt track; the next, it collapsed through a crust of earth into an endless pit of sticky brown goo, turning so sharply on its side that it almost flipped over. We all got out to wonder at the spectacle, shaking our heads. The strange thing was that the ground was hard and dry all around where the truck had sunk.

I guess I was expecting an open green pit like you see in the Tarzan movies, a menace that easily could be avoided with a simple turn of the steering wheel. This was altogether different. What makes quicksand so tricky is that the mushy stuff is hidden beneath a hard surface. It is completely invisible until you sink into it, and then it is too late. When you walk on the hard crust, you can feel the ground sink beneath your feet. It is an odd sensation, similar to walking on a trampoline.

Gerard had no choice but to give the order to unload the MAN, a task that would have taken a good deal of time on level ground. Removing

The hard, dry ground conceals the insidious quicksand beneath. Once in its clutches, the MAN must be unloaded to escape.

the MAN, canted over that way, was hopeless without lightening its load. He then left in the Volvo to scout ahead.

Once all the gear was unloaded, the real work began. Everyone fell to shoveling and jacking or chopping and hauling logs. It was fast and furious work, with no letup. With each pump of the jack handle, the jack sank deeper, and the brown goop would seep in from below as fast as the men could shovel it out. Now and then a man would sink and get stuck, and we would have to pull him out. When the jack reached its top notch, sinking uselessly in the mush, we laid a spare tire on its side on which to mount the jack, but even that was not enough. It took two truck jacks, working back and forth, to get the rear of the MAN high enough to begin stuffing logs under the tire and into the muck. As we soon discovered, however, it was like trying to smite a volcano with marshmallows: The hungry quicksand devoured the logs like candy. There seemed to be no bottom to it. So, we found ourselves in a race—a race against the rising ooze and the insatiable appetite of the quicksand. It was a race that we weren't winning.

The spare tire was soon buried three feet deep in the sucking muck, putting us back at square one. Everyone was covered from head to toe in quicksand, and muscles were growing tired. Rain started to pour around

7:30 P.M., so we had no choice but to give up and take cover for the night. Farouk took pity on me and let me sleep in the Land Cruiser cab with its roll-up windows to keep the pesky bugs out. Thankfully, there weren't as many to keep out as there had been in the swamps.

At first light we were in for a real disappointment. Not only had much of the previous evening's gains been erased, but the front wheel, which had been on solid ground when we went to sleep, had sunk to the bumper. We weren't sure where to start. While the men went to work on the lorry, Farouk and I took splash baths with a bucket and the water from a nearby stream and changed clothes.

We were covered in mud from the work in the quicksand, but I was most anxious to be rid of a week's worth of sweat and grime. In contrast, the average native has never bathed or showered in his entire life. Nor has a chance swim accomplished what a bath might do, for most Africans don't know how to swim. This is not at all surprising in a place where any body of water more than ankle deep can harbor crocodiles, hippos, and parasites, making swimming a sport that is hazardous to your health. Because of this, it is a fact that you often smell a native before you see or hear him.

Gerard returned in early afternoon, around the time we got the big truck pulled out. Though we had jacked both right tires up on stacks of logs for traction, it took the services of the winch cable, bound to the stout trunk of a nearby tree, to get the lorry out. Then came the chore of reloading the equipment and crates. We also had to use the winch to retrieve the spare tire from the sucking ground.

Once we got the truck fully loaded, the caravan moved on. Soon thereafter, the Bedford sank into quicksand, but it took only an hour or two to free it. Late in the evening we reached a place called Malay, an old campsite with several abandoned, half-dismantled buildings, one of which we slept in. As we lay in the dark, Gerard ribbed Farouk on his accent and chided him for his constant complaints of the difficulties he had faced along the trip. Gerard would yell out in the dark, as if he were Farouk talking, "You know, Bwahrna, by Garhd, mahn, I'm haveeng hard time."

"Barht, I'm taylling you, Gerarhd," Farouk replied, "thees queecksand is mingi sana. Eet's too mahch. Eet's making me crazy!"

"Bloody hell!" Gerard fired back. "The problem is chai. You spend all your time drinking bloody tea. Every time I turn around, you're off making another blankety-blank cup of tea! No wonder you are always late!"

"No, Bwahrna. I'm taylling you, eet's the queeksand! Eet is too mahch."

Typical preparation before crossing each creek.

As an apprentice hunter, Farouk had to put up with a lot, but it was part of the deal—like a private getting chewed out by his sergeant. Gerard is hard on him, I thought, but Farouk is lucky to have such a respected PH take him under his wing.

Gerard imitated him again: "Oh, yays, Bwahrna, the queeksand. Barht first I moost have my chai."

Then Gerard would laugh and I would laugh and Farouk would laugh, too. It was wonderful lying there in the dark, and I thought how lucky I was to be a part of it all. I had the privilege of seeing something that perhaps only a handful of people have witnessed. I would have a behind-the-scenes view of a safari operation, from beginning to end. The planning and strategy, the mechanics, the frustrations and headaches in dealing with a communist bureaucracy, the never-ending quest to find or weld or build the right parts and equipment, the unavoidable delays, the uncensored language and sentiments. The incredible amount of time, money, and energy it takes to pull off a successful safari in the bush, with everything against you—the elements, the government, and any number of unforeseen hardships.

We were up early, hoping to go twenty-five or thirty miles deeper into the Selous, for we had yet to reach Gerard's U1 concession. We had spent the last night in K4. He had permission from one official to use K5 if needed.

After spending half the day on a stream crossing, where the steep banks had to be chopped down with pick and shovel to allow passage, and after making a search of the rough terrain ahead in the Volvo, Gerard decided to cut the trip short and simply make camp within a few miles. The deciding factor was quicksand. Just past noon, the MAN sank in again, and it took three hours to extricate it.

While we worked to get the truck out, Gerard shot an impala for camp chow, and the cook roasted the meat on sticks propped about a small fire. I think it was Hemingway who best described the color of the impala's coat by comparing it to a tarnished penny. Impala are beautiful animals, and I love to watch them run and jump, often sailing a good thirty feet or more in the air. Soon, we plucked chunks of meat from the fire as each deemed them ready, holding the hot, juicy cubes in our fingers, blowing to cool them, and popping them into our mouths. It was a quick, late lunch, standing around the fire, and we were off as soon as the MAN was liberated.

Building Camp

Chapter 9

Roy Carr-Hartley flew in one day, accompanied by a TAWICO official named Bundala. At twenty-four, Bundala was just out of Mweka College and had never hunted in his life. (Well, he had hunted once, but more on that later.) Just dandy! Even so, in the government's eyes, and on every printed form required in the taking or processing of game, Bundala's name would appear as the PH of record. Gerard was considered the camp manager.

The young official arrived with a frown and a fierce crease in his brow, and I asked Gerard how he thought things would work out with this fellow. I knew that, at the snap of his fingers, Bundala could shut down our entire hunting operation for any reason.

"No problem," Gerard answered, with characteristic optimism. "When they are first appointed, they arrive arrogant, cocky, ready to throw their weight around. But after a few weeks, they realize how little they know and that we—the white PHs—have the pull with the clients when it comes to tips. After that, they settle down and are glad to have me in charge."

That day, just before dark, Gerard settled on what he determined to be the best campsite in the area—a breezy spot a quarter-mile from the Kilombero River. Looking at the virgin forest around us, it was hard to envision a campsite located where we were standing. The grass was head high, and thick undergrowth had claimed every inch of ground beneath the trees. I suddenly realized how much I took for granted when, as a client, I merely showed up at a completed camp. Roy, the natives, and I got busy with pangas, shovels, and scythes, which the men swung like golf clubs to cut the grass. Slowly, we began to clear a patch of ground, and we continued to work until it was too dark to see. By then, we had cleared only one small area of what would eventually become camp. Gerard dug out bottles of beer, and we drank them in the dark. Then we spread a tarp on the damp ground and went to sleep.

This campsite was in K5, and Gerard was worried that TAWICO might give him trouble over it. "I will tell them that U1 is not accessible for this part of the season and that I must have it, or I'll be forced to cancel my first two safaris," he said. "The problem is, Johnny, TAWICO already

Dawn in the Selous finds Roy and Nyamaiya clearing the long grass to make camp.

has their money—I paid them fifteen thousand dollars in royalties on the first safari—so they have little incentive to cooperate. Further, all the vehicles and equipment are mine—so what do they care if things get bashed up trying to make it all the way to U1?"

Gerard and Farouk left early in the MAN to retrieve half the fuel drums from the stuck Leyland. The Bedford, once its cargo had been unloaded, had fulfilled its purpose and was sent back to Arusha. The rest of us spent the morning clearing and preparing the campsite. There was a lot to do before the clients arrived five days later.

I took turns swinging the scythe back and forth like a pendulum, imitating the fellows' steady motion and cutting only a narrow swath of grass at a time. I realized how long it would take at this rate. The monotonous swinging soon blistered my hands, but I kept at it as long as I could. When the men took over, they cleared the thick green grass right down to the dark-gray earth below. After an hour or so, a square patch about the size of a living room appeared. Not a single twig or blade of grass remained, and the ground was level enough to play billiards on. This amounted to only one tent site, but eventually the entire compound would be cleared to the same standards. Gerard required his camps to be kept clear so there would be no mistaking an idle snake for a fallen branch and stepping on it.

When erecting the dining tent, not a blade of grass remains underfoot.

After clearing several more sites, we erected the mess tent and got two of the three client tents pegged in place, each on its designated patch of earth. In the process, I got to know Roy better. He was a solidly built fellow with a firm jaw, and he seemed quite down-to-earth. As Gerard put it, "Roy is the most unassuming, easygoing chap you will ever meet . . . until you make him mad. Then watch out!" Though twenty years his junior, I didn't want to cross him.

Roy had grown up in the game-catching business and was in command of a wealth of animal facts and figures, as well as the adventurous tales acquired during such an enterprise.

"We caught animals for zoos and ranches all over the world," he said. "Whatever they wanted, we would catch: lions, hippos, rhinos, you name it. We would help when Hollywood came to make movies of the wild herds or when they needed animal 'extras' in the background of a given set. We helped on the John Wayne film *Hatari.* He was a super fellow, that man."

Roy's family had developed a tremendous respect for the Duke. My bet is the feelings were mutual. Roy showed me a photo of his younger self, kneeling between two male lions, a hand on each of their manes. He had another photo of a full-grown rhino he could scratch behind the ears. You don't get up-close and personal with dangerous animals like these without knowing everything about them, without being able to read their body language, their every gesture and utterance. Not if you plan to live a long life, anyway.

Mauled by a Lion

Roy's stories brought to mind an incident Gerard had told me about earlier. Roy had had a close scrape with a wounded lion the previous season, and when I brought up the subject, Roy lifted his shirt and showed me the scars. He had been lucky—incredibly lucky. In the end, his intimate knowledge of animal behavior had saved him from certain death. This is his story:

Gerard's client had wounded a lion one morning, so Gerard and Roy set out after it on foot. A couple of hundred yards into the bush they heard a familiar roar that presaged an attack. Sure enough, the lion came straight at them, mad as hell. Gerard dropped to one knee—to get on a level plane with the charging brute—and fired. The lion rolled head over heels, and Gerard fired again, then again, and the lion lay still for good. But Roy, who was still standing, criticized Gerard's technique.

"You young blokes are wasteful of ammunition. Too quick to shoot, you are. The proper way to do it is to wait until the lion gets close—ten or fifteen paces, then shoot him once in the head, and be done with it."

"No way, boy!" argued Gerard. "I will shoot him as many times as I can. If he moves again, I'll shoot him again!"

He then shook his finger at his elder partner. "You keep that kind of thinking up, my friend, and one day a lion is going to make hamburger out of you."

Well, as it happened, the very next day it was Roy's client who wounded a lion. It was late afternoon, so Roy decided not to return to camp for Gerard's assistance. He set out on foot with Kipper, leaving the client at the vehicle. Like clockwork, things went much as they had the day before. The men were a couple of hundred yards into the bush when an alarm sounded: First the men heard a loud *"Rrruuuugggghhh"* that broke the stillness, and then the lion flew straight at them—again, angry as hell.

Roy was shooting an open-sight, bolt-action .458, a cartridge the size of your ring finger. This caliber is used for elephant, rhino, and buffalo and is the perfect choice when following up wounded, hard-to-kill, dangerous game like lion. He had three shells in the magazine, one in the chamber. As he had instructed Gerard the day before, he stood his ground and waited until the charging lion was within ten paces, holding his aim as steady as his adrenaline-pumped nerves would allow. He

Erecting the shower hut.

was aiming between the menacing, hate-filled eyes when he pulled the trigger. The gun went *click!*

Misfire.

As fast as he could he slapped another round in the chamber. But an adult lion is blindingly fast, covering a hundred yards in about three seconds. Ten yards would be just a blink. The big cat was on him before he could even get the gun to his shoulder. All he could do was point and pull the trigger as more than four hundred pounds of fury slammed into him. The shot went wild, grazing the lion's side.

Amazingly, Roy remained on his feet. As he struggled with the cat, he tried to keep the gun between himself and the chomping teeth searching for an easy target. Roy somehow managed to force the end of the barrel down the roaring lion's throat. Knowing that lion do not like loud human voices and are sensitive on the nose, he began yelling at the beast at the top of his lungs. At the same time, he hammered it on the nose with his fist while he clutched the rifle in his other hand, the barrel still in the lion's mouth.

"You want to eat me? Well, come on you big bastard! Come on and eat me!" he raged at the lion.

And where was Kipper during this entire escapade? The brave tracker was right there, knife drawn. He stabbed the giant cat in the ribs as it mauled his boss's partner. Kipper surely aced the test of a true tracker that day, not only standing his ground but coming to his PH's aid in the heat of battle. (After a few years of such encounters, a PH and his tracker are much like war veterans, men who have fought side by side and covered each other's backs during the worst of enemy engagements. The bond that develops cannot be bought or borrowed. It is irreplaceable.)

Remarkably, the lion suddenly turned and went. It took Roy a second to get his bearings—his glasses had been knocked off in the struggle—but once he did, he raised the gun and fired his third shot up the lion's rear as it trotted away. Instantly, the lion whirled and charged. Roy loaded up his fourth and final shell and shot the lion in the head at what he figured was less than two paces. As fast as Kipper could hand him shells, Roy shot the lion again, and again, and again. If the lion so much as quivered, he pumped another bullet into it.

"By the time I was done with it," Roy admitted, "the lion had so many holes in it, it looked like a sieve."

So much for the plan of waiting for a close shot. . . .

Farouk showed me the marks of the lion's teeth on the barrel. (Roy wanted nothing more to do with that gun.) The marks reached almost to the rear sight. A full eighteen inches of barrel had been rammed down the lion's throat. The fact that Roy had managed to hold onto the rifle throughout the ordeal attested to no small feat of strength. His only wounds were a claw through the hand, cleaving the tissue between thumb and forefinger, and a couple of claw marks on his belly, where the lion had removed the front of his shorts but luckily not his innards. He wouldn't have escaped that fate had the lion's swipe been better aimed.

Bundala Shoots His Gun

We made a lot of progress the next day and got the third client tent up, the kitchen area made, the shower bag hung, and part of a toilet hole dug. We had to abandon the digging when we hit rock. Around 2 P.M. Gerard and Farouk returned with a dozen fuel drums, which we unloaded and situated under a shade tree. Big shade trees made the site quite comfortable in the midday sun. From camp you could see the smooth, glistening surface of the Kilombero River.

We went out one evening to do a little scouting, and Gerard shot a wildebeest for camp meat. When we got up to it in the Volvo, it was still alive, and he let Bundala out to give it the *coup de grâce*. I was anxious to see this for a couple of reasons. First, Bundala had bragged to us about how much he had learned at the three-week course he was required to take to become a professional hunter. (I didn't mention to him that in

The thatch dining hut in George Angelides's Rungwa camp.

colonial days the white PHs were required to apprentice for three years.) Upon graduation from the course, he informed us, they were required to shoot a buffalo. When he told me how they hunted buffalo, I could hardly keep from laughing. The three graduates lined up, rifles at the ready, and, on the count of three, all shot at the buffalo. He proceeded to tell me that the wounded buffalo had killed his instructor!

The second reason I was anxious to see Bundala shoot was the condition of the firearm he had been issued. It was a beat-up, taped-together .458 that looked like it had been dragged behind a pickup truck for a week. He was provided a total of one shell. One! That is what the government game department had issued him to defend himself—not to mention helpless clients—from dangerous game. It was a joke. This reflected poorly on the Tanzanian game department.

Here is how Bundala shot the wildebeest: He clenched the gun awkwardly to his shoulder, tensed his whole body, and grimaced fiercely—he was outwardly fearful of the upcoming blast. After a lengthy aiming process, he shot the poor thing in—of all places—the face. We were in trouble! How did he expect to handle a charging animal, where split seconds and accuracy mean the difference between life and death? Gerard just grinned and winked at me. Then, in typical native fashion, Bundala swung the rifle 360 degrees, pointing the barrel at us. It is a problem I have noticed with most Africans. They hold guns like kids hold play guns and think nothing of pointing the barrel in your direction. That is not a biased comment but fact. (That is exactly how Gerard got shot in the stomach the next year with a .458, the story I recounted in my first book.)

That night Roy and Gerard ate shish kebab colon, which they considered a delicacy. I had tried it two years before and found it distasteful, so I passed. Instead, I had cold, sliced wildebeest tongue for lunch. It wasn't great, but you have to eat.

The next morning Roy and I went to scout the area, driving some fifteen miles one way. The going was rough and consequently quite slow. One of our tasks was to clear a road that had not seen traffic since it had been cut ten or twelve years previously. The old road was so overgrown with tree limbs hanging down and grass sprouting up that it was invisible for vast stretches. To make matters worse, the grass grew ten feet tall in places and was still too green to burn. So many trees had grown up in the road that there wasn't time to cut them all. If they were small, we simply ran over them.

Despite the tall grass, we did manage to see some wildlife: impala, wildebeest, hartebeest, eland, and two hippos. Both hippos, up to their ears in small ponds, emerged and trundled off when we drove near. One of them was a very large bull.

The critter that is most plentiful in the Selous is the tsetse fly. A vicious, biting fly that lives to suck your blood, the tsetse inhabits the long grass, the same long grass that was too green to burn that day. Swarming

It may not look five-star, but bush chefs manage to turn out amazing cuisine.

out to greet us, the flying menaces were everywhere, thicker than I had ever seen. They harassed us unmercifully. Their sharp bite feels like a needle slowly being jabbed into you. Sometimes they hit a nerve, and you swear that a small nail has been hammered into your flesh. It makes you jump and cuss and slap at the evil, armor-coated bastard. You can't kill it, either, unless you roll it across your skin like a raw pinto bean and, with real effort, pinch its body between thumb and forefinger until you hear a crunch. Then another one bites. And another.

They are a curse to humans, but, ironically, they are a great protector of wildlife. The tsetse fly is the only reason parts of Africa remain unsettled and unclaimed by natives. The tsetse fly carries sleeping sickness to domestic herds of cattle and goats. The wild game, fortunately, has developed immunity to the disease. Human encroachment is the greatest threat to African wildlife, but that subject gets little press.

I wasn't sure what trophy animals we would find in that spot, but there were certainly some trophy tsetse flies. By day's end, I had over a hundred bumps covering my back, legs, and arms.

Clients Arrive

Chapter 10

The three American clients arrived by charter plane two days later, and, had our first impressions of them been a good indicator, the safari might have proved a wonderful experience. For reasons that will later become apparent as the next few chapters unfold, I will call these Americans Rick, Ralph, and Dillon. Rick was forty-one, Ralph was in his mid-fifties, and Dillon was my age. They were all from Houston.

This was their first safari to Africa, and they were suitably excited. Their eager questions made me realize how much I had learned on my three East African trips. Their enthusiasm was contagious, flooding me with wonderful memories of my first safari with PH John Fletcher in Kenya.

After the clients had sighted-in their rifles, we were off for an afternoon hunt. I went with Gerard and Rick, standing in the back of the Volvo and scouting for wildlife with Kipper. My chances of spotting game before he did were slim to none, but it sure was fun to try. Soon we came upon a poachers' camp. If we hadn't looked closely, we would have missed it.

Only a few piles of leaves for beds and the remains of a fire were there to give it away. The coals were still smoldering, so we knew it was fresh. Perhaps the poachers had heard or seen us from the bush; perhaps they were even watching us now as we kicked at the leaf piles, looking for food, weapons, wire snares, or signs of buried tusks. To foil their operation, we would destroy or take anything we found. Regardless, once they saw our tracks, they would clear out of the area.

It is surprising how much heat we hunters catch for pursuing our sport of hunting game. We are, in fact, the true conservationists of wild game. The true culprits—the poachers—are rarely mentioned in the media or in discussions of wildlife conservation, especially on the topic of endangered or threatened species. Getting the word out on sustained-yield conservation is definitely an uphill battle but one in which we hunters must be relentless. If we want our children to continue to have the opportunity to participate in our sport, we cannot give up. If we want wildlife to remain intact, we must fight the battle—and win.

The tsetse flies were out again in swarms that afternoon, to the point that I had bites on top of bites. In a bizarre reaction, the bites began to swell and ache like bee stings. By the time we got back to camp, I felt feverish and achy, as if I had the flu. My unprotected legs had suffered the greatest number of bites, and were so swollen that it was painful to bend them. This had me rather puzzled. I had shown no reaction to tsetse bites in the Rungwa Game Reserve two years previously. Of course, I hadn't experienced so many bites all at once. Was it an allergic reaction, or perhaps poison in the bites? Whatever it was, the reaction put me down for a couple of days.

PH Maulings

After dinner that night, Roy told us the bleak story of an uncle who had been mauled not once but twice by a lion. This uncle had the misfortune to be killed by an utterly avoidable tragedy that should never have happened in the first place. This is his story.

"The client had shot a lion, and my uncle went up to check that it was dead—he put the end of the barrel in its eye. There was no reaction. As he turned to walk back, however, the lion came to life and jumped on him. The client bravely shot the lion off my uncle's back. But the shot did not kill it, and the lion now pounced on the client. My uncle staggered up, grabbed his rifle, and finished the lion for good as it chewed on his poor client.

"The lion lay dead on top of the client, and my uncle had just grabbed hold of the tail to pull it off him when the government game scout, who had been instructed to wait at the car, arrived on the scene. He had heard the commotion and had come running with a loaded shotgun. When he saw the dead lion, he completely panicked and unloaded both barrels into my uncle's back, killing him on the spot."

Roy's father had also been badly chewed by a lion. Talk to enough PHs, and you will find that most carry scars of the trade. A wounded leopard, buffalo, or lion are responsible for most. Hunting big game in Africa is fairly similar to the odds you face when gambling in Vegas: The house always wins. In this case, nature is the house. Keep at it long enough, and something in Africa is going to tag you. Gerard carries the scars from a leopard.

Here is the surprising thing, though. Ask any PH, and he will tell you that wounded game is not what he fears most. The most dangerous game is a nervous client with a loaded gun behind you. Sadly, this would prove true for Roy the very next season:

It happened while he was leading the son of a client to a lion bait. While they were creeping along the base of a rocky hill on their approach, a couple of lions suddenly appeared on a boulder above them. Startled, the young man panicked and fired his gun. The .375 softnose bullet passed through the trunk of a tree, fragmented, then hit Roy in two places: the back of the knee and the ankle. The wounds required several surgeries and took their toll on his ability to get around.

******

Unfortunately, the Americans didn't seem to appreciate how lucky they were to have a PH like Roy share his amazing stories. You couldn't hear stories like this in America, stories of Africa's magnificent beasts told by a man whose profession would be short-lived if the restrictive trend of the East African government continued. I, on the other hand, could sit and listen to Roy for days. But these clients were more interested in swapping dirty jokes, making up sick pranks to play on each other, and getting drunk on Safari Lager beer.

Dillon piped up that he had almost died a few weeks before and that he nearly didn't make the safari. While stopped at a gas station back home, he had been robbed, stabbed with a knife, and left to die. He opened his shirt to show the fresh scar from his chest to his belly button, the result of exploratory surgery to determine the extent of his injuries.

"Two black fellows came up and asked me for money for gas," he said. "When I wasn't looking, one pulled a knife and stabbed me in the back, then twice in the shoulder. They took the twenty or so dollars I had in my wallet, and then left me lying on the ground with a ten-thousand-dollar Rolex still strapped to my wrist! Next thing I knew I woke up in the hospital."

It turned out this assault was what had ended a three-day drug binge for Dillon. He had abandoned his wife and young child to party, snort cocaine, and chase women. He admitted he was going to have to change the way he lived. His dark eyes were glassy even now, the sign of a person who has done too many drugs. I nodded and told him it wouldn't be easy. I told him that the most important thing would be to avoid his old friends who still took drugs; otherwise, it would be very difficult not to relapse in a weak moment. While he agreed that he'd need to give up his friends if he wanted to stop the drugs, I wondered how much conviction was behind those words.

As the safari progressed, I was to see just how distasteful these three people would turn out to be. Of course, it takes all kinds to make the world go around, but as I watched the drama unfold in the days ahead, I realized how important it is to have a reliable, level-headed PH in charge of a safari.

Visitors of All Kinds

Chapter 11

The nights were generally quiet, once you tuned out the background clamor and cadences, but we were reminded that Africa runs on double shifts. Nocturnal creatures visit camp regularly. One night a hippo left me a large deposit beside my tent, no doubt protesting the placement of my tent in its feeding grounds. I never heard the enormous animal in the act, an arm's length from the tent window. What woke me was the loud, nonstop crunching of grass. It sounded like fabric ripping. My unconscious mind equated that with the sound of claws ripping through tent canvas, so it definitely caught my attention.

Other animals made no sound to announce their treachery; they crept in and out under cover of darkness like jewel thieves in the night. A pack of hyenas stole the meat grinder from the kitchen area, leaving no trace of their crime other than footprints and a few missing strips of biltong. You could hardly fault them for being drawn to biltong; after all it is meat.

Made from strips of game meat that is salted and peppered, biltong is hung to dry on strings tied in a web-shaped fashion from one tree trunk to the next. When a large antelope, like an eland, is killed, the cook's area abounds with biltong in the making. The dark maroon strips are as abundant and eye-catching as the pennants in a used-car lot. It is one of my favorite snacks while out on a hunt, easy to carry in a pocket or daypack.

Later in the trip, hyenas would chew holes in the doors of the Volvo, which had been removed and stacked against a tree. There was no telling what they wanted with the doors. Maybe some human or animal scent had remained on them. Regardless, it made one stop to think what power lies behind those fearsome jaws.

Lions and leopards generally skirted camp, but it was not uncommon to find their pugmarks around the fringe. Snakes also made their presence known, as did various antelope in their night wanderings. Elephants were the best at steering clear of camp.

Another type of invader struck the sixth morning of that safari. Gerard and Farouk both came down with malaria. Chills, aches, fever, and noticeable trembling. Fansidar seemed to knock it out quickly, for both showed improvement within hours of ingesting the medicine.

Nyamaiya prepares a bait, using branches to fend off roving vultures.

There is no question I would have suffered the same fate were it not for the regular course of preventive medicine I had been taking. Of course, taking such medicine year-round is not an option for anyone living in the region on a full-time basis.

An official from TAWICO, named Leek, arrived that afternoon by plane. He was the game manager of the Selous. He turned out to be a typical bureaucrat in his demands and unrealistic expectations. He joined us in the mess tent for a Coke, exchanged pleasantries, and then promptly dropped the bomb. He wanted Gerard to help build a ferry to cross the Kilombero River. There was to be no pay or other compensation, and the game manager gave no thought to how Gerard would conduct his safaris if he had to divert most of his time to building a ferry. Many Africans, accustomed to the miraculous methods of the white man, have

The Masai Plains appear endless.

no hesitation in asking for favors or demanding time—pro bono, of course. It is as if there is nothing a wave of a magic wand can't do or fix.

The official was asking, but his tone was demanding. Gerard said there was no way he could accommodate the official and conduct his safaris at the same time. Then came payback. Later that day, three game scouts hiked into camp with a handwritten note informing Gerard of the quotas in this block for the season. It was laughable: one lion, one leopard, one elephant, and no zebra. This was the quota for the entire season! A quota that would be filled with a single client—not to mention the prohibited zebra we had already taken—and we would have fifteen clients hunting this season.

Gerard pulled out copies of letters he had sent to TAWICO in January with his requested quotas and showed them to me. TAWICO's return letter to him stated there would be no problem but that the specifics had not been worked out. Neither could they tell him the exact date the season would open, not even when he had contacted them two short weeks before the clients arrived! Fortunately, it turned out the season would open on 1 July, as it had the previous year, but the game department had made no formal decision or announcement until the very last minute. Now, Gerard had just been handed written confirmation of the quotas he had requested months earlier, and the decision was a disaster—the result of revenge by some petty bureaucrat.

With the letters in hand, Gerard climbed behind the wheel of the Volvo and sped off, anxious to meet with the game manager and set things right. There was no reason for them to treat him like this. But, try as he might, there was no reversing their decision. What do bureaucrats care? They don't have to worry about clients' nonrefundable airline tickets that must be purchased months in advance for safaris that were booked two, even three years, ahead of time. Now well into the season, when little could be done about it, Gerard received this ridiculous decision on the quota.

Most likely the Selous game manager had darker motives. Perhaps it had been a large payoff by a competing outfitter to secure that block. Or maybe he wanted the area free of hunters so he could poach elephant at will without risk of detection or interruption.

Regardless, TAWICO's reckless actions left Gerard with no choice but to move camp to another hunting block. He decided on Masailand, where he had several open blocks and better relations with the game manager of that concession. Having to move camp is costly in time, fuel, and effort. It is one more headache for the modern PH in Tanzania, compliments of a corrupt and thoughtless government.

The clients took it reasonably well when Gerard explained that they could hunt different animals in the new block, including oryx, Grant and Thomson gazelle, and lesser kudu. These animals were not available in the present block. Gerard, however, was afraid his upcoming safaris would be canceled once his clients were informed that they could no longer hunt in the Selous as planned.

Ugly Americans

We loaded the MAN with as much gear as it could carry, and Farouk departed the next morning, piloting the massive lorry for Masailand. Everyone else remained to complete the dismantling of the Selous camp. Gerard and Roy were extremely busy packing and directing and attending to all the last-minute details. I tried to help out, so for dinner I roasted zebra and impala shish kebab over the campfire for everyone. What with the news from TAWICO and the behavior of the clients, the day passed in uncertainty and worry.

Like me, Gerard and Roy were fed up with the three American clients, and the safari had barely begun. In fact, things were going downhill quickly. Rick and Dillon would get drunk at night and yell at the staff, "Bring me another blankety-blank beer, n-----." They thought it hilarious that they could say the N-word and the Africans would have no idea what it meant.

Likewise, they showed little respect for the game they hunted. They talked about how they were "gonna let the blood run!" How they "want to shoot the blank out of a baboon just to see it explode!" They said "a real trophy is the animal with the biggest" male appendage. And on and on.

I will tell you their next stunt, which has no place in a hunting book except to make you aware of the behavior of some of our countrymen. When Rick shot a large eland, he cut the phallus off and had it "presented" to Ralph for dinner. Rick and Dillon fell apart laughing, while the rest of us just stared at them in bemusement. Their behavior reminded me of three sheltered teens turned out of the house for the first time, though it was really Rick and Dillon who were the instigators. Ralph just got pulled into it.

I was stunned to see what an African PH must contend with from certain clients. These particular clients, who were from Houston, were an embarrassment to me as a fellow American and, even worse, as a fellow Texan. It was a case of the "ugly American" in Africa. I would compare it to the busy executive or professional who, under constant pressure at work, cuts loose and lets all the steam out at once, going

(From left) Kipper with Daniel, a government game scout.

from one extreme to the other. On safari, it's almost as if he considers himself in a fantasy world where whatever he says or does won't matter. When he leaves that place, he can leave all his foolishness behind without consequences. There is no one to report his shocking behavior, no one to remind him of it around the water cooler.

But this was not just a case of letting off steam. There was something different about the behavior of these three—something immature, but also morbid. I couldn't put my finger on it, but Roy shed some light.

"You know, Johnny, there are two types of people who come to Africa. You have your hunters, and you have your killers. These fellows are killers."

We left early the next morning for Masailand, packed to the hilt in the Volvo and the Land Cruiser, people and gear on top of people and gear. It was a long trip, some four hundred and fifty miles from the Selous, every mile of it on dirt roads. For food we ate peanuts, bananas, and sugar cane purchased from local vendors in dusty thatched stands that lined the streets of small villages along the way. Lesaro—a former tent boy who was now a tracker in training, with lazy eyes that belied his hard work ethic—and Kipper, his mentor, showed me how to peel and cut stalks of sugar cane and place them in my mouth to chew and suck. It's no Hershey bar—eating one is more like chewing on a chunk of sweetened balsa wood—but, as the only source of sugar, it is very popular.

We drove until late afternoon, at which point we met the MAN at the designated campsite. We had limited time to search for a new site, so Gerard opted to use an area that PH Gary Hoopes had used the year before. It was near the town of Ndedo. We quickly erected two tents for the clients. The rest of us slept on cots with the sky above us.

Masailand

Chapter 12

The climate in Masailand was much cooler than in the Selous because of the higher altitude. Accustomed to the steamy Selous, I spent most of the next day shivering.

Again, we set to work building a campsite. While we were erecting the last tents and cleaning up the grounds, one of the younger natives sliced his finger deeply with a knife. The wound required stitches, a job that Roy would have performed in the remote Selous, but here it was easier to whisk the fellow to the local "dispensary," which handled minor first-aid problems.

The next day saw the completion of most of the camp, but the latrine was not yet finished. Building a latrine requires more involved construction. First, the men dig a pit some five feet deep. Next, they crisscross stout poles and lash them together atop the pit, forming the structure on which to mount the toilet. The toilet is a regular toilet seat bolted to the top half of an empty fuel drum with a hole cut in it to accommodate the dimensions of the seat. The men fashion a toilet-paper holder from two Y-shaped sticks jammed into the ground that support a wooden spool between them. The men erect poles and tie grass thatch in place to form the four walls of the small hut. Sealing the deal, they pour a square slab of concrete around the base of the drum to complete the latrine's floor. An overhead wire powers a light bulb hung from the latrine's thatched ceiling. This makes a flashlight unnecessary while the generator is running, which is usually until 10 P.M. Done properly and with the right chemicals, never does a foul odor emanate from the pit below.

That does not, however, preclude other problems with the latrine. Like critters.

Gerard told me the bizarre story of his father, Frank Miller, and a late-night trip to the john. He had just settled on the pot when a snake down in the hole bit him on the end of his you-know-what! Because it was too dark to see, he had absolutely no idea what kind of snake it was. Gerard's mother "rushed" her husband to the doctor. I say rushed because they were deep in the bush and many hours from the nearest town. When they finally got there, the doctor looked him over

A Masai warrior sporting traditional red-ocher braids.

summarily, and then said, rather matter-of-factly, "Well, it must not have been poisonous."

"How do you know?"

"Well, you wouldn't have made it this far if it was," he replied.

****** ******

In Masailand the dreadful situation with the three rowdy American clients went from bad to worse. Any chance of camaraderie was past—the PHs were finished with their drunken antics. Gerard and Roy were cordial in their presence but avoided them as much as possible, finding work in the kitchen, the garage, or the game shed. As if their behavior wasn't bad enough, both Ralph's and Dillon's shooting went to hell.

I went out with Roy and Ralph the following day to witness a massacre of sorts. Ralph made extremely poor kills on a zebra and oryx. In two attempted shots at a broadside target, he hit the oryx in one back leg and then the other. He then shot a zebra in the back leg as well. When such poor shooting occurs, the first thought is always to blame the gun—the sights must be off. But the answer soon came when Ralph went to finish off the zebra. Forgetting the safety was on, he flinched as if the gun were going to spring to life in his hands.

A flinching problem is hard to cure. The difficulty is that the flincher doesn't realize he is doing it. Tell him, and he will deny it. Only when the shooter recognizes the fault and applies immense concentration can he correct it. I have no statistics to back this up, but, in my experience, flinching seems to be more common among bird hunters. The reason for this, I believe, is that a shotgun does not require the same precision of aim as a rifle to connect with game. Perhaps it is more accurate to state that a shotgun, with its sprawling barrage of pellets, can better conceal an underlying flinch. What would count as a flinch in rifle hunting is often chalked up as a "miss" in bird hunting. You don't notice shot placement on a flying bird as you do an animal taken with a gun. A wildebeest you aimed at on the shoulder but hit in the rump stands out. Accustomed to blasting away in the general direction of doves and quail, bird hunters with the affliction fail miserably when it comes time to shoot a rifle at big game.

The African PH Learns from the American Novice

The next day we hung two baits, a practice Bundala had never heard of. He thought hunters just drive around until they spot a lion or a leopard. That might work, except the big cats of Africa are masters

Note the beautiful markings of the vulturine guinea fowl.

Black mamba!

at camouflage, and, in areas where they are hunted, you won't see them in the light of day except on rare occasions. It could work for lion in Rungwa or the Selous, where the lion have little contact with man, but never in Masailand. The Masai warriors are fierce cat killers and have no hesitation in hunting down a lion with spears. Especially a lion that makes the mistake of killing one of their bony cattle.

Bundala also didn't realize that clients seek trophy animals. Apparently, they skipped that little-known fact during his three-week professional hunter class. He thought any male would do.

"A bahffalo is a bahffalo," he said, a scowl of confusion creasing his dark forehead.

Bundala was raised in the confines of the city of Arusha. It was hard to believe he had spent twenty-four years in the heart of game-rich Africa, yet he had never seen an animal outside the zoo! Except, of course, for the buffalo on his infamous hunt after graduation. As we drove, he would point to animals he had never seen (not even in his college textbooks) and ask me their names.

"Gray duiker, oryx, gerenuk," I would tell him.

He shook his head in fascination and said, *"Ahh, ahh, ahh."* Then he laughed and shook his head again.

It was all a wonder to him. Slowly, he was descending from the pedestal he had arrived on. He was beginning to realize how little he knew about hunting, wildlife, or these odd white clients from across the sea. He now saw the mystical white PH as a guide who seemed to be at one with wildlife, reading the animals' every move like a cowboy reads his cattle or an Indian reads the tracks of a deer.

Bundala told me he could not drive a car. He did not know how. And he is the PH of record? Later, he tried to reach Gerard by yelling repeatedly into the handheld mike of the radio, unaware that one must first press the transmit button. I actually felt sorry for the clueless fellow. I gave him credit, though, for opening up to me. I figured it must be embarrassing to know so little about that which is in your charge. He was literally lost in this world of the professional hunter. It was ironic, but in a way I was his instructor. He asked me question after question, then continued to shake his head to the answers, uttering, *"Ahh, ahh, ahh."* Roy was too busy doing his job to be bothered with such greenhorn conversations. It was while Bundala and I waited for the hunters stalking game in the bush that we entered our question-and-answer sessions. He was eager to learn. I gave him that.

More Hunts in Masailand

The following afternoon we came upon an interesting construction near camp: a Masai water well that was hundreds of years old, according to Roy. We found it surrounded by several warriors and their herds of cattle, which were taking turns drinking. The entrance to the well had been gradually excavated over time into a sloping ramp that allowed the cattle to descend forty feet below the surface to a water trough carved in the stone wall at the bottom. The water was collected from a deep, dark crack in the rock beside the trough. Lean herdsmen with buckets disappeared into the narrow crack and descended a handmade ladder to the aquifer below. There, they handed up bucketfuls of cool water to be poured into the stone trough for their thirsty herds.

It was a fascinating discovery and the only example of a lasting architectural structure of their culture that I had ever witnessed. The Masai are a people who leave nothing behind. Their mud wattle huts and thornbush *boma*s disappear in a matter of years when abandoned. As far as I know, the Masai leave behind no written word of their history or culture, no pictures or hieroglyphs, nothing to remind future civilizations of their existence.

******

Back at camp that night, Gerard relayed in private an even worse tale of flinching. Aiming at a wildebeest, Dillon had hit a zebra that was unfortunate enough to be standing several yards to the side of it. The next day Dillon wounded a buffalo, which promptly disappeared into thick vegetation. Based on his poor shooting, I was surprised Gerard had let him attempt a shot on an animal that thrives on making hamburger out of poor shooters.

In any event, Gerard and Roy went in after it alone. Gerard soon found the bull waiting nearby ready to ambush the pair, and he placed a Weatherby .460 solid above the nose—to positively no effect. The stalwart bull vanished, and the chase continued in the thick bush.

From time to time the bull would hole up to watch its back trail, obviously in hopes of bushwhacking its pursuers. But each time the bull did this, Gerard and Roy, playing it wisely, were able to keep the upper hand. Every time Gerard caught sight of it, he poured lead into the black fiend. The stubborn beast continued to absorb slugs like a windshield absorbs flying insects. In the end, it took seven well-placed bullets to put the bull down for good. Seven bullets from a .460 Weatherby Magnum, the most powerful production cartridge on earth. There is a good reason why so many PHs consider the Cape buffalo the most dangerous of Africa's dangerous big game.

******

While driving that day, a black mamba some nine feet long crossed the road ahead of us. By the time we reached it, however, it had disappeared. We quickly decided to drive on. There are wiser things to do than to search for a mamba hidden in the bush.

A few days later, I went with Nyamaiya, Roy's head tracker, to build a blind at a leopard bait that had been hit a quarter-mile from camp. The four walls of a blind are built somewhat like the thatch walls of the latrine: whittled poles are set in the ground, with thatch tied to smaller cross-poles for complete concealment. The major difference is that one leaves the exterior of the blind a little ragged, sticking leafy branches here and there or piling brush against the walls to provide a more natural

Centuries of use have carved deep into this Masai water well. Bundala, Roy, Nyamaiya.

look. That evening Ralph and Roy had a long wait in the blind, only to discover that the leopard was a large female.

The following day Ralph shot a really nice impala, but he placed the shot too high in the shoulder. The bullet knocked the ram down, but the animal was simply stunned for a moment before it leapt up and dashed off at top speed. There was very little blood to follow, and what little there was ran out quickly, leaving only faint hoof marks on the hard earth to go by. But that did not slow a tracker like Nyamaiya. We tracked the ram at a good pace, covering a lot of country, but we never found it. Because it was not a fatal shot, the impala was still running an hour later.

"When an animal is hit high in the shoulder like that," Roy explained, "the bullet misses the vitals. The wound annoys and hurts, so the animal keeps running. I've seen them survive these shots. Find them months or years later with a bullet scar on each side."

That same morning we built another leopard blind near a large patch of sansevieria, a spiky desert plant that resembles a yucca, but with points so sharp and stout that it commands the attention of even the most stubborn rhino. The wicked plants gave Roy concern because the second thing you look for when placing a leopard bait is the type of cover the leopard will hide in if wounded.

A wounded leopard, unquestionably, is the most dangerous animal in Africa to follow up—if you consider your odds of getting tagged. The leopard may not be as likely to kill you as one of the other members of the Big Five, but because of its stealth and camouflage, it is the most likely to reach you with claw and fang and inflict damage, often before you even know it is happening. Following a wounded leopard in sansevieria would be tricky indeed, but in the end Roy decided the place offered the best chance at getting a leopard to feed, which is the first thing you look for when placing a leopard bait.

And he was absolutely right! That day at 4:20 P.M.—quite early for a leopard to put in an appearance—a large male scrambled up the tree, snatched one mouthful from the bait, and promptly climbed to the very top of the tree. Then, for no apparent reason, it suddenly spooked and disappeared, melting down the side of the tree like hot wax poured from a candle. Twenty minutes later, the wary leopard suddenly returned and climbed the tree a second time. When the leopard offered the right presentation, Ralph plugged it on the shoulder, and an amazingly good shot it was. The seven-foot cat dropped dead at the base of the tree, no follow-up shot required, which brought a sigh of relief from everyone in the hunting party. That particular hunt was a true success.

Farouk returned that evening from the Selous with nine drums of fuel and the other supplies we had left. The round trip had taken him an

A client's leopard in Masailand. (From left) Tracker Nyamaiya, PH Roy Carr-Hartley, and the author.

entire week. Gerard, of course, had to give Farouk grief on the length of his expedition.

"By Gahrd, Twangas," he said, calling him by his Swahili nickname. "Whar the hayl have you been? Whahrt you been dooing, mahn?"'

Farouk shook his head, smiling out of the corner of his mouth. "It's thee queeksand," he said. "We are hahving hahrd time, Bwahrna. We wude drive and get stuhck, then dig the lohrry out, then drive fifty yahrds and get stuhck again!"

"You hahving hahrd time, no?"

Gerard wouldn't let his apprentice get a word in. He was feeling better, finally over the malaria that had sapped his energy for days. Gerard grabbed the short Pakistani around the head and wrestled him about. It was good to have Farouk back. He was a jovial fellow, always ready to make a joke or a sly comment, but it was his accent and mannerisms that made his speech priceless. He was one of those fellows who could tell you a story about his walk down the street and it would crack you up—it was just the way he told it. He liked to talk, and I enjoyed hearing his stories, so I knew we would get on well. It appeared we would soon be spending a lot more time together. Gerard planned to use us to scout for elephants for the next clients.

A funny thing happened the next day. Ralph and Roy were pursuing a lesser kudu into the brush when they came upon Gerard and Dillon tracking the same animal. It turned out Dillon had shot at it earlier and missed. What a coincidence to run into each other in such a large area! It reminded me of Reggie Destro's story of the trophy elephant shot out from under them by another hunting party. Ralph later nicked a lesser kudu on a "gimme" shot ninety short yards away.

The three clients left for Arusha three days later, and it was a guarantee they wouldn't be missed by anyone.

******

If you step back to consider the grand scheme of things, I reckon snakes must have their place in nature; otherwise, why would they be here? Surely they must perform some positive and necessary function. Not being fully convinced of their merit however, we shot puff adders, black mambas, and spitting cobras whenever we had the chance. The puff adder is a sluggish, slow-moving snake that resembles a short, stout rattlesnake without the rattle. Combine the expert camouflage of its reticulated markings and its reluctance to move out of your way, and you have two traits that make it particularly dangerous on a continent where people travel mostly on foot. It should come as no surprise that the puff adder is responsible for killing more Africans than any other snake.

While I was in Kenya, PH Gary Hoopes had shared a couple of hair-raising snake stories about puff adders, including the time he stepped on one. He was searching a rocky hill for a wounded klipspringer, his eyes focused on the terrain ahead, when he stepped down from a rock and felt the earth squish beneath his foot. He shot up in the air as quickly as he could, just missing the potentially fatal strike that followed.

Another time, while sharing a tent with two fellow professional hunters, Gary kept hearing strange noises in the tent at night. When he asked his tent mates about it in the morning, they just laughed and said he was buggy. Three days later, Gary was taking a nap. He had rolled up his shirt for a pillow and placed it between the head of the cot and the canvas wall of the tent. When he awoke, he plucked up his shirt, only to find himself face to face with an angry puff adder ready to strike. It turned out the snake had been in the tent with them the whole while! Apparently the noise he'd heard at night was the snake crawling around the floor, looking for a way out.

The moral of that story is: Always keep your tent zipped, even when stepping out for something as quick as a shave or the brushing of teeth.

American Hunters Vindicated

Gerard had returned to Arusha not only to drop off the former clients, but to conduct a backlog of business and collect our next clients. He returned late that night with John Toomey and his wife, who were from Houston. These wonderful folks could not have proved more unlike the three hooligans who had just departed. They were polite, well mannered, glad to be in Africa, and ready to soak it all in.

Our next problems came from elsewhere. Gerard had the first serious trouble that season with his staff, and it came from someone who should have known better. While on an errand for Gerard, Kipper stopped at a local bar and proceeded to get liberally plastered. His local buddies then followed him out to the Volvo, and Kipper put on a show for them. He raced the vehicle like a bat out of hell and spun doughnuts around huts and other obstacles, burning out the clutch in the process. When he got back to camp, Gerard was steaming, to say the least, and fired old Kipper on the spot. Kipper had worked for him forever, but Gerard claimed he would send him back to town upon his next return—he was through with him. I figured we would have to wait for Gerard to cool off to see if he'd really carry through with the threat. In the meantime, everyone in camp was glum over the firing.

While Gerard was in town, a TAWICO official informed him that the game department was contemplating an immediate sixty-leopard limit for the country. If that limit were enacted, leopard hunting would be closed for the remainder of the season. How was that for a last-minute wrench thrown into the system? It brought to mind the changing quotas in the Selous, and this outsider had a whole lot of questions. Why can't these decisions be made before the season opens? Do the government bureaucrats making these decisions care nothing for the animal populations they are paid to manage? Do the officials simply like throwing their weight around? Are they really that terribly shortsighted, disorganized, and mismanaged? Or is it flat-out extortion—a scheme to produce additional bribes? Perhaps it is a mixture of each.

Regardless, it is evidence of an uneducated culture that does not think beyond the very short term. One wonders whether eventually they will make it so difficult for a professional hunter to operate a safari, and anger enough clients in the process, that the hunting industry will collapse, as it did in 1973 when Tanzania prohibited white PHs. Their actions would be less surprising were the country not desperate for foreign exchange. The safari business is one of the few avenues that brings in foreign currency.

******

Here are some notes from my journal as to my progress on this six-month odyssey:

It is a good thing I came to Africa with a few extra pounds, as I am getting quite skinny.

I am pleased to say that I've picked up a good bit of Swahili. I now understand much of the conversation between Gerard and the natives, and the men talk freely to me. They call me Bwana John. I don't know enough to discuss politics or religion (probably a good thing), but I know what animals they are talking about and what the plan is to hunt them and which way is camp—the important things, anyway. I've picked up quite a bit while riding in the back of the truck in their company. It is a phonetic language that is quite pleasant to the ear, unlike the harsh-sounding languages of Russian or German or Chinese. I now say jambo and habari and asante more readily than their English counterparts, hello, how are you, and thank you.

As I write this, a vervet monkey is scampering from tree to tree overhead, trying to impress me with his acrobatics, which he does. There are no hippos here, so you miss the snorts and grunts they make the whole night long in the Selous. There are fewer lion grunts and hyena whoops as well, a factor of our being that much closer to civilization

******

The Toomeys had quite a productive couple of days, collecting an oryx, a Grant gazelle, an impala, a gerenuk, and an eland.

The boys killed a small puff adder in camp one night. It was only two and one-half feet long but was still plenty of snake to send you on a one-way ticket to the next world.

When Gerard and I were alone, I mentioned to him Bundala's story of how the buffalo had killed his instructor.

Gerard broke into a laugh and shook his head.

"That's what he told you? That the buffalo killed his instructor?"

"Yeah."

"Ha! The buffalo didn't kill his instructor—the buffalo gored the instructor in the leg. What killed his instructor was a bullet through the chest."

"What!"

"Yes. I'm completely serious. The buffalo gored the instructor in the leg and went running off with him on top of his horns. The students tried to shoot the buffalo but hit the poor instructor instead. I knew that fellow—he was not a bad guy."

Gerard shook his head once more.

"Buffalo killed his instructor! That's a laugh."

Elephant Scouts

Chapter 13

There was a sequence of very early mornings for Farouk and me in our new role as chief elephant scouts. One morning we left in the early dark to check water holes for sign of elephant near the towns of Kibaya and Meridio. An earthen dam called Djoro provided a fair-size bull track. A water hole named Fundimagai, however, offered even better sign: four good bull tracks only an hour or so old, based on the steaming warmth of their dung.

The Kibaya dam was probably the largest in the area, creating a body of water that could rightly be called a lake. Around the perimeter were several respectable bull tracks, and from the top of a hill we radioed this information to Gerard in camp. An interesting sight was the solitary bull hippo that resided permanently in this lake. The old fellow was something of a legend. Apparently, he had lived here alone for years, miles from the nearest hippo. No one knew for sure how the famous hippo came to dwell here, but everyone had his own story.

Gerard speculated that the hippo migrated from Lake Manyara during a particularly rainy season and got stranded when things dried up. Farouk added to the mystique by claiming that the hippo was shot three years before by a thoughtless game scout. The hippo became deathly ill but eventually survived and thrived. And thrive he had—this water pig was enormous! The reason he had reached such abnormal proportions—or so the story went—was that he had had no females to work off his energy.

A local game scout later took us to a dam several miles from Kibaya. It was deeper in the bush than the other dams, and there we found numerous bull tracks. This was good news. There was no doubt now that we were going to find Mr. Toomey a bull elephant. It was simply a matter of time.

The most productive time to scout for elephant sign at water is before sunrise. Once the sun appears, another consumer of the precious resource arrives in force: local villagers. The first to arrive are women, who fill hefty clay urns and transport them home balanced on their heads. The muddy water, the color and opacity of chocolate milk, is used for their families' daily needs: drinking, cleaning, and washing. It is not water that you or I would choose to drink. It is the same water the wildlife,

Farouk and Lesaro stop for a quick bite while scouting for game.

cattle, and goats drink—and the same water in which animals relieve themselves. I thought drinking from the dam would be worse than drinking out of a ranch water trough, which is bad enough. I had shoveled the smelly black muck out of enough water troughs in summer jobs on the Callaghan ranch to know that I would rather not drink after livestock. The fact is, the dam water is the only water available to these folks. In the villages there are no water faucets, no plumbing, no running water of any kind. The locals have no choice and know no better.

In midmorning the men and boys would arrive with herds of swarming cattle and goats that quickly erased any elephant sign from the night before. On the bright side, they also left a clean slate for the collection of night tracks and sign the following morning.

The next day Farouk and I left in the early dark in the Volvo, ahead of Gerard and our clients in the Toyota. With the top and windshield removed, it was a cold ride to the T-junction, the turning-off point from the Arusha road to Kibaya. With my jacket zipped to the chin, I huddled against the blasting, frigid wind, but it did little good, and by the time we reached the T-junction a long hour later, I was shivering like a jackhammer and wondering if I was in Africa or in Alaska. We waited there in the dark for Gerard to catch us, neither of us looking forward to facing the cold winds again on the remainder of the trip.

Soon after the first gray light of day appeared, we came upon Gerard's empty Toyota on the side of the road. After a quick look around, we saw Gerard and the Toomeys stalking four greater kudu cows in the hills on foot. Apparently, there were two nice bulls that Farouk and I could not see from our vantage point, but it was still exciting to watch their stalk in our binoculars. True to kudu form, the bulls outfoxed the hunters and disappeared in the brushy hillside. Once the hunters returned, we continued our journey toward the Meridio dam, where I received a good lesson in trophy judging along the way. On the drive toward Meridio, Gerard took the lead and instructed us to follow a few minutes behind in case any jumbo crossed his back trail.

As we approached a big plain, I spotted the giant spread of horns of a greater kudu bull at the edge of the brush. The bull was staring at us but was far enough away not to be spooked. It was a magnificent sight. We radioed Gerard, who had already turned off toward the dam, and he responded, "On the way."

The bull continued to stroll along the brushy edge, and we waited, hoping it would stay put. In the distance, we finally saw the dust storm from the Toyota, which was coming toward us on the dirt road. When it neared, the hunters pulled over and climbed out. We watched them from afar as they stalked and eventually shot the wide-horned bull.

Back at the car, John Toomey was pleased to get the trophy and handed me a roll of Life Savers. A kind of tip, I guess. But I could see that Gerard was not entirely happy. Later, he informed me that the bull was still immature and should not have been taken, as evidenced by the second curve of the horns, which were splayed out. A kudu bull is mature, he explained, when the tips on the second curve have turned back in. He never got a good look at the bull while stalking it and had decided to rely on my assessment.

"But that is how you learn, kid," he said, flashing a grin full of white teeth.

And I resolved to be more careful when making trophy recommendations in the future.

Later that day, Farouk and I collected a local game scout, and together we climbed a tall hill to look for elephant. (The government employs game scouts to apprehend poachers—when the game scouts aren't poaching themselves.) The top of the hill provided a bird's-eye view and was a handy way to take in a lot of country and to learn its features quickly. We took up a position on a couple of boulders and stared out over the vast scrubland, hoping to glimpse a promising tusker gliding beneath the sparse canopy of acacias. We talked and drank the cans of passion-fruit juice we'd brought along for the hot, dry afternoon. Bored

The morning ritual: native women collecting water.

with sitting and waiting and watching, Farouk made a paper airplane out of a can wrapper and launched it off the steep face. It sailed far out, hovering on the updraft for a surprisingly long while before cruising to a smooth landing at the bottom of the hill.

Back at camp, we toasted Mr. Toomey's success. He had gotten a highly prized lesser kudu in the afternoon, and in the evening he had shot a beautiful leopard that measured nearly seven and a half feet.

Farouk and I were up and off in the wee hours for another freezing drive, but this time I was better prepared, bundled in layers from head to toe. At first light we made our rounds of all the water holes. We also went to a new dam, Upper Meridio, which a game scout from the town of the same name had shown us.

As we traveled between water holes, Farouk kept gazing at the endless plowed fields on either side of the road, shaking his head. This whole area had been thick forest, according to him. Few people lived in Meridio, and there were no women at the water holes in the mornings.

The natives' practice in clearing an area to farm is distressing. Every tree is cut down, leaving neither shade nor habitat for birds and wildlife. No hedgerows are left, no brush mottes. Nothing. Gerard claims that removing all the trees that way changes the climate, that the trees draw the rain, and when the trees are gone, the rain stops and the soil dries up. Areas in East Africa that were once lush and green are now scorched and brown, useless to man or beast.

Once again the plow and encroachment take the lead as the greatest threat to wildlife, responsible for eliminating more animal populations than the pull of the trigger ever would. Conservation-style hunting has never posed a threat to wildlife populations as a whole. In fact, just the opposite—it ensures wildlife's continued existence. Why is it that we hunters are the only people who seem to understand this?

Farouk pointed out of the window at the plowed land, at what once had been thick forest. "I sharht a one hoondred-twenty pouhnder right heer twehlve years ago," he said, proudly.

I had to whistle. That was quite an elephant!

In the heat of the afternoon, we came across a donkey sprawled on the ground, panting, its tongue flopped in the dirt. We guessed it was sick or had collapsed from heat exhaustion. The surprising thing was that no one had bothered to rectify the situation by moving it out of the sun, nursing it back to health, or finishing it off, if that was called for. The stream of natives trekking to and from the dam passed the stricken animal as you would pass a log lying in your path, often stepping over it and paying it no mind. At home, a sick animal would attract a crowd of hundreds. But in Africa, where life is cheap, where death is a factor day in and day out, where most kids don't survive to count their age in double digits, a sick donkey on the road brought only a fleeting glance from passersby. This was a good example of the fatalistic attitude maintained by most natives. If the donkey is meant to die, it will die. Karma.

"It seems cruel to leave it, but there is nothing we can do," Farouk explained.

Any attempt to revive the donkey that failed might be construed as murder, and the owner could claim extravagant damages. So the donkey was left to its own devices. It would recuperate and stagger home, or the lions and hyenas would find it that night and finish it off.

The next day was more of the same. After a deathly cold ride in the open Volvo, Farouk and I checked the Upper Meridio for elephant spoor, and there we found a promising track. Gerard and Mr. Toomey arrived later in the Toyota, and they followed the spoor into late afternoon but to no avail. This is the essence of elephant hunting. Searching long and hard for good, fresh tracks, following them through thick and thin, trying to manage your scent against a fickle wind, keeping your approach soundless on a twig-littered ground, and keeping your focus on a stalk measured in hours and miles. There are definitely hunters who get lucky, but most of the time you have to earn a good bull elephant.

That afternoon Farouk and I again went to the tall hill just west of the T-junction to scout the sprawling country below. The evening before, we had made it only halfway up the hill, running out of daylight in the process. This time we made an early start and climbed to the absolute peak of the steep hill, where we were treated to a beautiful sight: fifteen greater kudu feeding on the lower grasslands. The slanting sun gleamed off their sleek striped coats as the herd grazed casually along, at peace and unaware of our presence. One bull sported a worthy set of dark horns that corkscrewed up into the air, bobbing gently as it strolled along with its herd. It was a Kodak moment. Farther out, we could see the glistening water of some of the dams we regularly checked for tracks, but, search as we might, we saw no sign of elephant below.

While climbing the hill, Farouk and I received quite a fright. Having noted an uncommon amount of buffalo dung, we naturally had been on the lookout for these dangerous animals. You don't normally think of a steep hill as buffalo habitat, but the massive herbivores have no hesitation in climbing difficult terrain to get at good grass. Just as we passed a large patch of brush, there was an explosion of immense proportions. Broken limbs, branches, and leaves went flying in every direction, and sound thundered up from the destruction as if the mountain itself were erupting right in front of us. In the afternoon stillness, it literally sounded like a bomb going off, and Farouk and I jumped as if we were at Pearl Harbor and under attack.

Neither of us had a gun in hand, so my immediate thought was to look for a suitable tree to climb. I doubt I would have made it because the explosion came from such close quarters. As it turned out, we didn't have to climb a tree. The culprit was a greater kudu bull—perfectly harmless in this case, except for the fact that it nearly startled us to death.

Toward dark, from our perch on the hill, we saw Gerard's vehicle returning from Djoro and heading for camp. Farouk and I then descended the brushy hill to the Volvo, where Lesaro had remained to protect it against vandalism or theft by locals. Gerard had called on the radio, Lesaro said, and was worried about us because we had been gone so long. Truth be told, we actually had taken a long nap on the warm ground of the hill. I didn't feel bad about it, though. Waking at three in the morning, especially several days in a row, can make a fellow downright narcoleptic.

We were up early again and reached Upper Meridio at dawn, slightly delayed en route by a flat tire. This was by far the coldest drive yet. Though I was wearing Gore-Tex rain gear over my jacket and pants, the icy fingers of the rushing wind managed to find a way in and chill me to the bone. Once we arrived, however, the suffering seemed well worth it. We found two sizable bull tracks leading off from the shore of the dam. Gerard and Mr. Toomey arrived half an hour later to begin the long trek into the brush.

After several days of concerted effort, our elephant scouting and hunting finally met with success. It took more than six hours of difficult hiking and tracking in the thick stuff, but in the end Mr. Toomey got his bull—a fifty-pounder, which was not bad in those days.

While they were hunting, Farouk and I went to Kibaya to return a borrowed tool and to purchase some vegetables and other goods at a farmers' market. Farouk let me drive home from the T-junction. Steering and shifting gears from the right side of the vehicle was rather discombobulating and took constant concentration. We got to camp around noon, just in time for a well-deserved nap.

There was some bad news at camp. A black mamba had killed a Masai boy at the Masai water well I mentioned earlier. While the boy was drinking water from the trough at the bottom, the wicked serpent dropped on him from above. The snake bit him on the face and ear, and apparently death came quickly.

The African PHs' Favorite Big Game To Hunt

One of the great things about this trip was getting to meet so many African professional hunters in their element. These are folks who spend six months or more a year hunting full time. They are the best of the best, these professional hunters of East Africa. No other hunters on earth can match their hunting prowess, their knowledge of game, their guiding skill—at least no one from the civilized world. Throw in the remaining plethora of skills required of an African PH, and you have an impressive individual, indeed.

Of the twenty or so professional hunters I met on this trip, I put to each the same question: "What is your favorite animal to hunt?" Their answers were both surprising and nearly unanimous. In truth, I had expected lion or buffalo, my personal favorites.

"Elephant" is what they said.

Elephant?

Had I not spent a week hunting elephants in 1982, I would have been even more surprised. Before that experience, elephant hunting had sounded no more exciting than hunting a farmer's milk cow grazing in a field. What I had discovered, however, was that elephants hunted in the wild are nothing like the placid elephants that inhabit a game park. You can drive right up to game-park elephants and take their picture as they stuff grass and bark into their slack mouths and flap their ears with the intensity of a sloth on sleeping pills. But where they are hunted—especially where they are poached—elephants are a different animal. They are clever, stealthy, and nocturnal.

They are also dangerous.

A life-size replica of Kenya's Ahmed, famous for its symmetrical tusks.

If an elephant herd detects you from afar, its first defense is to run away. The big animals will dash off to the next country, and you will have a long walk back to camp. Everyone goes home in one piece. No big deal.

If, however, you manage to work your way in close before the herd discovers you, their strategy turns immediately to offense, and they crash through the brush, trying to trample and crush you. It is not dissimilar to the way you chase and stomp a cockroach scuttling across the floor of your garage. If none succeeds in trampling you, however, the lead female—the matriarch—will remain to locate you by scent with the end of her uplifted trunk, sweeping the air like a metal detector. Except her trunk is a hundred times more powerful. Her heart's desire, quite simply, is to catch you and kill you, beat you to a pulp against the hard ground or the nearest tree, or stomp you with one foot while she pulls you in two with her trunk.

Dramatic as that sounds, it is positively factual. In certain areas, the poor beasts have been so badly hammered by poachers that they detest man. Our smell alone can send them into a blind, killing rage. They absolutely despise us. We are evil to them. We are the devil, pestilence, and famine, all rolled into one.

That's what makes elephant hunting so exciting. But this answer inevitably leads to the next question. Why hunt them? Why pressure an animal that has been harassed to kingdom come by poachers and shot by the hundreds of thousands across the continent, where every animal with a tusk is a target—male, female, and juvenile? In a nutshell, the PH's sentiment is that the elephant is fighting a losing battle. In time, the poachers will win. Since every elephant will be poached anyway, they figure we hunters might as well be the ones to benefit.

But isn't legal hunting supposed to protect the game herds? Yes, it is. The problem in East Africa is corruption. The game departments are bribed to look the other way, or worse. Because of low pay and the great black-market value ivory commands, the very game officers who are hired to protect the elephants often give in to temptation and participate directly in poaching activities themselves. There is simply too much money at stake. The problem is similar to our fight against illegal drugs. We in America aren't close to winning that war, and the elephant's protectors in Africa sure haven't won theirs, either.

Hard as it is for antihunters to swallow this fact, professional hunters love the game they pursue. These men have a deep respect for the elephant in particular and are saddened by the indiscriminate bloodshed of poaching, saddened at the bleak prospects for this noble beast's future. If there were a way—any way—to halt the destruction, they would do it in a heartbeat. If they could push a button to end poaching, they would do it, just as we would like to push a button to end drug abuse. If a moratorium on legal elephant hunting would promise a positive impact, I believe they would vote for it in an instant.

In all probability, though, the loss of legal hunting would not help save the elephant. Witness Kenya's absolute mismanagement of their elephant resource by outlawing all hunting in 1977. Within ten years that country had lost over 90 percent of its elephant population to poaching! During this same period, the elephant populations doubled in Zimbabwe and South Africa, where legal hunting remained. The case for legal hunting is clear.

Sustainability is the key. Law-breaking poachers are anxious to shoot every elephant with a tusk—a practice that reduces the overall population of the herd and cannot be sustained because eventually you run out of elephant. A legal hunter, on the other hand, seeks out only the older bulls, most of which are past their breeding prime. Legal hunting is a practice that can be continued on a sustained basis because it does not threaten the viability of the overall population. Females and young remain to reproduce and build the herd. Also, legal hunting uses licenses and quotas to protect the number of elephant harvested. Most important, a portion of license fees provides money to local communities for projects such as building wells and classrooms. When the whole community benefits, the locals see a value in protecting the resource. Otherwise, they often regard the elephant, which regularly tears up crops and causes other destruction to the village and individual farms, as a nuisance that should be removed. To remain, wildlife must pay its way—an economic imperative as unavoidable as any law of nature.

In the end, the professional hunters' hands are tied. They have little political influence, and no one wants to hear their "white" solutions. At least no one in Africa. And least of all the black Africans in power who benefit financially from the trade in illegal ivory.

Still, it surprised me to hear that the PHs' favorite animal to hunt was the elephant.

Baiting for Lion

A couple of days later, Mr. Toomey shot two wildebeests for lion bait. With their bellies slit to spread the scent better, the carcasses were dragged one at a time behind the truck, along creekbeds and around the best "liony-looking" country we could find. Once we had located a suitable tree, I assisted Kipper (whom Gerard grudgingly had allowed to participate while under "house arrest") and Nyamaiya in hanging each wildebeest from a suitably thick limb. We took care to hang each carcass several feet off the ground—high enough so the hyenas wouldn't bother it, but low enough for an adult lion to reach it.

Borrowing Kipper's knife, I cut the rope and tied it fast to the rear leg of the wildebeest, leaving a proper double loop for the metal hook of the Volvo's winch cable, which we used to hoist the heavy animal to the waiting limb above. Balancing in the upper branches, Nyamaiya quickly secured the bait to the limb, tying off my double loop. I got busy and laid Kipper's knife on the ground, where I promptly lost it.

Kipper wasn't upset with me because Gerard had dozens of knives. A tracker uses the knife so frequently and in such demanding applications that he must sharpen it several times a day. Within a month, the metal is worn to half its original dimensions, and the knife is discarded and replaced. Unlike our hunting knives, which often last a lifetime, trackers' knives are considered disposable.

The next morning Mr. Toomey shot a fine zebra, which we skinned and hung for lion bait. On our way to hang it, however, a spitting cobra crossed the road ahead of us. It was so long and lean that I mistook it for a black mamba. Gerard jumped out with a double-barrel shotgun—the same sawed-off number he uses to follow up wounded leopard—and unleashed

(From left) We resemble a 1930s safari: Mrs. Toomey in a pith helmet, Gerard in Mr. Toomey's safari hat, and the author in a funky golf hat.

its wrath on the wicked fiend. Immediately after the first blast, the snake reared to face us, its head a full three feet off the ground. It flared its hood, threatening to strike us dead—or at least spit blinding venom at our eyes. A second blast in the face promptly ended its dastardly career.

We spent the rest of the day checking lion baits, which eventually brought good news. A male lion had fed on one of the wildebeest baits. A quick inspection of the bait revealed several long, ginger hairs from its mane. At this particular moment, though, the owner of those hairs was nowhere in sight. We had expected to find him close-by—lion often lie up in nearby shade to fend off competitor predators, such as jackals, hyenas, and vultures. Since this bait was high off the ground, however, virtually nothing but the lion could reach it. Perhaps he had wandered off to get an afternoon drink, visit a girlfriend, or engage in other feline business. Then again, he might have been studying us from twenty yards away, completely camouflaged in the undergrowth. A full-grown lion can practically disappear behind a sprig of grass. You really have to see it to believe it.

The next day there was still no sign of the lion. The sly brute had returned to feed at night—even at a distance, you could see that a good portion of the bait had been devoured. Extrapolating the lion's rate of consumption, Gerard decided we had better replenish the bait before it

The author with John Toomey and his wildebeest.

ran out and our lion lost interest. A roaming buffalo herd provided the perfect solution. Mr. Toomey stalked and shot a nice bull, and we hauled the massive animal to the site of the half-eaten wildebeest. The buffalo carcass ensured there would be enough meat to keep this lion dining for more than a week.

Two days later, however, we still could not get the wary lion to show itself on the bait in the light of day. This lion was quite the recluse, even by Masailand standards. In that country the cats have been aggressively hunted. This was a far cry from my experience in Rungwa, where a lion challenges you like a street punk in a leather jacket, cigarette dangling from its mouth. In Rungwa the lion are quick to make it clear that it is *you* who are on *their* turf.

Gerard decided we had best put up a few backup baits in case this shy cat continued its nocturnal feeding habits. On the way to a spot known as Laivera, we came upon a small herd of Coke hartebeests standing on the plains. When Mr. Toomey mentioned that he was tired of shooting, Gerard kindly suggested that I shoot. So they handed me his Remington 7mm Magnum with a fancy Zeiss scope—"the best money can buy," according to Gerard.

The herd eventually ran, then stopped at the edge of the brush, as antelope are prone to do, and watched us. Gerard glassed them for a minute, then said, "The one on the right, take him."

Because of the way they were all bunched together, I could see only the shoulder and head of the designated hartebeest, and I was worried that if I missed even slightly I might hit a neighboring animal.

"How far?" I asked.

"Over two hundred," Gerard answered.

I aimed on the animal's shoulder, held my breath against the pressure of an audience, and squeezed the trigger. The hartebeest bucked, ran about ten yards, and dropped. It was fun playing client. But mostly I was glad not to have botched the shot.

After hanging this hartebeest for bait, we came upon another herd out on the plains. Again, Gerard handed the gun to me, and I laid it across the rest and steadied it as best I could, for this herd was quite far off. Once Gerard had studied the heads and made his selection, I aimed at the top of the brown silhouette, at the ridgeline of its back, as Gerard instructed. The hartebeest dropped in its tracks, and Nyamaiya paced it off at 338 paces. Two hartebeest, two shots. Not bad.

On the way home I shot two guinea fowl for the pot, one speckled and one vulterine, the latter being fairly rare. The contrast of white speckled wings, a zebra-striped throat, and bright blue plumage underneath could

Time out for a picnic lunch.

Gerard and Mr. Toomey pose with the diminutive steenbok.

have made for a beautiful bird were it not for its ugly head—bald and vulturelike—hence its name.

Not far from where we had hung the second hartebeest, we came upon a lioness crouched on a small hill comprised of jumbled rocks. We circled the rocky hill, looking for her boyfriend, and, to our surprise, she remained put. In fact, she maneuvered around the hill to keep us in sight and growled her discontent at our approach. But there was no sign of a male with her. No tracks on the ground, either. She appeared to be an unescorted lady, which was rather unusual because lions, especially females, live and die in a pride. Most important, they hunt as a pride. Leopards may thrive on a solitary existence, but not lions.

We were off early the next morning to check our lion baits. There were no lions on our first three baits, but Gerard and Mr. Toomey spied a large male leopard on the zebra bait as they sneaked in on foot. Of course, Mr. Toomey already had his leopard, but catching sight of a leopard in the light of day is a rare and treasured event, license in hand or not. When we reached the second hartebeest bait, where the growling female on the hill had greeted us, we were rewarded with the magnificent sight of two full-maned lions. They were standing their ground, heads held high, drilling holes in us with their eyes. It was an impressive sight, indeed.

These two large cats and their girlfriend had eaten the entire hartebeest down to the hindquarters—a tremendous amount of meat in one night!

After a minute, the two lions turned and began to trot toward thicker brush. It was not an ideal presentation, a lion quartering away like that, but Gerard was tired of being outmaneuvered by these Masai cats. Once Mr. Toomey had a good rest, Gerard instructed him to shoot the lion with the better mane. The big cat went down, then gathered his wits and came right back onto his feet. Mr. Toomey quickly reloaded and shot him again, and the lion faltered. Then Gerard let him have one up the backside with the .460. A minute later, the lion went down, and Mr. Toomey stepped in close and gave the beast a final slug to finish him off.

But our adventure was far from over. Suddenly, the second male emerged from the brush and sauntered over to sniff his dead kin. This male was less than happy with the outcome. The angry cat growled and snarled, tossing his head at us. We shouted back, but the enraged lion refused to leave, no matter how much noise we made. We finally returned to the car, and Mr. Toomey took a video of the growling, snarling cat. To have persisted might have provoked a needless charge and ended in a bad result.

With the vehicle, we were able to coax the lion into the brush, where he remained, royally outraged, growling and hissing, but now

Gerard hands Nyamaiya the shotgun used to "deflate" a spitting cobra.

also completely invisible in thick cover. As we snapped quick pictures of Mr. Toomey's trophy, Gerard kept the .460 in hand. The lion, still growling in outrage in the bush, could have been on us in a flash if he had wanted.

At that point the lion squad upped the ante. Yesterday's female suddenly appeared on the scene, growling up a storm. It was plain to see she meant business, stalking in with her head low to the ground, tail twitching, clearly ready to charge. Gerard placed a bullet in the ground beside her to halt her threatening progress. The two cats finally retreated into the brush, where they kept up a fierce racket. We loaded the heavy cat in haste and were off to camp to call it a day. Mr. Toomey's lion measured 9 feet, 10 inches, from nose to tail. It was a very big cat.

The following morning we left camp particularly early because this was the last day of hunting for the Toomeys. We traveled far and wide in search of Tommies and buffaloes but found neither. The Thomson gazelles were almost nonexistent that year. Perhaps it was due to the drought. Perhaps it was something else. Game populations are not static; they move with shifting weather patterns and for reasons only Mother Nature knows. The one thing I knew for certain was that licensed hunting had nothing to do with it.

On the road we ran into young PH Simon Evans, who seemed as happy as could be with his new profession. He was grinning from ear to ear, his dust-covered face streaked in sweat.

Mr. Toomey kindly turned over his shotgun on the drive home, and I shot five guinea fowl for camp meat, which marked the end of a great safari on all counts.

Rungwa Game Reserve

Chapter 14

Masailand had been home for a month, but now it was time to move camp. Many of Gerard's upcoming clients had booked their safaris with the expectation of hunting in the Selous. That was what had sold them on the trip. The Deutsch family, ever on the quest to experience the richest game fields on the continent, was particularly keen on hunting in the Selous. We expected them in a few days. I had met them on passing safaris two years before and also on our ranch in South Texas.

Considering Gerard was not able to make arrangements with the game department to hunt in the Selous, he decided to take the safari to Rungwa. It was the next-best area available, in terms of the game his clients wished to hunt, and it would fulfill Gerard's promise of a remote camp.

Everyone was now quite familiar with the drill of moving camp. We pulled off the two-day journey to Rungwa without a hitch. Roy and I stopped at a place called Mwanagumbe to pick up two government game scouts, one for each hunting vehicle as required in the game reserve areas.

We arrived at Nicky Blunt's Rungwa #2 camp an hour after sunup and, finding him gone, made ourselves at home. Nicky and a German client drove in as we were finishing our breakfast in the thatched dining hut. They would be departing the next day, which would allow us to use this camp until we built our own.

"I need your help," Nicky said to me.

He then called out in Swahili to someone in the kitchen. Interested, I waited to see what was going on.

The black cook hobbled into the dining hut, his left leg stiff and swollen to humongous proportions. The culprit, it turned out, was a tiny snake, not two feet long, that had bitten him on the foot the day before while he was fetching water from the creek. Nicky could not identify the snake because the staff had so thoroughly crushed its head.

"It was either a green mamba or a boomslang," he concluded, as we gathered to examine the poor fellow's leg.

The cook was in great pain and winced with each step. He was quite lucky, though. Had it been an adult snake, he would have been with Allah by now.

Enrique Guerra with a superb Rungwa buffalo.

"Have you any spare antibiotic?" Nicky asked. "It would be very helpful in fighting off infection from the filthy fangs of the snake."

I had an extra dose and was happy to assist. But I was hesitant to hand over the full course at once, having heard accounts of natives swallowing a ten-day prescription in one gulp. Their logic was that if one pill was good, ten at once must be even better. It was not a lack of intelligence on their part, merely a lack of education, but the consequences of that lack of education in tribal Africa can be colossal. Throw some superstition and a little witchcraft into the mix, and it can be downright surprising what you take for granted when dealing with a primitive society. But Nicky assured me the cook understood.

Gerard arrived later with the good news that he had managed to acquire two additional leopard permits. I did not ask him how he managed it, and he did not say, but I knew it cost him dearly in funds, favors, or time. Nothing gets done cheaply or easily in Africa.

On the staff front, Kipper was still with us, but his salary had been cut. Like a court-martialed soldier stripped of rank, his head hung a little lower, and he spoke little, trying to keep a low profile around Gerard. When their paths did cross, Gerard cursed him loudly and bopped him on the head. Gerard wanted the whole camp to know that he was still furious with Kipper, that there were consequences for anyone who crossed the line. He wanted to put potential mutineers on notice and make them think twice before pulling an idiotic stunt like Kipper's. Once an esteemed member of Gerard's inner circle, Kipper would have to fight to regain everyone's respect and the full privileges of his former position.

The Deutsch party arrived two days later by charter. They were ecstatic to be on the safari. I knew it would be a fun group: the affable, animated Seymon and his lovely daughters Lisa and Debbie, twenty-one and twenty-three. (His wife and son could not make that trip.) As a family, their choice of annual vacation was both unique and exemplary. Some folks go to Disney World; the Deutsches go on safari. This marked Seymon's sixteenth African safari to eight countries. (Based on his vast safari experience, it was quite a compliment when he confided to me that Gerard Miller was the best PH he had ever hunted with. Period.) Seymon was a Laredo businessman and the owner of Joe Brand, a high-end clothing store. His most notable asset was a mind that never stopped spinning a mile a minute. He did not slow down, ever. He was famous for holding multiple conversations at once.

The other half of the party was Enrique Guerra, a Hispanic rancher and businessman from McAllen, Texas. There are some folks for whom you feel an instant liking, and Enrique was such a person. This was his first safari, an event he had been dreaming about for years. At 6 feet, 4 inches and weighing 340 pounds, he was a huge man. Any hindrance caused by his size was offset by a quick wit and a gentlemanly and genial presence.

Climbing out of the small plane, Seymon met us with twenty questions.

"Johnny, how are you? How is your family? What good trophies have you seen? What trophies have you taken? Did you meet Enrique? Enrique, meet Johnny. How about elephant? Seen any good bulls? Gerard, how is the generator I sent you? Is it working? Any problem with Customs? Johnny, how long have you been here? Did you hear what happened on our flight? Got lost. Have you had much rain? Are the roads good?"

Turning to the pilot, who was unloading their luggage, he continued, "Oh, let me help with that. Did you find the green bag? The one with our ammunition. Good, good! Hey, Gerard, you won't believe what Customs wanted to charge us on our personal items! Debbie, did you find your carry-on? Lisa, put this in the truck. Roy, good to meet you. Have you eaten? I'm starving. How far is camp?"

PH Armando Cardoza once told me, "That Seymon never stops—his mind is always turning. One day there was a problem with the shower bucket, and Seymon was all over it. 'Well, what if we hang it like this? . . . What if

Burning last season's dead grass results in tender green shoots that draw the Runowa

wildlife back in droves.

Enrique took this lion after a mock charge.

we hook a pump to it . . . add a section of pipe . . . I know, let's run a tube under . . . no, how about a cistern to collect the rain water. . . .'"

Seymon loved to solve problems, and the bigger the problem, the more delighted he was to assist. Solving problems seemed to keep his mind engaged. He was like a runaway train looking for track ahead—if he ran out of problems to solve, his mind would derail and crash. He was a wonderful person to have on your side, and I enjoyed working with him years later, when he leased our land for cattle.

The first day of safari is a magical event. It arouses feelings similar to those you had as a kid on Christmas morning. The overwhelming anticipation you felt when you first awoke and saw all the shiny presents under the tree. The pent-up wonder and excitement over each package with your name on it. On safari the events and sensations are spread out over a period of time so that you get to open a present or two each day. But that first day, that very first day, when the adventure is all ahead of you, takes the cake for anticipation and excitement. So, it was no surprise that with Seymon the excitement of the first day on safari was palpable in the air. Lunch was a festive occasion. There was fierce competition to get a word in on Seymon, who kept the table buzzing with anticipation and questions. Everyone was talking over everyone else, anxious for the adventures ahead.

After the clients got their gear stowed and sorted in their tents, both vehicles pulled out in opposite directions to see what the afternoon would fetch. I went with Roy and Enrique in the Land Cruiser. We soon found a herd of eland lurking at the edge of a *miombo* forest, and Enrique made an excellent shot on a fine bull. He was truly delighted and wanted to know everything about the antelope he had just harvested. He thoughtfully fingered the unique horns and dun coat, marveling at its immense size, which easily matches that of a Brahma bull.

Everyone appreciated his keen interest and respectful attitude, and, as a result, Roy was more than glad to accommodate his questions. Showing respect for the game you have taken is probably the greatest compliment you can pay a professional hunter. If Enrique had been forced to return home right then, for whatever reason, my guess is that he was the kind of fellow who would have declared the entire trip worth it.

This was a far cry from the three Houston killers on our first safari, who were asking what they could shoot next while the blood was still pumping from whatever animal that had just hit the ground. They seemed in a tremendous rush, as if trying to collect a certain number of items on a treasure hunt. To them, hunting was a game where winning depended on getting all thirty species available, and losing meant ending up with

Nyamaiya sharpening his knife.

This Rungwa hill is ideal leopard habitat—hence the bait in the left tree.

any lesser number. Quantity, not quality, was what counted to them. Rick illustrated their sentiment when he shot a beautiful kudu bull. The first words out of his mouth were, "Well, if we could only find a sable. . . ." He had no appreciation of the animal he had just taken; he was only greedy for the species left uncollected on his list.

Based on first impressions, Enrique was well on his way to being an ideal client. He was a helpful, cheerful, and interesting fellow who seemed to have been involved in a number of industries and business endeavors. Something he said really caught my attention. He told us he had been a millionaire several times and had been flat broke just as many.

A big-framed man, he leaned back with his hands on his hips and offered some sage advice: "Be nice to everyone on your way up, because you will see a lot of those same people on your way down."

My challenge was to spot game before Nyamaiya did. As with Kipper, I was up against a gold medalist. If you read my first book, then you know that Nyamaiya, a reformed elephant poacher, was a formidable hunter and tracker. To recap: He would read the ground the way you and I read the newspaper. He could tell you what passed this way and when, identifying the males, females, and youth of twenty antelope species. He read Roy's mind so well—and vice versa—that the two of them hardly spoke, knowing exactly what each wanted from the other.

Standing behind Roy in the bed of the truck, Nyamaiya squinted his eyes against the rush of the wind. *He must will animals into existence, I thought, for I swear they do not exist until he sees them.*

He hunkered down and tapped Roy on the shoulder, whispering in Swahili, *"Tandala hapa. Kushoto."* (Kudu here, on the left)

I stared, and a few seconds later a kudu materialized.

I would at least like to spot one or two animals on my side of the vehicle before he does, I thought. It happened, but only occasionally.

The next morning was quite successful. Enrique shot a zebra, a Lichtenstein hartebeest, and a beautiful black sable with ribbed horns sweeping back like two samurai blades above its regal head. Enrique took them all with well-placed shots and all before morning had ended.

We stopped for lunch at the foot of one of the rocky hills that dot this otherwise flat country. Afterward, Roy and I hiked to the summit, pausing midway to watch a pair of klipspringers scamper from rock to rock with the ease of mountain goats. These wee antelope, fitted with special hoofs that bite into the slick surface of the rocks, sail up and down the steeper grades, as surefooted as any roller coaster on tracks. They move quickly and unpredictably, flying about the rocky hillside

(From left) Roy Carr-Hartley and Gerard Miller.

like a swallow darts after insects in the air. This particular male wasn't a trophy in the horn department, so we simply delighted in watching their agile antics.

There was no telling what we might spot from the top of the hill—elephant, kudu, lion, buffalo, warthog—but in this case we saw nothing except endless miles of *miombo* forest in every direction.

A short distance from where we had hung half the hartebeest for leopard bait, we passed a worn termite mound. On top of this mound, as if on a throne, lay a lone lioness. After a brief poker-faced glance in our direction, her majesty turned her head away, paying us no mind, as if this hill of hers were on a busy city street where cars drove past every second of every day. Her message was clear in its arrogance: Our presence was such a trifle it required no scrutiny on her part. Gerard's warning from our first safari together came back to me: "These Rungwa lions are quite cheeky. You must watch them carefully."

At a water hole we counted forty-odd elephant, but there was not a single bull among them, which was about par. All we had seen in the area so far were cows and calves. The old gentlemen were wisely holed up in thick vegetation.

Gerard's crew was as successful as Roy's. The men were anxious to get baits up quickly because Lisa and Debbie were here for only a week. They collected a magnificent sable of forty-five inches, an eland, a duiker, and a hartebeest.

The next day our luck continued to roll right along. In the morning we came upon a pride of seven female lions at the hartebeest bait. There was also a young male, which we didn't see until we were nearly on top of it. A lion blends in unbelievably well in the golden grass. It's hard to believe that you can get within five paces of a full-grown lion in short grass and still not see it, but you can. We made a quick retreat so as not to threaten it into a charge. The lion was still young, as evidenced by the isolated tufts of mane on its chin, cheeks, and skull, which stood out like separate islands of hair.

Leaving these lions to their business, and hopeful that a mature male would put in an appearance down the line, we departed for the zebra bait, where we were delighted to find that half the carcass had been eaten. Not wanting to disturb the site or spread our scent, only Nyamaiya jumped out, and he confirmed that the tracks had indeed been left by a large male. In Masailand we had had difficulty attracting lions to our baits; here in Rungwa we were experiencing great success. It seemed we could hang a bait on just about any tree and fetch up a family of big cats. Yes, our odds were looking quite good.

A respectable Rungwa buffalo eyes us from the safety of a thick palm forest.

We had hung the zebra bait from a tree at the base of what was probably the tallest, steepest hill in the area. As we circled the rocky hill in the truck, I found myself wondering if lions ever climbed to the very top. Not ten seconds later, in answer to my unspoken question, the head of a female lion appeared above the crest.

There was no sign of the male who had left its tracks at the bait below.

Enrique was rewarded with quite a trophy that afternoon: a buffalo bull with a magnificent horn spread of 46 inches. He was elated, absolutely beside himself at the trophy he had collected. Enrique, we found out, was an exceptional shot. He put the bullet right where he aimed, and rarely was a follow-up shot required.

Throughout the following day we came across several small herds of gray elephant as they ghosted across gray earth through gray trunks of trees, blending into the gray terrain with incredible ease for an animal the size of a small barn. This elephant camouflage is not by chance. To ward off biting insects and to protect itself from the harsh rays of the equatorial sun, the elephant uses its trunk to spray mud and dust onto its hide, transforming itself into the exact color of the land it inhabits, be it red, gray, brown, or black. This is a perfect disguise for an animal of such size, and it is a bit startling in its effectiveness.

Climbing a bald hill, we discovered a poacher's shack on the summit. Built of thin, upright logs in the shape of a teepee, it had room for only one or two people. Roy guessed the poachers used the shack to "scout" the roaming elephant herds. Sure enough, as we torched it, we glimpsed a herd of elephant moving slowly through the trees. There were no bulls in this herd, but Enrique wanted to get some pictures. This led to the encounter of the charging cow elephant, which I described at the opening of this book. We got quite a fright from the animal kingdom, and it definitely took a few years off our lives. Frankly, it served to remind us who is the boss of the bush. Later, we encountered more elephant, including a small bull of some thirty pounds, and stopped to take photos—this time from farther away.

The rest of that afternoon we embarked on a campaign to spread fire throughout the land. From the roving truck we tossed lit matches in an attempt to burn as much of the lofty, lifeless grass as we could. Along the creekbeds, where the grass was tallest, the orange flames shot fifteen feet or higher. The heat, as if from a furnace, instantly scorched our faces, and black clouds of smoke pumped skyward.

"People are arrested for this back home," I told Roy, with a laugh.

"Why? Fire is a good thing," he said. "Except you'd best pay attention to the wind and where you light your matches, or you might return to find your camp incinerated! I know a hunter or two who have experienced that misfortune."

The burning of habitat is an age-old management tool. American Indians did it. Ranchers do it now. The fire clears out the old growth and makes way for the new. It stimulates dormant seeds beneath the soil and fertilizes future growth with its ashes. Nor does the fire harm most living trees, beyond a slight scorching of the lower trunk. Bright-green growth soon arrives without a sprinkle from the sky. The wildlife floods in to dine, making for a spectacular transformation.

As an added benefit, the hot fire also helps to kill a good percentage of the tsetse flies in the area, which lends particular satisfaction to the chore. I really do hate the vicious bloodsuckers.

The next afternoon Enrique took a beautiful roan, an antelope similar to the sable but with shorter horns. He confessed he couldn't get to sleep until well after midnight, his adrenaline still pumping from the front-seat view of the spine-tingling elephant charge.

First thing the next morning we checked the sable bait. We were in for a great surprise. At the site we found two male lions lying side by side in the shade of a tree. Ironically, one was quite large with no mane; the other was smaller but had a good mane, which made it the better trophy. At this point we were no more than fifteen paces from the two recumbent cats. The maneless lion suddenly crouched low and had that look. Just then, it sprang forth and charged us. It had made about

Seymon Deutsch and his daughters ready for a day afield.

Scouting for the nimble klipspringer antelope on the surrounding Rungwa hills.

Enrique continues his string of one-shot skills with this fine leopard.

two bounds when I did my best Nicky Blunt impression: I threw up my arms and shouted out in a booming voice. The lion stopped as if stung in the face, then retreated, and the male with the good mane stood up and turned conveniently broadside, watching us.

"Take him," Roy said.

Enrique shot the lion in the shoulder, and down the big cat went. And down it stayed—quite surprising for a big-game animal so close and on alert. It's one thing to knock down an unsuspecting lion from a blind in complete surprise. It's another to knock one down at fifteen paces when its adrenaline is up and it is looking you in the eye.

The larger, maneless lion, however, refused to leave. The big-bodied cat stood its ground and snarled up a storm at us, immune to further shouts and yells and mock charges. Finally, Roy had to place a bullet quite near it to get it to leave. Then came pictures and the joy of getting to inspect one of the Big Five up close—its teeth, its claws, everything that makes up the sheer awesomeness of the largest predator on the continent. Enrique was taking it in like a teen on his first date. You could tell he was attempting to soak in the memories of the hunt of a lifetime. These were memories he would have forever.

No question, it had been a great hunt so far for Enrique. But it had been an even better hunt for us, the guides. It was marvelous hunting with a client who shot well and enjoyed himself on the hunt, who put no undue pressure on the PH to perform, who was there to relish every aspect of the safari experience, from watching the cook prepare a kongoni stew to noting the skinners' field-dressing techniques. Enrique appreciated the foreign sights, smells, and sounds of Africa. He was humble and thankful. His ego was in check. He was not here to show anyone up. He had nothing to prove, no chip on his shoulder.

"As a hunting client, Enrique is as good as they come," Roy later confided. "It's unfortunate, Johnny, but today there are too many hunters who hunt with a rifle in one hand and a record book in the other. The animal has barely hit the ground, and 'Trophy Joe' is pulling a tape from his pocket to see if the horns will meet the magical number to get his name in 'the book.' His success and joy are measured by this one criterion. A real shame, it is."

In truth, nothing detracts more from the overall hunting experience than such behavior, especially for the other members of the hunting party. Trophy Joe hunts for the wrong reason: so he can return home and brag to his friends and business associates about how many "book" animals he collected. I believe hunting is a personal endeavor. It is between you and the animal being hunted. If you are hunting for anyone other than yourself, you should try another hobby. Like golf.

Three days later, we encountered a handsome lion at our buffalo bait, and Roy immediately radioed the location to Gerard. This was timely news for Gerard's hunting party, for they had just lost sight of a lion in the brush. The sly cat had crossed a riverbed and disappeared before they could get a shot at it. This was surprising—Gerard rarely allowed an animal to give him the slip, once he had made the decision that it was a trophy worth taking. He has a way of reading an animal's mind and knowing exactly where it is going—before it even knows where it is going. It is uncanny how he does that. I have often witnessed this performance of his when I swore the game had outsmarted us.

Gerard wasted no time in making his way to our bait. It goes without saying that they were successful in taking the lion, and quite a large lion it was. It had a splendid mane. Lisa Deutsch also took a tremendous roan.

The next dawn brought another incredible day of hunting. Enrique shot a greater kudu and a leopard. Debbie Deutsch shot a kudu at the impressive range of 400 yards and a bull elephant with 72-pound tusks!

While having lunch on our usual tarp in the shade of a tall tree, I pitched an empty can of sardines under a bush. This brought about an immediate raising of Enrique's eyebrows.

"If someone did that on my ranch," he declared, "I'd whip his butt."

The trophy lion at the top is king of the mountain.

But that's what everyone does in Africa, I thought. I never did it again, and I am now a rabid crusader for picking up litter in the wilds.

In the afternoon we encountered a couple of old buffalo bulls in tall grass and drove in close to take their picture. The gray scars of battles fought and won marred the black, crusty hides of these old warrior bulls. Neither was a trophy. Their horns were chipped and battered, the ends worn down to blunt stubs. The bulls were indeed old, but you could tell they still had plenty of fight in them. In fact, as we approached, they started to trot toward us, chins up, menacing eyes locked on their target—us. They were cantankerous—crotchety as old-timers with arthritis and ready to bash any intruder, harmless or otherwise. Bulls like these end up killing a wandering local in the bush—or a careless hunter!

We took some great pictures, but when the buffaloes got really close, Enrique put down his camera and said, "OK, Roy, let's get out of here!"

Roy yelled, and the old bulls turned and ran. It turned out they were merely inspecting us. But they had come on as if they were ready to climb in the truck with us.

What I would have given right then for a double rifle and a license!

At one point during the day I asked Roy what had happened to the game ranch his family had—the one that captured animals for zoos and motion pictures.

Lisa Deutsch took this tremendous common reedbuck.

Admiring the tusks of Debbie Deutsch's elephant.

"After independence, the blacks took it from us," he said, showing little outward bitterness toward what must have been a difficult event for his family. "Ran it right into the ground, they did. Nothing there now but the shells of the vehicles and equipment and buildings that they had no clue how to repair or maintain."

The next morning I went with Gerard's group to check the two zebra baits that Roy and I had hung at the foot of the same rocky hill from which the lioness had peered down on us. On our way we dispatched a nine-foot spitting cobra as it raised its threatening head. As we neared the hill, we heard a grunt—presumably a mating grunt. Soon our suspicions proved true, and we were favored with quite a sight. The lion couple appeared high above us. The male, however, was no ordinary lion. This lion was blessed with the most magnificent mane I had ever laid eyes on. A true MGM lion!

The hair of its mane was long, thick, and shaggy on top of the head and down the front of the chest. On the sides it was thick and golden, reaching far and deep to the absolute end of the ribs, like you only see on game-park lion. In broad daylight its mane positively glowed! There is no scoring system for a lion with a mane like that—which is just as well—but I consider that fellow a better trophy than 95 percent of what's listed in the record books, all species included!

Magnificently silhouetted against the blue sky, the king and queen stared down at us from their throne. It was truly a spectacular sight. They were calm and relaxed from their lovemaking and took our presence in with only passing interest.

Seymon, understandably, was salivating over the sight of such an impressive beast. He couldn't believe his eyes.

"Gerard, how much to shoot that lion?"

"What?" Gerard asked. "You can't shoot it. You've only one on your license."

"I know, I know—how much to buy another license?" he whispered quickly.

Gerard turned around in his seat to face him.

"The royalty alone is seven thousand dollars."

"Fine," he said, and began reaching for his gun.

Gerard held up his hand.

"Hold on, Bwana."

"Gerard, I really want that lion. I'll pay it. I don't mind."

"No," Gerard told him. "I'm saving that lion for Tony Sanchez, my next client."

"Find him another lion," Seymon laughed. "I want this one."

But Gerard remained firm. So we all just stared up in awe and watched the extraordinary pair survey their kingdom until they disappeared from sight and returned to their interest at heart.

I could not have dreamed up a better note on which to end a safari.

Alone in the Bush

Chapter 15

The next stage in this adventure involved spending a week in the bush as the sole white man in camp. There was a hiatus between safaris, and Gerard and Roy had returned to Kenya by charter, first having dropped the clients in Arusha. That left me alone in the bush. My first order of business was to return to George Angelides's camp, now vacated of PHs and clients, to complete some errands for Gerard before continuing on to his Rungwa camp, where I would await his return.

I was still not fully adapted to driving on the opposite side of the vehicle. Only by a conscious effort did I manage not to collide with the trees growing close to the narrow road. Upon my arrival in Angelides's camp, I asked the cook to prepare dinner for me, as well as breakfast in the morning.

"*Hapana chakula,*" (There is no food) the cook said. He added that there was no food for breakfast the next day, either.

"*N'dio chakula!*" (There's plenty of food) I argued.

I knew there was because I had seen lots of food that morning before I taxied everyone to the airstrip to catch the plane.

"*Hapana chakula,*" he repeated, and threw up his arms helplessly.

I beckoned him toward the kitchen area. Though he was still hobbling, his leg had improved dramatically. I must admit I was rather huffed at the ingratitude he was showing the fellow who had provided him scarce antibiotics that had possibly saved his life. In the kitchen area I pointed out meat, rice, and onions. He made me a wonderful meat curry out of no food! The next morning eggs and sugar magically appeared. I have no doubt that George's men were planning to treat themselves to this fare, then tell George that Gerard's group had eaten it all!

Once back at Gerard's new camp, which I hoped would be our permanent camp for the remainder of the season, I worked with Willie, the slow-moving but friendly tent boy, stringing lights around camp. At night I slept with a shotgun beside my cot, just in case. Some hyenas lurked into camp late one night, but they slunk off the minute I unzipped the tent and poked my head out.

That week there was little to do with the PHs and clients gone. Bored, I kept wandering into the kitchen area to see what the men were up to.

The camp headman, Abdi, was there. He was dressed in his regular dark blue, short-sleeved shirt and shorts, the ever-present white fez atop his graying head. Admittedly, Abdi had slowed with age, but there was no question he was still the best skinner alive. A deliberate, meticulous fellow, he could work magic in the turning of mouths and ears of the various game animals he skinned, never nicking a hole in the thinnest of hides, even on the smallest dik-dik. His hands were uncommonly smooth and soft from handling countless greasy pelts, and his watery dark eyes, though not as sharp as they once were, had yet to fail him in the taxing, close-up inspection required in his work.

He shared some adventures from the old days, but, unfortunately, many were lost to the language barrier. I encouraged him to continue, understanding bits and pieces, and nodded and laughed and shook my head where appropriate, taking my cue from the others, who were listening as they did their work—what little work there was to do during the hiatus.

One tale in particular caught my attention, and Gerard subsequently confirmed its veracity. This chilling incident occurred when Gerard was a mere two years old, and it happened in a hunting camp run by his parents, both of whom were professional hunters. One day a pride of especially aggressive lions wandered into camp while both his mother and father were out hunting with clients. The lion proceeded to roam the campgrounds, making a complete mess of the kitchen and foodstuffs. A quick-thinking and much younger Abdi tied Gerard to his back and carried him up a tree to safety.

When the insistent cats eventually eyed Abdi and his young charge high in the tree, they approached and began to circle beneath them. Soon the lion attempted to climb up after the pair. Luckily, the lions couldn't make it more than ten or twelve feet up the trunk before losing their footing or balance. But the persistent creatures refused to leave. Abdi had to remain in the treetop until Gerard's parents returned and chased the lions off with their guns.

This reminded me of an unsettling account Gerard had once told me. It also happened while he was an infant, but this time he was on his parents' farm. One night his parents heard an odd noise in young Gerard's room. Fortunately, Frank Miller, Gerard's father, made the decision to investigate. Can you imagine his shock at the sight of a grown leopard perched in the open windowsill above his son's crib? With the quick reactions intrinsic to his profession, Frank promptly grabbed a firearm and killed the leopard. The spotted culprit turned out to be a female cat—old, hungry, and missing most of her teeth. A desperate situation had left the animal little choice but to seek out an easy meal.

Gerard's new camp in Rungwa starts to take shape.

One morning I awoke to both a headache and a sick stomach. After some probing in the kitchen, I discovered that the staff had failed to boil the drinking water. Gerard leaves camp and procedure goes all to hell!

As the day progressed, my condition improved, but later that night I got a fright in the form of a disturbing call on the radio. An American, apparently a stranded client of a safari company, was calling for help from camp. *What is a client doing on the radio?* I thought.

"Ugalla One? Come in, Ugalla One!"

Static.

"Ugalla One, this is Ugalla Two. Come in Ugalla One!"

"Go ahead, Ugalla Two, this is Ugalla One. Over."

"What is happening? We are alone out here. We don't know what to do. Are you sending someone for us?"

There was panic and urgency in the voice.

What in the hell is going on?

"Yes, Ugalla Two—we copy. We are sending someone for you. Just hold tight. Who is this? Over."

"This is Bob Brown—we are really upset about this whole thing. What has happened to our professional hunters?"

"Mr. Brown, just hold tight. We are sending someone as quickly as we can—over."

Later, Gerard came on the radio. There was real concern in his voice.

"Johnny, is everything OK in camp? Over."

"Yes. Over."

"No problems, then? Over."

"No, everything's fine. Over."

"Very good, then. Very good."

There was a pause.

"Listen, Johnny, there's been some trouble. I need you to pack your bags and be ready to fly out on the charter coming in three days hence. Over."

"What's happened? Over," I asked, stunned at this turn of events.

"Uh, can't say right now, Johnny. I'll explain when I get there. See you tomorrow—over and out."

The next day my stomach was fully recovered, and I anxiously awaited Gerard's return, very curious to know what had happened to cut my trip short. When Gerard arrived by Range Rover that afternoon, he quickly told me what had transpired in the Ugalla camp.

It was scary stuff—something right out of a John Grisham novel. Two truckloads of soldiers toting machine guns had arrived in the Hunters Africa camp and had arrested three Portuguese professional hunters. The soldiers arrested another PH in town. Once they had bound the hunters and loaded them into the military vehicles, the soldiers drove off, leaving the three American clients to their own devices, without explanation, in the middle of the bush. The problem, Gerard had heard, had to do with foreign work permits, which are hard to come by. These PHs either didn't have them or had bribed the wrong officials to get them. Either way, the PHs were now in jail and in big trouble.

A worried look came over Gerard's face.

"When they come to our camp, check your passport—see how long you've been here. We'll have a hard time convincing them you are not working for me."

"But I'm not! You haven't paid me."

"Right. But try to tell them that. Dubanya, the game commissioner, told me he is coming to check our camp!"

I was quite depressed at the news. I did not want to cut my trip short. If Gerard felt I was not safe, however, I had no choice but to go. I just hoped the soldiers wouldn't cause trouble for Roy.

PH Adelino Pires and Fiona Capstick wrote about this incident in their book, *The Winds of Havoc*. It was Pires, his son, and two friends who had been arrested. They were tortured, interrogated, and held in solitary confinement for five months—until the president of Portugal secured their release. It turned out the arrests were not related to work permits but were at the instigation of a co-worker who had spread false rumors about them because he wanted them out of the picture. The book sheds light on the difficulties of working in Africa and recounts Adelino's troubles in one African country after another.

Gerard also mentioned that he was having ongoing trouble with TAWICO. The government claimed it had not received his fifteen-thousand-dollar check, a check that had cleared Gerard's bank. Even when Gerard showed TAWICO officials the canceled check, they refused to believe that the trouble lay with their own bank. The ultimate insult came when they threatened to cancel his safaris unless he wrote them a new check!

What a bunch of—well, I had better not say.

Perhaps it is time for me to return to civilization, I thought.

This incident made me realize that I did not have the patience to endure such incompetence. But there was more to it than that. After four months, I realized that I did not have what it takes to be an East African professional hunter. Not that I had seriously considered that prospect except in my daydreams. In any event, as a direct result of my trip, my respect for these talented, dedicated, hardworking, and resourceful men had multiplied tenfold. I will always hold them in the highest regard.

Luckily, I encountered no trouble in leaving the country a couple of days later. As it turned out, I would return next year to hunt as a client in the Rungwa camp I had helped to build that trip. How lucky is that?

Part II

Botswana and Zimbabwe
1986

Leopard

Chapter 16

The Kalahari Bushmen came to a sudden stop and pointed at the large leopard paw prints in the sand, conversing in their peculiar pops and clicks. Professional hunter Terry Palmer and tracker Kuna joined in the huddle. Jim Speece and I anxiously awaited their verdict.

"This is last night's track," Terry said, excitedly. "We shall follow it up." Thirty-something, our Botswana PH was trim in build, bronzed from a profession in the sun, and outfitted with a pair of the brightest blue eyes you have ever seen.

This was an exceptional development for two reasons. First, it was our first full day on safari. Second, having hunted the reclusive cats exclusively in blinds—a rather boring method—I was quite excited about the chance to participate in tracking them up, the extraordinary technique employed in the Kalahari. Little did we know how exciting things were about to get.

Kuna and the Bushmen spread out in formation and tracked ahead of the white Land Cruiser. Twice Terry got out to track with them, while I drove the vehicle. At this point Jim was in the passenger seat, manning the video camera. Around 5 P.M. we discovered a smooth depression in the sand, where the leopard had spent the night. Forty-five minutes later, with only half an hour of daylight left, we knew our odds of catching up with the leopard were growing slim. At six o'clock, however, the tracks indicated the leopard was running, which meant it had heard us or seen us and was quite near. Soon we got more than we had bargained for.

Jim climbed into the back with the .300, and Terry took over the wheel. I stood beside Jim with the camera over my shoulder and filmed. The Bushmen were now running ahead of us, and after a few minutes, they too climbed on board. Perched on the spare tire fastened to a rack above the cab, Kuna directed Terry with a stick pointed down at the windshield. The tracks were now fresh and plain to see, even for us on top of the truck.

Here I should mention something about Jim's gun. Although our trip to Africa had gone without incident, Jim's .300 Winchester had met with misfortune on the flight. A substantial blow, evidenced by the sizable dent

First day in the Kalahari: Jim Speece prepares to board the "White Elephant."

in the plastic case, had left the fore-end of the wooden stock shattered in two. Apparently, the bolt of the accompanying .458 had smashed into the stock with the force of a ball-peen hammer. Fortunately, Neville Peak, Hunters Africa's managing director, had come to the rescue. A liberal amount of epoxy and duct tape did the trick, though the result certainly wouldn't have won any beauty contest. This was a painful lesson illustrating why a metal case is far superior to a hard plastic one. The good news was that the accident had not affected the accuracy of the gun.

At 6:10 P.M. we got a brief glimpse of the leopard. It was a big one. Despite its size and the scarcity of the brush, the wily critter vanished in an instant. We followed but lost its tracks. Terry circled the brush in vain, then circled again and again, until I was so turned around I had no idea which way was which and which tracks were which. Somehow he and his men knew, and, a minute later, we sighted the spotted cat loping two hundred yards ahead. Terry hit the gas, swerved around a bush or two, and just managed to close the gap as the leopard entered a thick patch of cover. The frantic driving, though unavoidable, didn't make my job of filming any easier. Holding onto the roll cage with one hand, balancing the camera in the other, I tried my best to keep the leopard in the viewfinder.

Camp and the arid Kalahari landscape, as seen from the air.

Fifty yards away, the leopard ducked behind a small bush. We stopped at thirty yards, and out it came in full charge! The leopard was getting closer and closer as I was filming. I kept expecting Jim to shoot, all the time thinking, *Why are you waiting?* But he never did. He had thrown the gun to his shoulder and pulled the trigger, but nothing happened. It turned out the gun had jammed.

At this point, based on the leopard's speed and trajectory, I was preparing myself for the up-close and personal meeting on top of the truck with Mr. Leopard. Fortunately, the leopard veered to the right at the last instant and ran alongside the vehicle. I filmed the angry cat as it ran by, no more than an arm's length below me, and I shouted out to discourage it from coming up at us, which leopard are prone to do.

(Three months later, that is exactly what happened to my good friend Dr. Richard Allen and his family. It was the very first morning of their safari, and they were hunting with PH Willie Engelbrecht in this same area. A big leopard pounced into the back of the truck, not once but three times. The trackers pulled his young daughter out of harm's way, and the cat unleashed its fury on Richard's arm, sinking its long teeth into the bone. A far cry from the welcome to Africa they had expected, it was a warning of how quickly things can go from bad to ugly on safari.)

Terry whirled the truck around, and we watched the leopard dart behind another tree before Jim could get a clear shot. Now the big tom was really angry—growling and hissing—and when we got closer, it came straight for us. This time Jim's gun was in working order, and he made a great shot. The leopard was sprinting, legs pumping furiously in the soft sand, grunting its discontent and preparing for what would surely be a leap into the truck. Its eyes were fixed on us like a target, and I was sure the leopard was about to land in our lap when Jim's gun bellowed.

The bullet slammed into the blinding flash of fur, hitting the leopard solidly between the shoulder blades, no more than an arm's length from the front bumper! The close blast crumpled the leopard in midstride, and it piled into the brush guard with a thud. But the cat was not ready to give up—not by a long shot. Enraged, the cat prepared to attack.

In the next instant, the leopard began to climb and claw and chew at the metal grillwork. It was trying to exact revenge, trying to find human flesh to sink its teeth into. The cat's fury pumped up its waning strength, and I was concerned it would climb for us any second. Just then, Terry suddenly backed up the truck, and the leopard lost its grip and tumbled to the ground. Surprisingly, the spotted cat nimbly regained its feet and started toward us again. I thought, *When is this nightmare going to end?* and began shouting, "Shoot! Shoot!"

Hot on the tracks of a leopard, Kuna can jog for miles in 110-degree heat.

Jim's leopard charged the truck not once but twice.

Jim's gun had jammed—again—and I held my breath as he fiddled with it to make it work. Luckily, the leopard took only three or four steps before it collapsed. Even in its dying breath, its golden eyes were locked on ours, and you could tell it wanted to rip our faces off.

We all got out to admire the big cat, now lying calmly in the sand, quite the contrast to the fire-eating devil of a moment ago. Seven feet long, the leopard had sharp, colorful markings, and the yellow splash of the setting sun made for several hasty but outstanding photos.

The real surprise came in playing back the video in the viewfinder that night. We found that the charges had occurred much faster than we had realized at the time. The first charge in the video took all of three seconds from start to finish; the second one, even less. This fact stood in sharp contrast to the footage recorded forever in my mind. While the charge was in progress, time seemed to slow to a crawl, and it seemed to take ages for the leopard to reach us.

Despite Jim's excellent shot in the heat of battle, the gun's failure lends support to the African PH's strong distaste for semiautomatic actions. The fact of the matter is that semiautomatics are unreliable. They should have no place in hunting dangerous game, a situation where reliability counts for everything. Take them deer hunting, take them target shooting, but don't take them to Africa. End of story.

We arrived at camp late and, after showers, dinner, and celebrations, did not get to sleep until well after midnight. What a day!

It was amazing how quickly my trip to Botswana had come about. Until Jim Speece called, three weeks before the safari, I had no idea I'd be going there. His wife had had to cancel, and he had called to ask if I would like to accompany him as an observer. I had yet to visit this interesting country, so the safari would be a special treat, and I had wasted no time in booking my flights.

Jim and his brother Conrad were good friends of mine from the Dallas Safari Club, an organization that has introduced me to a number of close friends over the years. Jim had hunted in North America and Mexico, but this was his first safari to Africa. An anesthesiologist by trade, he was an avid outdoorsman and was quite excited about experiencing the sights and sounds of Africa. Besides the leopard he had just taken, he would be hunting lion, buffalo, and a plethora of plains game on this twenty-eight-day adventure.

Comets and the Kalahari

Chapter 17

I stepped outside my tent around 5 A.M. and searched the night sky for Halley's Comet. The constellations Orion and the Southern Cross stood out splendidly, but the light from the quarter moon overpowered the night sky, banishing any chance of sighting the famous comet.

Camp was situated at the south end of a large pan—a shallow watering hole that was currently bone dry. The larger pans are named and used as landmarks, and this one, "Jackie's Pan," was named after a Frenchman named Jacques. At dawn I slipped on jogging shoes, shorts, and a T-shirt and ran around the circumference of the pan, a distance of five miles, or what I would come to call the "Killer Kalahari Eight K." The scenery was beautiful, the temperature perfect, and the sunrise magnificent. I must admit my eyes did roam the landscape for wayward snakes or crouching lions. Fortunately, the only animals I saw were a few springboks and gemsboks, and surely they wondered what this crazy white man was doing.

Once out hunting, we made a reconnaissance drive, mostly in one direction. Terry wanted to determine where the game was concentrated, an event that changes with the seasons. For those of you who have not visited the Kalahari, the four seasons there are hot, hot, hotter, and hottest. Only the hardiest of animals can survive in the Kalahari. There is little to eat, and water is as scarce as Gatorade at a posh restaurant. We did not expect to see a tremendous number of animals here, but those we did see had real trophy potential. We encountered gemsbok, steenbok, and a few wildebeest and red hartebeest. But Terry paid them little attention. He was chiefly interested in locating lion spoor.

By early morning, the sun grew hot. We wound our way on and off dirt tracks through the desert scrub. I felt right at home riding in the bed of the truck, where I had spent most of my time on my last Tanzania trip. In truth, I prefer riding there. You see a lot more game from the back of the truck, and standing is more comfortable than sitting, especially in rough terrain. In back with me were Kuna and the two Bushmen.

The Bushmen are a fascinating people. Standing less than five feet tall, they sport high cheekbones, flat faces, and narrow, slanted eyes

(From left) The author and Terry enjoying a beer around the campfire—not often done before dark.

that hint at oriental origins. Surprising, too, is the light color of their skin—the color of creamed coffee.

Subjected year-round to the harsh sun of the Kalahari, one would expect these desert denizens to be the darkest of all Africans, for there is no hotter place on this half of the continent. As a tribe, the Bushmen are expert hunters, existing almost exclusively on the animals they harvest with bow and arrow. Theirs is not the fancy weapon of the modern-day archer but a simple device crudely crafted from whittled stick and string.

Later that morning, Jim made a fantastic two-hundred-yard shot on a steenbok, an antelope no bigger than a Texas jack rabbit. Despite its small size and the large, well-placed bullet in the chest, the steenbok took off at a dead run. The Bushmen sprinted in pursuit and, after a couple of zigs and zags, finally pinned it down. We got a chuckle out of that—no disrespect to our quarry intended. Every animal, once its adrenaline is coursing, is capable of amazing stamina and strength. Even the tiniest of creatures becomes Superman.

An important aspect of every hunt is the camaraderie that develops among the members of the hunting party. I was glad to find that we were in good shape on that front. Jim Speece was about as friendly and easygoing a fellow as you could meet, and Terry's accommodating and amenable disposition rounded out the group quite nicely. That night we told joke after joke around the campfire, laughing so hard we were all in tears. Terry had the best one, but it is not fit to print. What a shame, for it was quite good.

Lion

The next day was more of the same: driving established tracks and making new ones in search of lions or their spoor, and pausing now and then to scrutinize the trophy quality of the gemsbok and springbok that peppered the desert floor.

Early on, Jim spotted a tremendous python coiled beneath a bush, and we all got out to look at it. Suffering from jet lag or some other affliction, I grabbed the giant snake by the tail and tried to pull it out into the open for further inspection. It was much stronger and heavier than I had anticipated, and only with real effort did I manage to drag the fifteen-foot serpent into the open. The snake, understandably, was not exactly pleased with this arrangement. Jerking its head in my direction and issuing a loud hiss, it made a dash at me. I let go immediately (for no other reason, of course, than suddenly remembering some other pressing business at hand) and took a couple of quick steps in retreat.

Glancing over my shoulder, I noticed the Bushmen running away at top speed. I guessed if I were their size, I would have run, too. In all seriousness, I believe the snake, given the chance, could have made a meal of either one of them. After taking some pictures, we drove on and abandoned the snake to the process of recoiling its cumbersome body. Most puzzling of all was what a python was doing in the middle of the Kalahari! The python is a jungle-loving forest snake. Even Terry had no explanation.

By day's end, we had covered an amazing amount of country, logging 137 miles on the odometer. We encountered a number of lion tracks, but all were female.

We were back in camp late, and Terry decided to change strategy.

"We can cover more territory if we make spike camps the next couple of nights. So pack a small bag, and we'll be off in the morning."

At 8:30 A.M. we pulled out of camp, loaded with more than enough gear for spike camp. The rear of the truck was full, and so was the second truck Kuna drove behind us.

As luck would have it, less than an hour later, we crossed the spoor of two male lions, along with a female companion. The men quickly unloaded the gear from the first truck, and Jim climbed on top with his .458. I set up the video camera beside him, and the Bushmen set off

Terry and Jim evaluate the tracks of two male lions.

on foot after the beasts. A little after 10 A.M. we sighted the two males trotting ahead of us in the scrub. Terry gunned the Toyota to narrow the distance. (Regrettably, a passing branch yanked out the power cord to the video camera, and we caught no more of the hunt on film.)

As we neared the big cats, we could see that the lead lion was easily the better of the two. It had a tremendous black mane—a rare and highly sought-after quality in a trophy lion. Manes aside, they were both great brutes in size. Watching the muscles work beneath their taut skins as they trotted in front of us was a sharp reminder of the immense speed and power possessed by the mighty cats. They are killing machines, no doubt about it. Designed to slaughter prey that outweighs them by several multiples. Designed by nature not to take prisoners. Designed for complete and total success at what they do. Killing, killing, and killing.

The second lion soon turned off to the side, and we continued past it. The first lion eventually circled behind a small bush and became instantly and completely invisible. The four-hundred-and-fifty-pound cat remained camouflaged until we made our way around the other side. At that point, the king stood up and made a mock charge. It stopped at forty yards, and Jim shot it square in the nose. A perfect shot! The magnificent beast dropped to the ground, dead still.

As Jim and Terry approached, however, the big male suddenly came to life. As the lion struggled to rise, Jim quickly shot it in the chest, and

A beautiful black-maned lion for Jim.

the lion went back down. The lion continued to growl, so Jim stepped around to get a better shot from the side. As Jim placed a final .458 round in its chest, ending the chase for a black-maned trophy, things turned a little interesting.

Standing in the truck, Kuna and I had a clear view of the entire proceedings, and fortunately so. Right then, Kuna yelled out in warning. The second lion was stalking the hunters! Jim and Terry made a hasty retreat, and an instant later, the crafty lion appeared in the open, not three paces from where the men had just been standing.

You could almost read the disappointment on the lion's face. There is no question the cunning feline had taken a roundabout route and used strategic clumps of brush to conceal its approach. Its plan, pure and simple, was to make a surprise attack. Finding its human quarry out of reach, the fearless cat approached and sniffed Jim's lion, then simply sat and stared at us, challenging us to make the next move.

"That was close!" said Jim. Then, after a moment, "But what a great video this would make."

"Yes," Terry said, "but if we leave to retrieve the video cord, I'm afraid this lion might claw or chew up your lion."

When several shouts did nothing to dislodge the second lion, Terry decided he and Jim had best return to the car. Given the lion's surly attitude, there was no reason to risk provoking an attack, an event that might require a needless killing in self-defense. I'm sure a mountain of bureaucratic forms would have been required to justify the shooting to the game department, but that was not Terry's motivation for holding back. A cool head in the heat of battle kept us from doing something we might regret. Another cool head belonged to Jim. Here he was on the fourth full day of his first safari, and already he had been charged by two of the Big Five. You never know how someone will react in such a situation, but it should have come as no surprise that Jim, a doctor and a Vietnam vet, displayed such steady nerve.

In the vehicle we circled the lion and honked and hollered at it, but to absolutely no effect. Terry instructed Jim to shoot beside the animal. The thunderous shot failed to budge the big cat. It simply ignored us. After fifteen minutes of these raucous proceedings, the lion finally lost patience and wandered away. We returned to Jim's lion, but there was no skinning it there, not with an angry cat hanging about. So we loaded the lion into the bed of the truck by hand—no easy task—and, as we did, Kuna spotted the second male returning. We could not have timed our departure any better.

We soon rendezvoused with the other truck waiting beside our mountain of gear. Congratulations went all around, and there we took pictures of the magnificent cat. But the real trophy was the mane. The hair was particularly long and thick, 80 percent of it jet-black. A super lion! Jim could return to Africa twenty times and never find a better one.

So much for spike camp!

Lesser Game

In the afternoon we encountered our first flock of guinea fowl, and Jim shot five of the twenty-odd birds. They were curiously tame and reluctant to fly, unlike the wild guineas I had experienced in East Africa. There, you had to be an Olympic athlete to bag one for the pot.

The next day Jim made a nice, quick shot on a gray duiker before it could dart off, as the sleek antelope are prone to do. Either you shoot them quickly or you watch them dash off with the speed of a greyhound, darting here, then there, making a running shot nearly impossible. We looked for kudu all day but found only a lone female. Other antelope were scarce, too, so Terry decided a move was in order. We would leave the next day for Massatang Camp, about one hundred and twenty miles away. So far, the camaraderie had been fantastic, the weather hot (except at night), and the trip wonderful.

The next morning I set my alarm for 4:30 A.M. to have another look for Halley's Comet. To my continued surprise, there was no sign of the

Jim and PH Terry Palmer enjoying lunch on the go.

fireball anywhere in the sky. Having seen the elliptical glow with the naked eye outside Dallas city limits, I had hoped for a better sighting in Botswana. The Southern Hemisphere was supposed to provide the best view.

The comet has special meaning for me because my great-grandfather Fred Rarick had observed it in 1910, the last time it passed near Earth. He was twenty-five (my age at the time of this safari) and was working as a telegraph operator for the Pennsylvania Railroad. He once told me that he wanted to live to see Halley's Comet again. He almost made it, too, passing away in 1981 at ninety-five. So I decided to set the same goal for myself—to see Halley's again in seventy-five years. I wondered where I would be and who would be there to see it with me.

We left camp after breakfast, and the sun quickly grew hot. The harsh rays seared my forearms, raising pink welts—the same rash that had occurred the day before. Even fifteen-factor sunscreen was no match for the ruthless Kalahari sun. Ten hours in it was just too much for this fair-skinned hunter.

Among the more interesting creatures we encountered were the bustards, and we encountered all three varieties: the greater, the lesser, and the black-bellied bustard. The greater bustard is a large, prehistoric-looking bird that stands three feet high. The feathered crown at the back of its head gives it the appearance of a pterodactyl.

On our way to the new camp, we stopped at the general store in the small village of Hukuntsi and met the owner, Pam. I was impressed with the merchandise. The small store had quite a variety of foodstuffs and supplies: sardines, mussels, vegetables, toothpaste, deodorant, and the like. Pam and her husband were the only whites in town, so these goods were for the blacks to buy. Nothing like that existed in the impoverished country of Tanzania. The couple obtained their water from a twenty-foot well, but water at such a shallow depth was scarce. Pam invited us to her house, where she served Lion Lager beer. It was good. No, it was great! There is nothing better than a cold beer on a hot day.

We arrived at Massatang Camp in time for dinner—hot, dusty, and travel weary. It is one thing to be hot and dusty while hunting, but it is altogether different to be hot and dusty while traveling between camps. The latter really saps your energy because there is little to do but stare at M.M.B.A., as the old-timers called it—miles and miles of bloody Africa.

Hardy Kudu

Chapter 18

We were off early one morning to an area where it had rained the day before—a rare event in the Kalahari, to say the least. The sandy ground was damp, making new tracks easy to read.

By midmorning, we found and were following the fresh track of a greater kudu bull. An hour later, we spotted the big antelope two hundred yards away in a gap in the brush. But it had already gotten the drop on us. Facing us, it looked absolutely majestic with its powerful neck, white-striped face, and dark, corkscrew horns. Terry studied the bull with his binocular, but the horns were obscured by the shade and branches, and he could not properly judge them.

"I think he's all right, but I'd like to get a better—"

The kudu turned its great head and, with one leap, disappeared in the brush.

"Yes, he was a good one."

Of course, then it was too late.

The kudu's behavior reminded me of a trophy whitetail, which is a master at monitoring you from a concealed position. If I've experienced that situation once hunting a trophy buck, I've experienced it a thousand times. Once you realize it's a good buck, it's gone. But that's hunting—real hunting, the best kind of hunting. That's what makes it exciting and challenging and keeps you coming back to hunt the same species year after year. If the trophy buck simply stood there and let you whack it every time, it would be a collection or a shoot, anything but a hunt. And you would quickly lose interest.

We went to the spot where the kudu had disappeared, and the trackers began pursuit on foot. The Bushmen and Kuna took turns jogging two at a time on the tracks of the bull. While two were tracking, one sat on the tire over the cab, directing Terry with a stick. I kept expecting to see the kudu any minute, but minutes soon turned into hours, and still there was no sight of the hardy antelope. Just deep, cloven-hoofed tracks in the sand.

In the end, the spiral-horned antelope led us on quite a chase. We went over twenty-five miles per the odometer, a distance I would not have thought possible. If it was an impressive performance by the big antelope, it was an even more amazing feat for the trackers. Switching off as they did, I figure they each ran a total of sixteen miles. Unbelievable! The temperature had to be one hundred and ten degrees in the sun, maybe more, and Kuna, who was forty, was the only one sweating.

The Bushmen wore brown jumpsuits and thick wool hats, but not a bead of sweat appeared anywhere on their bodies. It astounded me—I was dripping in sweat after my daily jogs in the early morning cool. It was a fine demonstration that the Bushmen are truly at home in the desert. Just think what they could do if they didn't smoke! The funny part—no, the insulting part—was that they would jog with a cigarette clenched in their teeth!

At three o'clock we spotted the kudu some six hundred yards away, but it vanished once more into the brush with two leaps. We could not catch it. An hour later, Terry called an end to the chase because we were quite far from camp. Then he displayed the amazing talent of a topnotch PH. He simply turned off the fresh track we had made and aimed the vehicle toward camp in a straight line through the brush. How he could even begin to find the way back I'll never know. It was similar to elephant hunting, when, after winding this way and that for hours through the thickest labyrinth of cover you can imagine, it is time to quit, and the PH simply points to indicate that camp or the truck is "that way" and makes a beeline for it. I would give anything for a little of that talent.

The last of the ride to camp was quite cold. It was after 8 P.M. when we finally arrived, all of us bushed and beat from the hot sun, covered in dust and dried sweat. A shower in the brisk air was just the thing to revive me from my zombie status.

The tractor arrived the next morning with water. Our water supply was quite low, and we were glad to see it. The two Pittsburgh hunters before us reportedly had taken three showers a day! I'm sure they were even less accustomed to the heat than we Texas boys.

Desert Practicality

The next day Jim had quite a successful hunt, starting with hartebeest. We found a bachelor herd of three males that would not stay put. This resulted in a twenty-five-minute stalk through patchy bush, making it difficult for Jim to get a shot. The chestnut-colored animals, when stopped, were skilled at using the intervening cover for concealment, and they had a way of milling about and huddling up so that you couldn't tell which head went with which body. Finally, we got a break, and Jim took a large male with a well-placed shot.

Jim with a magnificent gemsbok. Note the tape holding the gunstock together.

At noon we spotted several gemsboks, one of which displayed outstanding headgear. We pursued the herd, and eventually the big-horned one afforded Jim a broadside shot, though it was a long one. Unfortunately, Jim had a poor rest, and he shot over it. The gemsbok bolted, and another mad chase on foot ensued. But we were supremely outmatched, and soon the trophy gemsbok was nearly out of range.

As the gemsbok made for the hills, the only shot offered was at its rear. With three seconds left on the clock, Jim's only option was a Hail Mary pass. He threw the rifle across the shooting sticks, took a quick breath, and made a fantastic shot. A quick follow-up shot rolled the large antelope in the dust. It was fine shooting at a fine trophy. The dun bull had beautiful, thick, straight horns measuring 39 inches. A super gemsbok.

Butchering the gemsbok brought a lesson in desert practicality. Having spent several months on the Dark Continent, I knew all too well that no part of a hunter's animal goes to waste in Africa, that every scrap is eaten, every piece of hide used, but what the Bushman did next I would never have imagined. He sliced open the gemsbok's belly with a knife and rolled out the ample stomach. He made a slit in the bulging organ, reached a hand deep into the opening, and scooped up a palmful of the malodorous contents. It looked like green salsa, the same green crud that brings a gag reflex when a hunter gut-shoots an animal by mistake and gets a whiff when field-dressing it. The Bushman then clenched his hand in a fist, squeezing green juice into the palm of his other hand. He lifted the liquid to his lips and eagerly slurped it up. In fact, he squeezed and slurped until he had extracted all the moisture from this particular fistful of pulp. Discarding the soggy remains, he repeated this procedure several times, drinking what barely amounted to a cup of liquid.

The idea of drinking intestinal fluid may seem utterly repulsive until you stop to think how limited are the Bushmen's options to acquire water in the Kalahari. Then it makes a lot of sense. It is a matter of practicality—the ultimate in practicality. In the desert every ounce of liquid, no matter the source, must be utilized. The Bushmen's first commandment is "Thou shalt not waste water." Murder and adultery are way down the list. In fact, they can ignore the other nine just fine. But without water, they would all promptly perish.

Being the gentleman that I am, I welcomed Jim to go ahead of me for a drink. Strange thing, it turned out we are both gentlemen, and neither was willing to go first.

We pulled into camp in midafternoon, the tail end of the truck sagging noticeably from the weight of the large antelopes. But we didn't dally long. At 4:30 P.M. we left to find a springbok, an animal only slightly smaller than a pronghorn. Two hours later, we had seen only three. The day before, there had been several hundred in the area. As I have said many times before, don't ask me how, but somehow animals know when you are after them!

Then, as the light of day was swiftly receding, we spotted a herd of seventy or so near camp. Terry would have preferred more time to make a better approach, but we were running out of shooting light. So we did the best we could, trying not to spook any in the herd, for spooking one springbok is as good as spooking the whole herd.

After some posturing, Jim got into position, and Terry scouted for a trophy head in the binoc. Terry had just located a nice male and communicated its location to Jim when the whole herd suddenly turned and sprinted past us. That didn't slow Jim. He kept track of the large male and shot it as it hit full speed a hundred yards away. The sprinting antelope tumbled in a flurry of dust, and Jim ran up to finish it off.

The springbok sports on its lower back a peculiar display of white hair called a ruff. The ruff, standing in sharp contrast to the tawny coat, can be raised and fanned at will. The ruff now stood at "attention" on the back of Jim's springbok, even in death, and remained erect throughout our picture shoot. Eventually, the ruff folded and disappeared beneath the tan hair of the rump.

Jim was as happy as could be. We had had quite a day, and the safari had been very successful. All that was left to hunt in this area was kudu.

In camp the moonless night sky made a perfect backdrop for our continued search for the mysterious comet. Near the bright band of

Our Bushman tracker takes a drink from an unlikely place: the stomach of Jim's gemsbok.

the Milky Way we noticed a familiar clump of stars that on a previous evening we had all agreed was a globular cluster. Tonight it appeared farther apart and a bit more elongated.

"No!" we both exclaimed in unison.

What do you know—this was Halley's Comet! We had observed it for several nights without realizing it. How unimpressive it was, for all the hype. It was nearly as visible with the naked eye in Dallas.

We left camp early the next morning and stumbled onto a male kudu's tracks at 10 A.M. We followed them, but when we caught up to the kudu forty-five minutes later, it turned out to be an immature male. The rest of the day we saw several female kudus and their young but no fresh tracks of males.

That evening we arrived in camp bushed and beat. This was our last day in the desert, so we called it quits on kudu in the Kalahari. The next day we would leave for the Okavango Swamp—"The Land of Many Rivers."

The Okavango Swamp and Botswana PHs
Chapter 19

The charter plane arrived on time the next morning. After a quick packing job, we lifted off for the frontier town of Maun in the northern part of the country. Upon arrival, we had lunch at the nearby Duck Inn, where we were joined by Terry's wife, Mirva—a lively, friendly sort—and his mother and father. I quite enjoyed meeting Terry's father, Lionel Palmer, a well-known and respected PH. We shared our favorite safari books and talked about the authors.

"I took Wilbur Smith on safari," Lionel told me. "And I ran into James Mellon in the Nairobi airport."

The author of *African Hunter,* Mellon spent years collecting every conceivable species of African game, as well as game around the world.

"Young Mellon was strolling through the airport with a rifle slung over his shoulder. 'Going hunting?' I asked him.

Jim riding safari style.

The enormous dry pan beside camp, also known as "Johnny's jogging track."

"'Yes,' he said.

"'Where?'

"'Don't know yet.'"

Don't know yet! That was unheard of. No one just showed up in Africa to hunt—not in the past few decades, anyway. You made the arrangements months or years ahead of time, before you ever set foot on the soil. Those three words spoke volumes to anyone familiar with the process of booking an African safari.

Then we got on the subject of Capstick and other writers of hunting literature.

"He's here now," Lionel said. "He's in the country making some film or other."

Then I confessed to my own interest in writing. I'm sure Lionel thought, "Oh, great, another flake come to write about Africa."

"It's funny," I told him, "that it's often guys like me who write about Africa, while professionals who know the most, like you, don't."

He got a good chuckle out of that.

On the way out of the restaurant I ran into Willie Engelbrecht, another famous (or infamous) PH, depending on who's telling it.

"How are your mom and dad?" he asked. "And, by the way, I saw that kudu of yours at the Dallas convention two years ago. Impressive as hell!"

After a leisurely lunch, we boarded the plane and left for James's camp, situated in a delta of the enormous Okavango Swamp. As we neared camp, pilot Mark Morgan dropped the plane to only a few hundred feet above ground, and we saw great numbers of game below: red lechwes, elephants, buffaloes, hippos, and a leopard or a cheetah (couldn't tell which). Unlike the Kalahari, this lush area of the country supports high densities of wildlife. At the edges of the water, red lechwes gather in fantastic herds that spread far and wide.

Sitatunga, Sable, and Kudu

Once we had landed and got our gear settled in camp, Terry was anxious to be off in the "White Elephant II," his twin Land Cruiser, to see what we could find. Tsessebe and red lechwe were everywhere. A good sitatunga dashed across our path and disappeared into the safety of the swamp before we could stop, much less get it in the binoculars. That was an encouraging sight because sitatunga was the prime trophy in this area, and one that Jim was most anxious to collect. We decided to try for that one tomorrow. It would have been anticlimactic to drive

The ruff of Jim's springbok remained erect for some time after death.

The labyrinth of swamps that makes up the Okavango, as seen from the air.

around the bend and simply bushwhack a trophy sitatunga. The proper sitatunga hunt features many long and fruitless stalks through thick bogs and reedy swamps. Anything less would feel like cheating. I think most hunters measure the true success of a trophy hunt by the disappointments and hardships experienced in the quest. Trophy hunting is one endeavor in which the end does not justify the means. In other words, getting the animal is not the most important thing. How you get it is.

Staring up at the stars that night proved a humbling experience. We discovered the three of us stank at astronomy. Were our hunting skills as bad, we would still be stumbling around the Kalahari, trying to bag our first trophy. What we had thought was Halley's Comet a few nights before was not. After much searching, we finally did spot it. The elusive mass of ice and dust was just to the left of the Southern Cross, as a friend of Terry's had indicated at lunch.

In the morning we visited several "sitatunga trees," strategic tall trees hunters use to spot sitatunga feeding or moving about the swamp. To reach a couple of these trees we would have to trek through shin-deep water in the flooded flats. (I was glad for nylon-sided boots. The water squished right back out, though my feet remained damp all day.) With the skill of a spider monkey, Terry climbed high into each of the spotting

142

trees to have a look beyond the tall reeds that blocked our view from the ground. Here and there were shallow flooded patches in the reeds, and it was in one of these open patches that we had hoped to sight a sitatunga and make a stalk.

Despite our efforts that day, we saw none.

Jim shot a huge hyena in the afternoon. Hyenas are protected in Tanzania, and this was the first one I had seen up close. An arm's length away was close enough! The spotted animal reeked of death. Dining primarily on putrid carrion, hyenas are the junkyard crew of the animal world, performing the necessary but unpleasant task of cleaning up what other predators leave behind. Most noticeable were the bulbous, solid-black eyes, which must provide exceptional night vision. The torso of the hyena is unusually large, and its back legs are unusually short, giving it a droopy hind end and the odd, rocking horse gait. My first impression remained the same: The hyena is butt-ugly, and that is a charitable description.

Despite the hyena's repulsive odor and unsightly features, I considered it quite a trophy. Perhaps trophy isn't the right word. Maybe a unique find is more accurate because it is so rare to see a hyena in the light of day. After nine months in Africa, I could count on two hands and a foot the number of hyenas I'd observed. It was satisfying finally to see

"OK, we got all the luggage aboard—now, where do we sit?"

Terry glasses the swamp for sitatunga, using a ladder that is carried from tree to tree

firsthand the critter responsible for making the familiar *whoop, whoop* in the African night.

That night, as we sat around the campfire swigging Ohlson's beer, munching tuna-and-cracker hors d'oeuvres, and chatting over our adventures, I reflected how wonderful this was and how splendid I felt. It was one of those moments you wish could last forever. Your body and mind are relaxed, and your soul is at peace with the world. This sense of calm was due in part to the physical exertion of the hunt, in part to the day's exploits, and in part to the aftereffects of the adrenaline surges brought on by our endeavors. But it also had to do with the fire itself. There is something deep inside us, something from our caveman days, that craves watching a night fire. Sitting around a campfire is more therapeutic than a visit to the shrink. The dancing, crackling flames are both mesmerizing and hypnotizing. They work magic that no doctor or scientist can put a name to. If the happy, blissful feeling that comes from watching a campfire could be bottled and sold, it would fetch billions. It would put the alcohol and drug industries out of business.

When we finally turned in to our tents, I fell into a deep sleep. But it didn't last long. A hippo feeding beside my tent made such a racket that it kept me awake much of the night. I guess I could have gotten out of bed and tried to shoo it off, but I had as little experience shooing off hippos in the dark as I did locating comets in the sky. So I stayed put.

We left for spike camp after a quick breakfast. The White Elephant was packed to the hilt with gear, leaving tracker John and two additional natives to balance themselves on top. We drove along the grassy, green flood plains toward the Okavango, seeking an area that had reportedly been teeming with game last season. But we found the place bone dry and consequently devoid of wildlife, so we backtracked a few miles and tried another direction.

Late in the afternoon we discovered a small water hole, home to a family of spur-winged geese. John and one native lit out on foot at top speed. They chased down five of the large goslings, which they carried proudly back by the necks, grinning at their catch. Terry told them to release three, and we kept the other two for dinner.

"Breeding stock," Terry asserted, and rightfully so.

Terry's assertion summed up what sport hunting is all about. Harvesting animals on a sustained-yield basis is what makes hunting work for the hunter and the hunted—both equal parts of the equation. It is nothing less than the same equation employed by Mother Nature. There is one major difference, however. When it comes to harvesting prey on a sustained-yield basis, animal predators are limited by their physical ability. Man, with his modern weapons, is limited only by conscious self-restraint.

Because of our inherent advantage, it is incumbent upon hunters to set reasonable limits when afield, especially where reason dictates a more conservative take than the regulations. For instance, there is no law to prohibit a group of hunters from shooting fifteen quail out of a covey of eighteen, but I believe doing so is irresponsible. Many will tell you that 80 percent of quail succumb to natural causes each year, anyway. And that may be true. Quail, like rabbits, are at the bottom of a food chain, but they are a necessary part of that chain, and others depend on them. But I will tell you that leaving three quail creates havoc with the viability of covey dynamics. Three quail does not a covey make. Don't leave three and walk away thinking you are doing the quail any favors. With that attitude, a person might as well shoot all eighteen because the three left probably aren't going to make it.

We made camp under a cluster of trees a couple of hundred yards from the water. (The word camp is perhaps an exaggeration; camp consisted of a ground tarp with three thin mattresses laid on top.) After a tasty dinner of baby goose, we retired to the mattresses with an eye on the dark storm clouds that threatened on the horizon. We lay in the dark,

The smile after a successful day afield. Time to return to camp, for there's no room for more trophies.

It doesn't take much to make a fly camp—a fire and a couple of chairs and you feel right at home.

watching spectacular displays of lightning and listening to the mounting thunder. Rain was on the way, but I was thinking of something much more forbidding. Before turning in, Terry had shared a couple of tales that weren't exactly the kind of bedtime stories I wanted to hear.

"A lion ate a tourist camped near here," he said, rather matter-of-factly. "The family woke to the terrified screams of their daughter. A lion had wandered up and taken her by the head. The lion dragged her out of a sleeping bag while the rest of the family screamed and yelled and threw things at the cat, but the lion couldn't be distracted. It simply dragged her off in the night and began to eat her. There was nothing they could do but listen in horror."

His next story was about a lady tourist who went to wash at the stream in front of a game lodge. She was never seen or heard again. The life insurance company required proof of death, so the rangers killed several large crocs in the area and cut them open, but they found nothing of her inside. Whatever animal got her left no trace of the crime.

Just after midnight, it began to rain, and Jim and I pulled a tarp over us. It kept the rain off but made for hot and muggy sleeping. Sleep did not come easy, especially after I heard the roar of a lion in the distance and remembered Terry's bedtime story. The constant rumble of the big cats did little to relax my guard. I must admit I lay there with ears and eyes on full alert until the need for sleep overwhelmed me.

We awoke wet and tired at sunrise and had a quick bite to eat before setting out from spike camp on a very successful day. An hour or so later, a bull sable appeared in the woods. It proved difficult to collect in the thick undergrowth, playing hide-and-seek with us for some time. Either it was out of range or it was in range but hidden behind trees or clumps of brush. Regardless, we were unable to get a clear shot. Then the wary sable would dash off and disappear, and we would have to start searching all over again. It was slow work, but Terry was persistent. We crept through the thick tangle, making as little noise and movement as possible, and it surprised me each time we made another sighting. But it was always just a piece of the black antelope—its head, leg, or rump—we saw disappearing into the vegetation.

Eventually, the bull made the mistake and presented a shoulder. Jim got in a shot, and as the sable dashed off, he followed up quickly with another. We pursued it immediately, running as fast as we could. After a winded chase, we glimpsed the black bull trotting forty yards ahead in the thick bush. Jim fired the .300 once more and brought the sable to a standing stop. All three were good shots, but the sable was extremely tough. We closed in, and at fifteen feet Jim shot the bull twice again. Incredibly, the sable remained on all fours. The black bull, literally dead on its feet, was pumped with enough adrenaline to power a jet engine. Nothing short of a spine or brain shot was going to take it down. Ribbed horns swept over its back like two samurai swords and were just about as lethal, so we refrained from closing the distance between us. Finally, the sable collapsed, and Jim made a final shot in the shoulder. That was one tough animal.

We dropped the sable at spike camp, and Terry informed the men that we would return to James's camp after lunch. I was not looking forward to another sleepless night, so I was glad to hear it. A tent is no obstacle to a hungry lion, but at least the sound of shredding cloth provides a warning.

In late morning Jim shot a nice reedbuck in the tall grass of the flood plains. After loading it, we returned to spike camp for lunch.

On our return to James's camp, a large kudu bull stepped from the bush as we neared the swamp. Jim jumped out and shot it smack in the shoulder. Unlike the smaller sable, it ran only a few yards and dropped, stone dead. Go figure.

And big it was. It took all of us to load the great antelope onto the truck, the back of which was piled high with gear and game, all covered by a slick tarp. We almost had the bull loaded twice atop the tarp when it slipped and crashed to the ground amongst us. Luckily, the big horns didn't bash anyone. You read about dead buffalo killing hunters, but I never thought it would happen with a kudu! On the third try, the kudu stayed put, and the men lashed it down. Now loaded to overflowing, the truck headed back toward camp with us looking like a band of gypsies. The weight seriously tested the limits of the springs along the way. Once there, I stripped off my sweaty, grimy clothes and headed for the simple joy of a hot shower.

We left camp after breakfast and an early jog. We hadn't gone far when Terry suddenly slammed on the brakes. There, in the middle of the road, was a long black mamba, its head hovering three feet off the ground. It stared at us as we came to a sliding stop in front of it. Tracker John, who had been sitting above the cab, just about did a backflip as he retreated into the bed of the truck and landed on top of Jim. Aware of the mamba's aggressive nature and being closest to the snake, he figured he'd be the snake's intended target. Fortunately, the lightning-quick snake opted not to attack. Instead, it disappeared into the undergrowth beside the road.

I chucked sticks at the brush while Terry stood ready with a shotgun. But the wicked snake never showed.

At 1 P.M. we came across fresh buffalo tracks. Terry took a quick look and nodded in excitement. We started after them on foot. While the Kalahari had offered dry heat, the Okavango specializes in the oppressive, humid variety. It was a hot and muggy trek through the mopane forest. Visibility was twenty yards at best, and we did our damnedest to keep quiet. Suddenly, several dark shapes loomed in the brush. They were no more than twenty paces ahead, but it was impossible to see a complete set of horns, much less a whole buffalo, in the thick foliage.

The shifty wind was no help, either. The buffalo saw us or smelled us and abruptly went crashing through the brush, raising a cloud of dust that hung in the damp air like fog. Terry shook his head in disappointment, and we followed them again. But we saw nothing of the black beasts except the spiraling dust left behind as they raced away.

An hour later, Terry pulled up and said, "Forget it!" He removed his cap and wiped the streaming sweat from his face. "We'll never get near them with this fickle wind."

A supply truck drove into camp that evening while we were sitting at the campfire. It was driven by eighteen-year-old Peter Henning, a gofer for Hunters Africa. Gofers run errands and shuttle supplies from camp to camp as necessity arises. Interestingly, he was a sixth-generation

Setting up the radio antenna in the bush to check in with headquarters in Maun.

white African. He joined us for supper, and we all retired by 9 P.M, though Peter didn't get much sleep. He was off at 3 A.M to deliver eggs to another hunting camp. At 7 A.M he returned to our camp for breakfast and awaited his next orders. Such is the schedule of an aspiring PH!

Before heading to far-off buffalo country the next day, Terry decided to check the sitatunga trees. It was only a five-minute walk to the first tree. The tree itself sprouted from the crown of a large termite mound, which prompted the question: Which came first, the termite mound or the tree? Probably the tree. Both Terry and John climbed the metal ladder we had left leaning against it a few days before. A second later, Terry came clambering down, his blue eyes as big as doorknobs.

"Remove anything that is not waterproof," he whispered, digging in his pockets.

I laid my coat and daypack on the ground, and Jim did likewise. With Terry in the lead, we dashed beyond the termite mound toward the Kwando swamp, parted the thick reeds that grew at the edge, and plunged into cool, murky water that came up to our chests. We soon had to stand on our tiptoes to keep our heads above water. The bottom of the swamp turned quickly to mush, sucking us in ankle deep, then shin deep, and finally knee deep with each searching step. It was a real struggle to keep our balance on the mushy bottom and not slip under the surface. The water was the dark color of over-brewed tea, full of lily pads, underwater stalks and vegetation, and, of course, hippo dung. The area was also full of crocs, so you would be right if you guessed we were keeping an eye out for the wily devils and hoping not to get dragged under suddenly. Fortunately, most of the crocs we had seen so far were in the larger, open bodies of water, but they clearly traveled throughout the entire swamp. In the deeper parts, Terry and Jim had to hold their rifles over their heads, as the actors do in the old Tarzan movies.

We clambered out on a narrow strip of land, navigated our way through thick, eight-foot reeds that blocked our view in all directions, and reentered the water, crossing another chest-deep tributary. We did this two or three more times, all the while getting closer to our prize. We made slow progress, trying to keep quiet, trying not to splash water or break reeds underfoot. Glancing back at the lookout tree, I was surprised to find that we had traveled only a couple of hundred yards. It seemed much farther.

The next dry land was an island that had a dirt mound in the center with a bush growing out of the top. We could not have designed a more perfect blind or shooting platform had we the tools and time to do so. Peering through the leaves, we were met with a splendid sight: a magnificent sitatunga bull feeding in knee-deep water one hundred and fifty yards away. Steadying the .300 on a firm branch, Jim took advantage of our concealment to wait for a good presentation. When the spiral-horned antelope finally turned broadside, Jim shot the bull in the shoulder. It jumped and ran, and Jim placed a second shot up its rear—the only shot offered—which brought the bull to a stop. A third shot dropped it into the swamp.

Terry threw his cap to the ground and broke into a great grin. He slapped Jim on the back, and everyone shook hands and roared at our success. The sitatunga is a rare and highly sought-after animal, so this was quite a triumph. We trudged through knee-deep water to the spectacular antelope, where another celebration took place.

Terry pointed out an interesting feature of the sitatunga: elongated, splayed hoofs that are used to negotiate the mushy swamp bottom. We dragged the trophy to dry land and took plenty of photos, then returned to camp. A change into dry clothes felt especially soothing because the weather that day had been overcast and cool.

Buffalo

Then we went right back out in search of buffalo. Young Peter came with us, thankful to be hunting and away from errands for the moment.

A pack of fearless African wild dogs.

Along the way, Jim collected a good impala. The herd had spooked at
the sight of us and disappeared in the bush, so Jim and Terry went after
them alone, making this the first animal of the safari shot in my absence.
I considered myself quite lucky to have been present on every hunt until
then. A stop in the shade for lunch featured fresh roasted impala liver.

As we packed up the lunch box, the sky darkened and a few drops
began to fall. There was no question it was going to rain, but the sky held,
as if determined to save it all up for once. Nevertheless, we pressed on
through the mopane forest. Soon we crossed the tracks of a small herd
of buffalo, and everyone got out. Jim and Terry checked their loads and
ammo, and a game plan was whispered back and forth. Just as we set
off, it began to drizzle. When the drizzle turned to rain, Terry instructed
the rest of us to stay put, and he and Jim pushed on ahead. While we
waited, the sky opened up and the heavens poured! We couldn't hear
a thing except the rain pounding on our heads and on the broad leaves
of the surrounding mopane bushes. The rain was so loud I doubted we
could hear Jim and Terry shoot, much less hear a whistle for us to join
them. Patiently, we waited there in the downpour.

Finally, tracker John indicated that we should follow. I was hesitant
to do so. First, I did not want to stumble into the line of fire. Second, I
did not want to intercept their quarry and blow the whole hunt. Either
was a real possibility, given the weather and the terrain. You couldn't

hear a thing in the pounding rain, and we couldn't see but a few yards in any direction while navigating the narrow openings that meandered around the thick mottes of trees that made up this forest.

Standing there in the rain didn't sound like such a great idea, either, so we pressed on. Soon we found the hunters themselves taking shelter under a large tree. The buffalo, they said, had given them the slip, but Terry was not about to give up. We huddled in silence, shaking our heads or rolling our eyes at the rain that refused to quit. No one spoke a word because, for all we knew, the buffalo could be a few steps away in any direction. At the first break in the storm, Terry and Jim carried on alone. We had just reached the truck when the dark clouds poured a second time, and we took cover inside the vehicle. Some time later, Jim and Terry arrived, soaked to the skin, the water pouring off their hat brims and bodies as if they were statues in a fountain.

The buffalo were the victors that day.

The two-and-one-half-hour drive back to camp was, in a word, miserable. Standing in the rear of the Land Cruiser, Peter and I were hammered by the driving rain. I figure it was the equivalent of standing on the bow of a ship in a hurricane, the water pelting us from every angle. I must say my Gore-Tex jacket proved invaluable. I was dry from the waist up, soaked from there down, and quite cold from the rush of the wind. Peter was completely sopped. He must have been freezing, but he never complained. An apprentice PH knows what he is in for.

After changing into dry clothes for the second time that day, I went to visit Jim in his tent. Still chilled to the bone, I took my gas lantern as a source of heat and huddled around it. Jim was busy drying all his gear and oiling his guns. Pretty soon Terry and Peter joined us, and we spent the evening swapping jokes and listening to the rain pummel the taut canvas. Terry and Peter had us in stitches with one joke after another.

The next day we finally continued our quest for buffalo. The rain had wiped the slate of all tracks and made the search for fresh ones that much easier. Early on we found the spoor of a large herd of buffaloes and set out after them, prepared to be out all day. When tracking an animal, especially in thick cover, you never know how long a particular hunt will last or how far away it may take you.

As luck would have it, we sighted the black beasts less than twenty minutes later. But the wind was erratic, and we could not get a good look at the bulls before they went crashing off. This scenario repeated itself several times. We would sneak up to the herd in the thick bush, and the creatures would catch sight or sound or wind of us and thunder off like locomotives through the underbrush. After a couple of hours of this, Terry took my suggestion and left me waiting behind with two natives. Six people walking through the bush was just too many. Three would make half the noise and half the movements.

The strategy paid off. About twenty minutes later, I heard the first of sixteen shots. (No, that's not a typo.) After the fourth or fifth shot, the two natives and I glanced at each other, and on each successive shot thereafter we would shake our heads in amazement. The shots just kept coming. Whatever had happened, the hunt had not gone as planned, but as long as we heard shooting, I knew that at least one of the hunters was still alive.

There was a period of silence. Then *boom!* The sixteenth shot was so close it made us jump, and I wondered, *What the devil? Has the buffalo worked its way back to us?* After the first shots, the herd had stampeded quite near us, and I figured the wounded bull was following the herd. The sixteenth shot turned out to be tracker John, shooting in the air, trying to locate us.

He led us to the dead buffalo and our spent-looking hunters, and we got the full story. At the first shot the bull had run off in the thick mopane bush. The hunters followed the blood trail, but when it led into a particularly dense patch of bush, Terry called a halt. After looking around, he decided they should climb a tree and take a look ahead. It was a wise decision. Sure enough, they spotted the bull. It was circling back, relentlessly seeking its pursuers. The bull continued several times to circle their position. From high in the tree the hunters took shots at

Jim and bush pilot Mark Morgan fueling up for the flight out. Little did we know we'd be heading into dangerous cloud cover.

the circling bull through sporadic openings in the bush. But the big bull absorbed bullets like a sponge absorbs water. Like a zombie, the stubborn beast seemed impossible to kill, and it just kept circling, determined to find and destroy our heroes.

Eventually, the bull dropped dead. There were too many holes in the hide to try to figure out which shot was which or in what order. As I have said before, buffalo are just plain tough. You really have to witness the punishment a rugged, determined old bull can take in order to believe it.

"Another case of lead poisoning," Terry concluded.

Terry sent tracker John to retrieve the truck, but it took him forever to navigate the thick mottes. It was late afternoon before we heard the car approaching. When we got up to flag it down, we made a surprising discovery. The road was no more than five yards from where we sat! It had been completely hidden in the thick bush. Had we seen it earlier, it would have saved John more than two hours of battling brush to reach us. The good news was that it saved us substantial time on the return drive.

Terry used a neat trick to load the buffalo, something I had not seen before. Holes were dug in the sand to accommodate the rear tires, thereby lowering the bed of the truck and saving each of us a hernia, even with the buffalo cut in two. There is no such thing as lifting half a buffalo by hand, but with the bed lowered we were able to "roll" each half in.

We arrived to quite a celebration in camp that evening. Everyone knew how hard we had worked for this bull. After a festive dinner and the retelling of the day's adventures, we turned in early for a good night's sleep.

Eland

In search of eland the next morning, we discovered an abandoned village. The grass-thatched huts showed signs of neglect but offered no explanation as to what had happened to the inhabitants or why they had chosen to leave.

At midday we stopped at a likely looking field to try our hand at a bird drive. Jim and Terry stood ready at brush line, shotguns in hand, while I drove the field and tried to push the scurrying birds in their direction. The birds finally flushed, and Jim shot a couple of Swainson's francolin as the birds sailed overhead.

Back at camp, Terry told an interesting story of a black American client who wanted to mingle and get to know the African blacks. The client figured he would have a lot in common with them. After a couple of weeks, however, the fellow realized how little, besides skin color, he shared with the African natives. He shook his head and said, "Thank God for slavery!" Obviously, he was quite thankful his ancestors had made it to America.

I started the next day with a five-mile jog, but I found the Okavango terrain more difficult than the hard, flat pans of the Kalahari. The sand is softer and deeper and swallows your feet, making you struggle as if running in place, and I knew I wouldn't miss it one bit when we left. We spent most of the day bird hunting, and Jim and I had a grand time shooting six crowned guinea fowl. While driving, we spotted another mamba on the road, but we couldn't get a shot at it. The sighting did little to increase the comfort of my early morning jogs.

(Two weeks later, I would visit a snake park in South Africa to see what nasties I had missed in the bush and to get a closer look at the ones I had seen. It was amazing what a difference a quarter-inch of glass made; I could thump my chest at them, look them eye to eye, and tell them what I thought of their mothers, all without fear of retaliation. Behind glass, snakes appear as harmless as hamsters in a pet store.)

Later, Jim collected a zebra, and we had a quick lunch while the trackers skinned it. Hordes of hungry vultures hovered in anticipation. The instant we drove off, the big, dark birds descended upon the skinless carcass. They had appeared out of thin air, gliding in from all directions. Some landed with a hard thud, so eager were they not to miss out; others waddled up anxiously to the carrion and plunged in beak first, tearing, pecking, ripping, gulping. The hunched gray birds soon numbered in the hundreds. With the skill of piranhas, they devoured the remains, finishing the sizable animal to the bone in less than twenty minutes! It made quite a video. It was startling to see how quickly the zebra's existence was wiped from the face of the earth. One minute an animal of several hundred pounds was lying there, and the next there was nothing left but a tattered skeleton—every scrap of muscle, tissue, and organs gone. The vultures were like a school of sharks in a feeding frenzy. It made me wonder if the ghoulish birds ever sustained casualties from the misaimed beaks of over-eager comrades.

The next day we awoke to a low-lying fog that threatened hunting visibility. Fortunately, it lifted to reveal an overcast sky. In late morning we came upon a pack of twenty or so African wild dogs. Little larger than a coyote, these rare canines bear an interesting coat. The fur, similar to that of a calico cat, is a medley of mottled colors and patterns. Outfitted in black, white, and tan markings, each coat has a unique pattern. The dogs sport big, Mickey Mouse-type ears, but any resemblance to the fun-loving mouse stops there.

Considered one of the most effective predators in all of Africa, wild dogs hunt as a pack, though not all running at once. The cunning beasts take turns chasing their prey, the tiring animal handing off his pursuit to the next, rested, dog like a baton in a relay race. Using this tactic, they can drag down an animal twenty times their size. Exhausting and overwhelming it in numbers, they tear at their prey like wolves, pulling the insides out, ripping off chunks of meat, literally eating the doomed victim alive. Watching a film of the massacre is enough to turn a hunter's stomach. So much for Mother Nature!

I must admit to an eerie feeling as I watched these fearless predators. It was if they had never encountered a real threat. Undaunted, the tranquil pack lazed about as we drove up to them. They did not budge except to sniff the vehicle as it passed. Terry could have stuck his hand out the window and scratched one under the chin. In fact, as we drove away, the whole pack started to follow at a trot! Maybe it was the smell of zebra from the previous day that attracted them. Maybe they thought we were food. Whatever it was, it felt like something out of a Stephen King novel. I can promise you this: The wild dog is one animal I would rather not meet on my morning jog.

On our quest for eland, the largest antelope on the continent, we came upon a village of thatched huts. We stopped to inquire if the natives had recently seen the antelope, but they hadn't. After a quick lunch near the village, we put in a lot of miles and saw lots of game, but there was no sign of eland that afternoon.

On the return to camp, Jim made a nice one-shot kill on a red lechwe at the edge of a swamp. The henna-colored antelope is built heavier in the rear than in the front, with long, sweeping horns that bounce above its back as it gallops in the swamp. It is quite a sight to watch a whole herd dash about in the shallows. The rocking forms appear to be running on top of the water, and the water is where they prefer to stay. So they tend to dash from one end of the shallows to the other, keeping a comfortable distance from you all the while.

We were excited to find fresh eland tracks the next day but had no luck in catching up to the animals. This was not surprising, for the eland is fast-moving, capable of covering countless miles in a day. On the return trek to the truck, a tsessebe appeared in the distance, and Jim made a splendid shot from over two hundred and fifty yards. We loaded the dark antelope in the truck and had not gone far when Terry glimpsed a lone wildebeest. After a careful stalk under a clearing sky, Jim finally collected the funny-looking animal. Surprisingly, the wildebeest proved to be a most difficult trophy to collect on the safari. The species was really wild in Botswana, and it ran like mad at the first sight of us.

The only animal left for Jim to hunt was the elusive eland, so Terry decided we had best move to a camp situated on the Kwando River. This move would also accommodate hunters on a bird safari who wished to use James's camp in our stead. After lunch, we packed our gear, said good-bye to the staff, and left for the new camp. It was hard to believe we were on the eve of our last day on safari. A safari is a little like summer vacation is to a kid: It is over before you know it.

On the way to the new camp we stopped to try our luck on a few doves flying over the perimeter of the swamp. The few aerial acrobats we managed to get made spectacular appetizers before dinner.

Terry had in mind a spot where we might happen onto eland. Sure enough, we found some good tracks, but, after an hour of following them, the massive antelope winded us and ran. The wise creatures ran consistently downwind, making it impossible for us to make an approach. We returned to the truck and carried on but saw no more fresh tracks on our last day of safari.

The hunt might have been over, but the adventure surely wasn't.

Last-Minute Adventures

The next morning we were off in a charter plane with Terry and Mirva, who had decided to join our sightseeing trip to Victoria Falls. While on a stop in Kisame to clear Customs (a tin shack on the side of the runway), I introduced myself to a familiar-looking fellow awaiting his own charter.

"Pat Carr-Hartley," he said.

"Any relation to Roy?" I asked. I had not seen Roy since my 1984 trip.

"He's my brother!"

Small world.

"How is he?"

"He's good, but his leg isn't. The part of the bullet that lodged in his ankle is giving him fits. He's going to the States to have it removed."

We chatted until my plane had clearance to go.

"Tell Roy hello."

"Will do."

Once back in the air, a large cloud of smoke appeared in the distance, rising from the plains. It was the kind you might expect to see from a sizable brush fire. As we neared the rising smoke, it became apparent that it was not a cloud of smoke at all but a fantastic plume of spray looming above the Falls. Pilot Mark Morgan circled the gaping chasm in the earth, treating us to a bird's-eye view of the nearly bottomless spectacle and the voluminous water of the Zambezi River plunging from the edge and disappearing into it. I rank this natural phenomenon in my Top Ten list of nature's spectacles. It is not to be missed when traveling in the area.

The Vic Falls Hotel is a grand, white, colonial-looking structure. The hotel appeared to have been well kept since independence (despite a few mortar pockmarks, courtesy of Mozambique rebels across the river), and the staff was notably friendly. It was a welcome contrast to my experience in Tanzania. Lunch was a copious buffet on the grand patio, a bargain at five Zim bucks (one dollar equaled one and one-half Zim bucks). The food, imported from South Africa, was quite good. We sat at tables in the shade while a band of locals, dressed in white, beat out island tunes on concave metal drums. The combination of bubbly, uplifting music, the Falls roaring in the background like a big surf hitting the beach, and a cold beer in hand made you feel as if you didn't have a worry in the world.

After lunch, we wandered down to the Falls and the various lookout points that descend partway below. We passed a statue of David Livingstone, who in 1855 was the first European to discover the falls. I was surprised that it had not been demolished or removed (or even renamed) during independence in an attempt to erase any trace of the white man's presence.

I mentioned the plume of spray that looms above the falls. Actually, it is a permanent rain cloud, created by the plummeting water and the

Victoria Falls from the air

The mighty Victoria Falls.

resultant spray that rises into the air. Whether it is the height of the falls or the sheer volume of liquid plunging into the abyss that produces this phenomenon I do not know, but the cloud is a perpetual presence, showering constant rain wherever the predominant winds happen to push it. It makes for a unique sight: blue skies in every direction except for this one dark cloud hanging at the mouth of the falls.

With that day's wind, the dark cloud enveloped our trail, and the lookout points became wetter and wetter as we went. First it was misting, then drizzling, and finally there came an absolute downpour as we entered the interior of the cloud. I drew my Gore-Tex coat over my head as we entered this stormy stretch, but it did little good—the rain seemed to come at us from all directions.

You never know what the day will bring in Africa, and our next day was no exception. The sky was overcast as the charter lifted off toward Maun, but it hardly appeared threatening. Not long into the flight, however, the clouds thickened and transformed into a solid cloud bank, which formed a distinct ceiling above us. This was not a concern until the ceiling began to descend, forcing the pilot to make a corresponding drop in altitude. The lower we flew, the lower the cloud cover dropped, and soon we were flying down in the bottom of a valley, and the dark sky had swallowed the hills around us.

The problem was that a plane without instruments must remain in sight of land at all times. Once you ascend into the clouds, you can't come down without the risk of smacking into the side of an unseen hill. In such a case, it is a matter of having enough fuel to outrun the clouds. Compounding our predicament was the fact that airports and other safe places to land are not exactly a dime a dozen in that part of the world.

The pilot was looking frantically about. Abruptly, he glanced over his shoulder.

"I need everyone to look for a break in the clouds, NOW!"

His face was ghostly white, his expression the scariest thing I had witnessed on safari. We were in trouble. He was not panicky, but you could tell he was deeply concerned. The charging elephant, so to speak, was in his sights and quickly getting closer.

We were now cruising only about one hundred feet above the treetops. Animals on the hillsides were actually above us, watching us fly past below them. Herds of sable and eland and giraffe whisked by. Everyone was searching anxiously out the windows for a break in the clouds, but there was none to be found in any direction. The daunting sky was solid as a metal roof, and it continued its relentless efforts to press down upon us.

Up ahead, the valley split around a cloud-masked hill, and Mark had to decide whether to go left or right. This turned out to be the first of several splits. He had to make this decision again and again as the winding valley continued to fork. A while later, he announced we had missed the airport.

"We've gone too far."

When we reached a spot wide enough to accommodate a U-turn, he shouted, "We're turning back!"

Now we were skimming the treetops, and the clouds continued to drop, threatening to shroud the entire valley in fog. The trees whizzed by—literally a few short feet beneath us—and I knew that a downdraft, any downdraft, would finish us off. I kept expecting to hear the wheels catch a limb—we were that low! It was a terrifying experience. It was similar to being a passenger in a car and seeing an eighteen-wheeler coming head-on at you and having the overwhelming sensation you would have to grab the wheel and spin it left or right—anything to miss certain death. Likewise, I desperately wanted to grab the controls of the plane and point us up, even if it meant going into the clouds.

"Look for the airport!" he shouted. "It should be somewhere up ahead."

Jim and I glanced at each other—there really wasn't much you could say. We immediately turned our attention to scanning the misty terrain. Pilot Mark had to work through another series of forks in the valley. And then we got lucky.

"There it is!" he announced, pointing through the windshield. "I see the airport."

Minutes later, we landed at the Vic Falls airport, and I know the feeling was unanimous: No one had ever been so glad to be back on solid earth. After climbing out, shaken and queasy, we each took in a big breath of fresh air. Poor Mirva was sick to her stomach. There really was only one remedy. We headed straight to the Vic Falls Hotel bar, lined up on stools, and downed two or three beers in a row.

Sometimes You Gotta Earn 'Em*

Chapter 20

All they could see of it was the black tuft of its tail twitching in the shadows of the brush. Somewhere in the tangle of scrub was a pair of angry, almond-shaped eyes watching them. The twitching tail told them that. And the roar—the bloodcurdling roar that had stopped them dead in their tracks. The noise rumbled through them like thunder. Judging by the paw prints they were following, it was as big as any male lion gets.

Tom Anding switched off his rifle's safety and braced for the forthcoming charge. PH Darrik Littleton stood rigid and grim-faced, while the two trackers—Bani and Smash—were stooped, squinting masterful eyes at the brush. Visibility in the mopane scrub was forty feet at best. The men swapped fleeting glances: *Can you see him?*

But no one could see the five-hundred-pound cat that was attached to the whipping tail. The brush was that thick.

The constant growling was growing louder. The vibrations rumbled through their bowels, down into the deepest recesses of their bodies and spirit—right down to the secret places where each man buried his fear in an attempt to keep calm.

"Get ready," Darrik warned. "He's going to come for us just now!"

Tom searched frantically in the scope, trying to find the lion that was promising to charge. But even with a scope, all he could see was thick undergrowth—and, through a small gap, the tail that was stirring up little dust clouds from the ground.

This is it, he thought. *This is why you came on safari. This is the hunt you wanted so badly and for so long, the one you heard about from all your friends who have a lion, the hunt you even dreamt about at night. So get ready. But this sure the hell isn't how your friends got their lions. No, sir. What ever happened to stringing up a bait and waiting inside a blind for a lion to show? A layer of thatch between you and those teeth and claws, a stool to sit on, a steady rest, and all*

*First published in Dallas Safari Club's *Hunters Quest,* March/April 1990.

the time in the world to catch your breath and shoot. What the heck ever happened to that?

******

It wasn't as though they hadn't tried to bait a lion. In Zimbabwe's Kazuma Forest during the first two weeks, Tom had been successful on everything but the cats, which were the prime objective of this fourth safari. Baiting for them just flat hadn't worked. They had hung baits till it made them sick, yet none drew the slightest nibble from the king of beasts. Darrik was at a loss. They hung more baits. They baited here, they baited there. They baited along rivers and they baited in the open plains. They baited every liony-looking place they came across.

But still no lion came to feed. Not even a passing paw print to tell them a lion had noticed their work.

The key to the problem lay with the Botswana game department. It had culled a number of elephant in a bordering park just three weeks prior to the hunt, and, consequently, the lion were so stuffed with the convenient fare that they were not the least interested in the baits. In two weeks of hard hunting—hunting from sunup to sundown, from one end of the concession to the other—the men had not so much as glimpsed a shootable male.

Frustrated, they decided to explore fresh country. They raced to the Ngamo-Sikumi concession to try for the obstinate cats. Raced, because instead of shooting new baits, which take days to develop the rank odor worth fetching a lion, they had decided to cut down the old ones and take them along. They figured that if they traveled at less than breakneck speed, the horrible stench of rotting meat would waft into the cab.

With only a week left, Darrik decided on a new approach. After checking baits early, they would head to the water-filled pans that dot the mopane forest and search the perimeter for pugmarks. They did this for six days straight, and each day they followed fresh tracks. But after hours of difficult tracking, they were disappointed to find either immature males or males with poor manes. These treks in thick bush often ended in intense confrontations when they came upon lions quite suddenly and at rock-throwing distances that tested the cats' fight/flight range.

Each time, the men were forced to stand their ground. To withdraw could provoke a charge. As a result, they endured threatening growls, menacing displays of dagger-sharp teeth, and startling mock charges until the lion grew weary and wandered off in retreat. When hunted in this manner, it was evident that the lion had every advantage.

They were now on day twenty of twenty-one, and it seemed the cats had given Tom the slip again.

But that's hunting, he thought. *You can't plan it like a job. It doesn't work that way. You may start out with Plan A to hunt lion, but before you've gone a hundred yards from camp, you cross a good buffalo track, so you set out on Plan B. Then a fifty-six-inch kudu appears—the same devil that gave you the slip last week—and, of course, you take off after him, and now you've ended up at Plan C. You can't just say, for instance, that today you are going out to collect a lion. In fact, it's often the reverse. It seems the harder you try to find a particular animal, the less likely you are to find it. They always pop up when you least expect them. Leave the guns in camp and mosey with a camera to snap pictures of the local bathing hippos, and that's when the biggest bloody lion you've seen in your life wanders out in the clear.*

******

Everyone was excited about the lion track they had found this morning at the edge of a pan. Placing his splayed hand upon it, Tom found there was ample room around it, and Darrik said, "Christ, that's a bloody big brute."

But the tracks soon led into thick vegetation, the kind that gives a big-game hunter nightmares. Because the Zimbabwe game department did not allow prescribed burns, the forest undergrowth was chest high and treacherously thick. As they inched from each likely place of ambush to the next, their progress slowed.

"I think you'd best put a solid in the bore," Darrik told Tom. "You'll likely have to shoot through the brush, and I don't trust a soft not to break up."

Darrik whispered instructions to Bani and Smash on either side of him. The trackers were moving their heads about to peer into the brush better. Sinewy thin, they looked as agile as cats themselves, ready to spring into action at the blink of an eye.

When the trackers slowed to a stalk, Tom knew something was up. He had spent enough days with them to read their body language. They often slowed when they lost a track in the spoor-littered forest or came upon a new track. But this was different. They were watching the brush ahead intently—perhaps even more intently than they watched the ground. And their proceedings had grown cautiously deliberate. Their voices gave over to whispers, then hand signals. Their faces wore the strangely mixed expressions of both the hunter and the hunted. Everything about them said the lion was quite close.

Tom Anding and his trophy lion—the culmination of four safaris and a lot of hard work.

Then the lion cut loose with a roar that shook the forest, as described at the beginning of this story.

"He's coming for us any second," Darrik cautioned. "Tom, I'm afraid you're going to have to shoot him on the charge."

Tom had read somewhere that a lion could cover one hundred yards in less than four seconds. Tom thought, *This is a fraction of that distance. What I have to do is this: Shoot the instant he appears, then work the bolt as fast as I can, and shoot at the center of the gold blur leaping at me. Palm the bolt and slap it shut. Don't finger it. And just keep shooting.*

Then came the thoughts that come to every big-game hunter facing this situation. *What if I botch it? What if I screw it up and shoot him in the gut? On the bright side, maybe it will bring him to a stop and give me time to shoot him a second or third time.*

But he had read too many accounts to believe that. When the lion came, he would have to stop it with the first shot. On a charging lion, there is rarely time for a second shot.

But still no lion came, just the constant roaring that had a way of curdling your stomach. It snarled the most gruesome threats and vows.

"Try moving to your left," came a whisper at Tom's ear. "You might see him."

Carefully he sidestepped, his gun at the ready, his finger on the trigger, until a tiny gap appeared in the brush. Filling the gap was the very big head of one very angry lion. *How would you like to have that monster sink its teeth into your chest?* thought Tom.

The lion was closer than he had expected. It was crouched no more than a dozen paces away, staring him down, its yellow eyes boring into him through the scope of the gun, its shaggy head taking up the whole lens. The lion's glare had a way of melting his insides. There was no bluff in its eyes. It mocked him. It called him a sheep. Standing his ground, Tom was forced to draw on inner resolve—forced to draw upon the same grit that propels soldiers out of trenches and into enemy fire; a cowboy out of the chute atop a bucking bull; a fireman into the blazes to rescue a child. Drawing a breath, Tom steadied himself, placed the cross hairs between the lion's angry eyes, lowered his aim just below the chin, prayed, and fired.

All at once the forest went dead silent. It went from a deafening roar to absolute stillness—a frightful contrast. Now the only sounds Tom could hear were the ringing in his ears from the blast and the sound of his heart knocking to get out of his chest, as the four men anxiously awaited the result. When first shot, a lion usually jumps in the air or whirls around once or twice before departing. This lion did none of that. It simply disappeared.

Unlike a moment before, with the constant roaring and the tip of the tail in sight, they now had no idea where it was, which was even more unsettling. The men exchanged blank looks, waiting, listening, staring. Tom's first inclination was that he'd missed it clean, that the noise from the gun had startled and silenced the lion.

They waited.

Darrik gestured for Tom to stay put, and he crept to the right, trying for a glimpse of the cat that had suspiciously vanished. As Tom waited, the gun grew heavy in his hands. Unconsciously, he let the barrel drift lower.

Smash (presumably nicknamed for his driving record), who in two weeks had yet to say a word in English, suddenly whispered, "Hold your rifle up. Get ready to shoot!"

It had the desired effect, sending a shiver up Tom's spine and stirring the hollow in the pit of his stomach.

Just then, Darrik turned with a smile.

"Well done," he said. "I can see the old boy lying on the ground. Work your way toward me, Tom, and plant another in the shoulder for what we refer to as 'life insurance.'"

This last-day leopard completed the Big Four for Tom Anding.

Tom did, and the lion made not the slightest flinch. The first shot had finished it dead.

On further inspection, the solid had traveled the length of the lion's body, resting just beneath the hide on one hip. In fact, the bullet had suffered so little deformity that Tom's first impression was that it looked good enough to reload. Of course, he had other plans for it: It would live out its retirement as a keepsake on the fireplace mantel at home. There it would remind him of what he considered to be one of his finest hunts. It had to do with earning it. As a sheep hunter who had battered his body over hill and dale in pursuit of a Grand Slam, Tom knew the meaning of earning an animal.

And this one, by God, he had earned.

"Here's what got our friend riled up," Darrik said, rolling over the heavy cat. Several gashes in the lion's hindquarters had festered and swelled painfully. "The ol' boy's must have been defending his territory against other males. They scratch each other up something terrible. Must have hurt like hell to walk. I was doubtful we'd pushed him that hard. It was pretty clear something else had stirred him up."

Then they paced it off. Thirty-seven feet.

There was quite a celebration when they arrived in camp. But it was cut disappointingly short because they had only one evening left in which to try for the smaller, stealthier cat.

They left straightaway for the leopard blind that had become their regular afternoon retreat. They were fortunate that a big male was feeding, but, so far, it had remained a phantom. They knew the cat was real from the pad prints left at the base of the tree and the substantial portion of meat missing from the bait on the previous nights. Their problem, quite simply, was that the cat refused to show itself in the light of day. As a result, the men had fidgeted away untold hours in the blind.

It was frustrating. As a sheep hunter, Tom was used to equating effort with success. The harder you worked, the more sheep you saw. The more sheep you saw, the greater your chance of finding a good ram.

But leopard hunting, Tom found, doesn't work that way. No amount of physical effort can produce a leopard. You are at the mercy of the leopard, who decides when it will show. If you've done your homework in hanging the bait and building a blind, there isn't much else you can do. If the leopard wants to feed, it will; if it doesn't, it won't. It's that simple.

So they went to the blind each afternoon and waited.

The lengthy stints in the blind weren't always uneventful. Punctuating the afternoon stillness were the sounds of other forest dwellers: the screech of a belligerent baboon, the lonesome query of a francolin, and the doglike bark of a reedbuck. Each evening, a lone hyena would lope in and eye the bait overhead. After circling and deciding it was hopeless, it would hump away in search of other fare.

Late one afternoon, an elephant paid them a visit. It was during that brief stillness when afternoon gives way to dusk and when the calm before the sounds of insects and other night creatures prevail. The elephant made a surprising amount of noise as it approached. Leaves and twigs crackled beneath its feet, and its stomach rumbled with indigestion. These sounds, magnified in the momentary silence, were nothing more than a curiosity, a break in the monotony—until they realized the elephant was heading straight toward them.

They could not see outside the thatch walls of the blind, except what lay beyond two tiny peepholes in line with the bait. Their ears were left to determine the elephant's location. Soon the elephant was quite close. Suddenly, the flimsy blind began to shake as the elephant bumped and rubbed against it. It was using their blind as a scratching post!

Darrik made a gesture to keep still. They sat motionless, waiting to see what would happen when the elephant caught their scent. The guns clutched in their hands were little better than sticks. Tom had a .340 Weatherby loaded with softs, and his PH had the standard wounded-leopard repellent: a 12-gauge shotgun with 00 buck. At best, they were good for making a lot of noise. Having taken a large bull on a previous trip, Tom knew what it takes to bring the big beasts down. Anything less than a .458 and you're just going to make it mad.

Luckily, the wind was in their favor, and the elephant wandered off after satisfying its itch.

Since this was their last evening, Darrik decided they would stay all night if they had to. When he sent the car off, he instructed the others not to return until morning—unless they heard a shot.

The hunters watched the light of day dwindle as the sun dipped behind them. Soon it was dark, and no leopard had appeared. The men stretched out on the sandy ground of the blind, dozing in turns, and waited.

They waited the whole night, listening to wild night noises, stretching wait-stiffened limbs, and staring at stars overhead. Nothing tests one's imagination like the sounds of an African night. Each sound strikes your imagination like a match strikes sandpaper. Vivid pictures pop into your head—pictures of the lion that might fancy a taste of your flesh, the surly rhino without a recent trampling to its credit, the deadly snake returning to its den and mistaking you as a threat. To say it was the longest night of Tom's life would be no exaggeration.

A hand clasped Tom on the shoulder just before dawn. Tom sat up and slipped the gun barrel through the peep. A big male leopard, spotted and wary, was crouched on the ground beneath the bait.

Its face had the same go-to-hell expression the lion had had.

The cross hairs found their mark, and, an instant later, a fiery blast filled the scope.

At the shot, the leopard bounded and vanished into the brush.

Now came his PH's concerns: "Could you see it clearly? Were you steady?"

"Yes, I think so," was all he could say.

It was still plenty dark. Unsure where or how well the leopard was hit, Darrik thought it best to wait for the car.

While they waited, Tom played over the whole thing in his mind. *How was my aim? Could I have pulled the shot? I held smack on the shoulder, but what if he were angled away and I just clipped him? Wouldn't that be a dandy way to end my safari? Regarding your tip, Darrik, I've left you a fine leopard mauling.*

When the car arrived, they climbed on top and started slowly into the brush toward the spot where the leopard had last been seen.

Unlike its bigger cousin the lion, a charging leopard would give you no introductory roar, no warning to let you know it was coming. There would be just a spotted blur, with the surprise and speed of a shark bursting from beneath the surface.

The going was slow, all eyes alert and everyone whispering and pointing and guessing. Then Darrik's shotgun flew to his shoulder, and everyone tensed. Just as suddenly, he lowered his weapon, and cries rang out as they spotted the almost imperceptible form stretched out in the tall grass.

The big leopard was quite dead. Tom's shot had been true.

As the trackers loaded the handsome cat into the car, Tom turned to watch the warm, coppery glow of the morning sun spreading into the waking forest. This had been quite a day. Today's leopard and yesterday's lion marked the end of Tom's lengthy quest to collect Africa's Big Four.

So now you know why they make it a twenty-one-day safari. In twenty days, you would have gone home empty-handed, my friend. You need the extra day to make sure of the cats.

And no one can say Tom didn't earn them.

Part III

North America

Mountain Marathon[*]

Chapter 21

B y our seventh day of hunting in the Muskwa Range of British
Columbia, I had been yanked and tugged and pulled over so many
mountains that my feet were turning Benedict Arnold on me.
Already my big toes had turned a solid, traitorous black, and they were
definitely winning the battle in uniting the smaller ones against me. I
did sympathize with their mutiny, since each of the past few nights I had
promised them they would stay in camp the following morning.

I had lied.

Each morning I reckoned the day would prove different. As I lay
shivering in the predawn dark of the tent, my aching body reluctant to face
the morning cold, my mind would stray to wishful fancy: *Perhaps today
we won't have to hike far from camp to find a record-book ram grazing in
a nearby meadow. At a "can't-miss" range of fifty yards, I bet he allows
me plenty of time to get set up in a steady, comfortable shooting position,
too. And he won't run at the slightest sight or sound of us.*

If you are familiar with North American sheep hunting, you know
this kind of thinking indicates one of two things: Either I had developed
altitude sickness or my rebellious toes had affected my brain.

Each morning, while stumbling through the meadow, I would realize
that, of course, no foolhardy sheep awaited me there. I would awaken
slowly to the fact that the day actually promised pain and exhaustion, and
treacherous climbing from one peak to the next, and struggling through
timber and willows anxious to tangle my wearied legs. From sunup, the
day promised more than twelve hours of this punishing treatment before
it would allow me to trudge my battered carcass back to camp.

But the day also carried a rumor. If you listened carefully amidst the
pain and exhaustion of its promise, you could hear the rumor. At times
only faintly, yet its whisper remained. Each day rumored that a trophy

*Previously published in DSC *Hunters Quest,* July 1987, and *A Hunting Heritage: Fifty
Years of Shikar-Safari Club International*, Andrew B. Phillips, editor, 2002.

There is no easy way to circumnavigate a Muskwa mountain like this one.

ram lived somewhere in the mountains you were hunting. And the rumor went on to suggest that if you looked long enough and hard enough, you just might earn a chance at taking it.

The rumor kept me going. That and the fact the trip was fully paid for.

✱✱✱✱✱✱

The sun shone bright, and the sky remained unusually clear and blue on this seventh day. It was not nearly as cold as it had been on the previous August days. In fact, I actually started to sweat while climbing in the sun or nervously traversing a crumbly shale cliff. The latter forced me to clutch and grasp my way from handhold to handhold until I could reach safer terrain. If the physical effort wasn't enough to make you sweat, the sight of the mountain falling away from you for hundreds of feet below surely was. Yet, when I paused to catch my breath, the wind invariably found its way to the dampness coating my skin, which would soon start my teeth to chattering if I didn't quickly push on.

By one o'clock and our break for lunch, it appeared that the rumor would end just that—a rumor. My guide, Marlin, and I ate our packed lunches high atop a muskeg-covered ridge, where the endless stretch of country was laid out before us in all its rugged splendor. Canyons and valleys worked their way through the land below like the creases in an old man's palms, and the surrounding pewter peaks jutted patiently into the sky, anticipating the approaching snow.

Munching the last of his second sandwich, Marlin leaned forward, planted his elbows on his knees, and meticulously scanned the opposite mountain with his binocular. My guide was not in pain; he was invincible. To him these rugged mountains were little more than gopher mounds, and after a week of hunting with him, I had deep suspicions that the fellow hailed from Planet Krypton.

At 2 P.M., the momentary sanctuary of lunch and rest over, Marlin appeared to be contemplating something grave. It had taken us seven hours to reach this spot from camp, and I knew we had no choice but to return by the same route we had come. Starting back now would put us into camp around 9 P.M.—already a longer and harder day than I had expected.

"There might be some sheep over that next ridge," Marlin put forth, lowering his binocular and pointing in the opposite direction from camp.

I wondered if, besides being Superman, he might also be crazy.

"Let's go have a look."

He was crazy.

At least I've got the gun, I thought.

Admittedly, with most of the day gone and the pain escalating in my feet, the rumor lacked the power to revive my interest. But Marlin, impervious to the physical limits of us regular mortals, persisted in his original fancy. Granted, the ridge did not appear all that far. But the perilous cliffs that intervened clearly had my attention.

"You want me to cross those?" I asked.

He nodded, then muttered something about "a piece of cake." Maybe he didn't realize my legs were undergoing an active rebellion. And suffering through a common cold with the accompanying aches and chills, not to mention hacking up green stuff every so often, certainly didn't help matters. After some debate, I conceded to him that even if I knew a ram awaited me over that ridge, it would take a miracle for me to summon the strength required to struggle up it.

After I said that, Marlin took off at a jog for the ridge. Just to spite me, negotiating the scantiest of goat trails, he practically jogged his way across the crumbly shale cliffs. He did slip once or twice, making my heart skip, but each time he righted himself instantly. Essentially, he made it over and across the deadly obstacle with no more difficulty than you or I would encounter in crossing a downtown street.

Bruce Jenner has never met Marlin.

My nimble guide continued at a trot, hardly slowing up on the steep ridge, then disappeared over it. I waited. Minutes passed. Some time later,

The mountains of British Columbia are humbling terrain, indeed!

Marlin reappeared atop the ridge. I half hoped he brought good news; my feet didn't. Whatever the case, Marlin was in a hurry. He came running down the ridge toward me. Did he see a ram? Or maybe an elk in the timber far below? Or is he simply in a hurry to get back to camp?

Marlin dropped on all fours in the muskeg beside me, catching his breath and appearing more human than he had at any time before.

"Five rams," he gasped. "Couldn't tell how big . . . didn't want to scare 'em. . . . One looked pretty good."

My feet cringed at the report, but my heart leapt. Luckily, I still made the decisions. I emptied my packsack of all its gear, as Marlin had instructed, then slung my gun over my shoulder. *Marlin has spotted five rams,* I thought excitedly as I followed him toward the shale cliffs, my feet sinking in the spongy muskeg and the excitement spreading through me like a fire in a high wind. Much more than a rumor, this was a firsthand account! Through Marlin's sighting, a ram seemed vaguely tangible now—no longer a mere concept but a real critter with hair and horns.

Push on, I told myself. *Try your hardest to keep pace with Marlin.*

As we neared the shale cliffs, the craggy faces glared mockingly at me. I had learned that, firm as the rocks appear, many would inevitably pull free from the mountain or crumble in my grasp, clattering off to nothingness below. Fortunately, I wasn't thinking of the perilous cliffs ahead but of the rams Marlin had spotted somewhere over that ridge. And my thoughts were suddenly filled with "ifs": *If I did not take too long to get there and if the sheep did not hear or see us, if they did not move off, if the wind did not shift and betray us, and if I could tackle the lengthy shot—then maybe, just maybe, along with the aches and pains (and missing toenails), I just might have a sheep to take home.*

I knew our chances were slim with so many "ifs."

Rocks did, in fact, pull free from the cliff face, and others crumbled, but in the end my will at least to glimpse those five rams won out. Minutes later, we crested the ridge, hunkered over to avoid skylining ourselves. We fell prone against the down slope. I was gulping at the thin air like a fish out of water. Marlin wet a finger and held it up. A quick nod told me that the fickle mountain winds still blew in our favor.

After motioning me to stay put, Marlin slithered forward on his belly to steal a closer look. He brought the binocular up to his eagle eyes. Nothing. He inched forward and looked again. Then again. Finally, he turned and motioned me ahead. There he whispered the discouraging news.

The sheep had moved. He couldn't see them five hundred yards below where they had been a short while ago.

Damn, I thought, *one "if" failed.*

We stalked and crawled another two hundred yards down the mountain until we came to a ravine that grew into a canyon farther below. Split almost evenly down the middle by sunshine to the left and shade to the right, the ravine also offered a choice of grade: treacherous to the left, death wish to the right.

I sighed when Marlin cut for the left.

Stopping within a few yards, Marlin peeked over a small boulder and watched below for what seemed like hours. I desperately wanted to have a look but remained tucked into a ball behind an adjacent boulder as instructed. The last thing I wanted to do was to sabotage the operation by doing something stupid like revealing our presence to the very animals Marlin was working so hard to locate. Eventually he turned from the binocular and reported, "I see two rams about six hundred yards below."

I couldn't believe my ears!

"Is either one legal?" I asked.

Here I should mention something about the hunting regulations in British Columbia. Only full-curl rams may be taken; in other words, one horn tip must rise at least flush with the bridge of the nose. The regulations also prohibit the taking of a ram less than eight years old. So before you can even think about pulling the trigger, you must fully assess the ram's curl and determine its age by counting the darker rings in its horns—a task much easier said than done on a live animal at some distance.

"Can't tell," he said, thwarting my growing elation. "They're too far."

Marlin then crawled in retreat to a shallow depression. There he explained that if we continued down this same side of the ravine, the sheep would surely spot us in the sun. (He had earlier warned me how alarmingly my rifle barrel gleamed in the sun.) He felt our only chance was to hike back up the mountain, then descend the steeper side of the ravine in the shade. I had to agree, despite the instant uneasiness I felt when I glanced at the harrowing features of the terrain in question. Luckily, there wasn't time to think it over and chicken out.

With new resolve, I scrambled after Marlin, clawing my way up the incline on all fours. In places the slope grew exceptionally steep, a factor that would have made the climb impossible were it not for the firm handholds provided by the muskeg. When we reached the top of the ravine, my apprehensions were soon confirmed. The descent on the shady side of the rift was tricky, indeed. I caught myself holding my breath time and time again as I fought for traction and purchase on the unstable landscape. A fall would have been—well, a fall was out of the question.

Large bowls and drainages offer rams a tactical view and provide escape routes.

As we descended the widening gorge, I wondered if the sheep had moved off. *Had they heard us? After killing ourselves to get there, would we even find a legal ram among them?* The anticipation was overwhelming, more so than I had experienced on any previous hunt. By now, I was so wrapped up in the excitement that I paid little heed to the steepness of the canyon walls, or to my throbbing feet, or to the roughness of the rock surface that lacerated my bare hands. None of that mattered now: Only the sheep somewhere below us mattered, if they were still there.

Eventually, we encountered several large protrusions, or knobs, that had formed in the canyon wall. Each knob allowed a view around the side of the mountain only as far as the next knob. As we mounted each, Marlin would glass ahead for sign of the rams. Five or six times we did this, but each time we saw no sign of sheep.

Crawling over yet another knob, stomach flush against the mountain, Marlin suddenly froze. He motioned me still. He retreated a few feet, shook off his pack, and dug out the spotting scope. My heart fluttered, for I knew this meant he'd spotted sheep. He placed the scope atop the hump and glassed. Minutes crept by.

When he beckoned, I scampered up beside him, my gun at the ready.

"They're in the shade," he whispered excitedly, pointing. "Down there. Can you see 'em?"

I raised my binocular, expecting sheep to jump out at me. Disappointed, I saw only canyon wall. In the mountains, distances are tricky—especially to flatlanders—and I didn't know how big they should look at that distance. That threw me.

Then a head turned.

The movement brought their whole world instantly into focus: five Stone sheep rams masked in the shade of a sheer rock face. They were standing at alert but currently unaware of our presence. At that moment, just the sight of the magnificent beasts made the effort all worthwhile.

Marlin strained his eye through the spotting scope, trying his best to judge their horns, but the light was poor in the shade, and it proved frustratingly difficult. A moment later, one of the rams moved out of sight behind the rock face. Marlin continued to scrutinize the four left. Noticeably disgruntled by the poor light, he informed me that one of the four might be legal, although the one that had just stepped behind the rock face was possibly the biggest of all. He suggested we wait. That was fine by me—my heart needed about a month to slow down.

Marlin then asked if I had a steady rest. It was ironic—for all I had cussed it, the wall of the canyon made an excellent rest. I couldn't have done better at the shooting range back home. And the four rams stood about two hundred yards away, a very reasonable distance for sheep hunting.

If the fifth ram would just show itself, I should be able to take it. We waited. Then the largest ram of the four decided to wander behind the rock face as well. It appeared that luck had sided with my toes and was quickly turning against us.

While we waited on the mountainside in silence, my eyes roamed the canyon. I noticed a small, sunny patch beyond the rock face and a little higher up. Before the sheep could completely disappear around the far side of the mountain, it looked as if they would first have to cross this sunny patch. But I had learned how deceptive the Muskwa landscape could be. An unseen gully or half-a-dozen hidden trails might afford an escape for the sheep. Even if we were lucky enough to have one of the rams cross this sunny gap, it would have to stop and pose like a Cover Girl model for Marlin to judge it and for me to take a decent shot.

Marlin estimated the gap at nearly three hundred yards, not as easy a shot, and I could feel the wind on my face blowing stronger from down canyon. *Could the wind throw my shot?* I wondered briefly but kept silent. During the day's hike, had some twig, pine needle, or other menacing object found its way into the barrel of my gun? I prayed not.

Unexpectedly, the fifth ram, looking as confident and brave as a quarterhorse stallion, strutted into the middle of the sunny patch and stopped, broadside. With the shade on their horns Marlin couldn't get a good sighting, but now, in the sun, he saw at once that this ram was a monster!

"Shoot him!" he said hastily. "Hold in line with his shoulder and just below the top of his back."

I sucked in deeply and squeezed. *Bang!* The ram bolted quickly out of sight, seemingly a complete miss. The second ram then dashed across the sunny opening and disappeared.

"You think you hit him?" Marlin asked, rather skeptically.

"I don't know. He was gone so fast I couldn't tell."

Half a long-awaited minute later, the second ram reappeared and came running back toward the other three rams, all of which were now startled and standing in bewilderment beneath the rock face. They stood stone still, their heads cocked and listening. With all the echoing, they were unable to locate the direction of the shot.

The fifth ram did not return.

This was a good sign, or so Marlin said. "They usually stick together," he explained.

Concealed behind the knob, we waited another ten torturous minutes, giving the ram time to stiffen up—assuming it had been hit. Marlin felt

The culmination of hard work and determination.

that if we rushed, the sound of us clambering after it might push the ram to hell and gone or cause it to leap blindly into some near-bottomless chasm. (This very thing happened to a doctor we met later in the trip. His first shot went high, taking the ram in the flesh of the neck, and before he could drop it with a second shot, the ram sailed off an eight-hundred-foot cliff. They found it the next day, but the tips of both horns had been shattered in the fall, knocking off no telling how much in length. Despite that loss, the horns still taped close to forty-one inches apiece!) We watched the four remaining rams—a beautiful sight in itself—and they soon started at a fast clip down and around the mountain beneath us.

Finally, we began our pursuit. But the steepness of the dry ravines carved into the canyon wall proved difficult. Once or twice I had to lower my gun to Marlin before I could work my way down to him. Then, while climbing another stretch, a grasped root pulled free of the earth, and only by clutching a stronger root with my other hand was I able to prevent a tumble.

Eventually, we found ourselves in the sunny patch where the ram had stood when I shot. I felt like crossing my fingers as we hurried across the lightly sloping stretch of ground near tree line. My eyes searched the mossy ground for signs of blood, but I saw none. And I glanced ahead as the backside of the mountain came into view. Nothing. My heart sank. Had I rushed the shot? Or had the wind perhaps thrown my bullet?

Mountain Marathon

Then, thirty yards away in a small patch of willows, I caught sight of an upturned horn. We ran up to it and found the big ram dead. Still not fully believing it, Marlin and I jumped into the air and began to shout. We must have looked a sight up there, dancing around that mountainside with our fists over our heads and roaring at the wilderness.

Despite the "ifs," I had done it. I had succeeded in collecting an animal more challenging than I had ever imagined—a big-game animal that I would readily classify as my worthiest opponent. And what a monster it was! After the required drying period, the big ram measured 176³/₈", making the Boone and Crockett record book. It also turned out to be the biggest Stone sheep taken in 1986, as recognized by the Foundation for North American Wild Sheep (FNAWS).

After taking some photos, I had cooled a tad from both the excitement and the retreating, late-afternoon sun when I realized that now the real work would commence. We must carry the head, cape, and as much meat as possible back to camp. While Marlin quickly butchered the ram and stuffed both packsacks to their fill with meat, I was reminded of the many hostile miles that lay between us and camp. It was then that I understood I had a marathon ahead of me.

Balancing the forty-pound ram's head on top of his forty-pound pack, Marlin started around the mountain toward camp. I had found his pace difficult before; it now fell nothing short of grueling.

Luckily, the snow fell after this hunt. (From left) The author, guide Marlin Watson, author's dad, and guide Mike Green.

Guide Marlin with the author's ram of a lifetime.

We cut around the mountain instead of climbing back up the canyon wall. Not only was the canyon too steep with our heavier burdens, but that route was less direct as well. Marlin confessed, however, that he had never tackled this side of the mountain, and we certainly saw no trails. It was rather a forced gamble; we could easily find ourselves at a dead end. And, with darkness approaching, spending the night out would be our only option—for even invincible Marlin believed that hiking in the mountains in the dark was suicide.

(His partner, Mike Green, had told the story of a guide and his hunter who had tried to make it back to camp one night on horseback. When his horse came to a sudden stop and refused to go forward, the guide continued to kick it until it stepped off into nothingness—what turned out to be a sheer cliff, killing them both.)

The backside of the mountain steepened as we gained altitude in search of a route back, and the willows grew thicker with each step. The harder I struggled to keep my balance, the harder the willows fought to pull me down.

When we came to a sheer crevice, Marlin sighed and in a resigned voice said, "Looks like we'll be spending the night up here."

We continued up along the edge of the crevice until we came to a small saddle at the top. Here we met with luck and soon found the familiar trail leading to the shale cliffs, though it was still questionable whether we could beat the sun getting over the last mountain. I dreaded the sight of the shale cliffs, especially with my extra load, but all I could do was sneer back at them.

With hope and a prayer I somehow made it past.

To have slipped and died would have been the easy way out. Then the largest mountain by far would not have been looming up at me in the failing light.

I mention the following for comparison purposes only (well, perhaps also to brag a little). I was twenty-six years old and ran five to nine miles a day. I had run a marathon of twenty-six miles. Understandably, I was no rookie to endurance, exhaustion, or physical pain. But to get back to camp that night involved drawing on reserves of strength I never knew I had.

Several times while lumbering up that last mountain, I collapsed on my seat and gasped for air. I did this whenever the urge to vomit built to more than just a threat. Superman Marlin, now dripping in sweat himself, would stop and talk me into climbing another fifty yards.

"It's only a little farther," he would coax.

The convex bow in the mountain helped immensely because I could see only tens of yards above me at any given time, and with each step I could promise myself that the next fifty-yard stint would take me to the top.

Ultimately, I made it. But I'd be willing to wager that climbing the last three hundred yards up that last mountain with fifty-plus pounds on my back was more painful than open-heart surgery without the anesthetic!

But that was OK. Most important, the rumor had proved true.

Hunting Caribou in Alaska

Chapter 22

A lot can change in three years. In September 1989 I'd had a great hunt in the barren grounds of Alaska with Frank (as I will call him in this story), a respected outfitter. His guides were topnotch, and his camps were well kept and well run. Three years later, when I returned for a repeat adventure with my dad and five friends in tow, we were in for a true disappointment. Frank had fallen into the bottle, his staff had departed, and his entire hunting operation had gone to hell.

Dad and I had swapped a white-tailed deer hunt on our ranch for this hunt, so perhaps we had less to complain about than did our friends, who were paying full fare for a guided hunt. It's one thing to ensnare yourself in a bad hunt; it's another when you trouble a friend.

The bottom line was, there were seven hunters in camp and only two guides, neither of whom lived up to even the most liberal definition of the term. The guides turned out to be a couple of Missouri knuckleheads who were hunting for free in exchange for guiding us Texans. On two weeks' leave from work, they were here to hunt first, guide second. We quickly discovered they knew even less about caribou hunting than we did. When one guide pulled me aside and his first question was whether I had any "pot," I realized how dire our situation was.

We couldn't count on Frank or his copilot, Robert, as guides because they were more interested in guzzling whiskey and swapping Vietnam and plane-crash tales in the supply tent than they were in hunting. Sad to see, Frank's hands now shook noticeably in the morning until he got his fix: Never food for breakfast, mind you, but a mug of straight whiskey. The wiry fellow had lost weight from a frame that didn't have weight to lose. When asked about fly camp, he'd stick his bearded face out the door of the mess tent, glance at the gray sky, and announce, "Weather's too bad to fly." By lunch, he would be slaphappy drunk.

On other days he would taxi his plane to the end of the "airstrip" and back, only to climb out and pronounce the weather too bad to fly.

"Well, let's hunt around main camp."

"Can't hunt. Been in a plane today," he would say, citing the Alaskan law prohibiting hunting the same day you are airborne.

Though I seriously doubt the law applied in this case, since the plane hadn't even left the ground, it was hard to argue with his logic. You don't want to hunt with a drunk, and you certainly don't want to fly with one. Frank and Robert couldn't guide any day they had touched a plane, which was most days. We just shook our heads and vowed to make the best of a bad situation.

Our friend C. K. Lawson ventured out early the first morning with one of the knuckleheads. Having lived in Germany and the northeast, C.K. was accustomed to cold-weather hunting and was well prepared for whatever Alaska might dish up. Years later, he would survive a plane crash and hypothermia on a hunt with a different Alaskan outfitter.

C.K. and his guide hiked all day, up and down and over the rolling tundra, seeing little in the way of caribou and nothing in the way of a shootable bull. On their return that evening, however, they spotted a bull crossing the airstrip near camp.

The knucklehead threw up his binocular and said, "Damn! That's the monster we saw the other day at camp!"

C.K. studied the bull.

"Are you sure? He doesn't look like much to me."

"Yeah. That's him. Shoot him!"

It was a long shot at three hundred yards, but C.K. was a crack shot. With a good rest, he dropped the bull with a single pull of the trigger.

When they approached the downed animal, it was readily apparent to C.K. that this was not the "monster" bull but an immature bull that should not have been taken. He couldn't hide his disappointment. First, C.K. was the type of hunter who would rather return home empty-handed than shoot an immature animal. Second, despite his restless nature, he was a hunter who craved the full experience of the hunt and, as a result, was in no hurry to fill his tag. In more than thirty years of hunting on our ranch, many was the time C.K. encountered a monster buck on day one of the hunt, only to pass it up because he just couldn't bring the hunt to an end on the first day. Since this caribou had claimed his one and only tag, I knew the outcome was doubly disappointing for him. Fortunately, he found a solution that would allow him to continue to hunt caribou, albeit vicariously.

According to the next day's plan, Frank would fly C. K., Dad, and me to fly camp. C.K. would fish while Dad and I hunted. We had to take separate flights because of the confines of the tiny plane. A Piper Cub is hardly bigger than some of the kites we flew as a kid. As another example of the diminutive size of the plane, C. K., who was the first to fly out, could not fit his bag on the plane with him. Frank said he would have to fly the bag separately. Hesitant to part with his gear, C.K. agreed to allow this only when Frank assured him it was the only way.

Our friend's concern turned out to be well founded. On the return to camp, the weather turned ugly, and Frank decided it was too dangerous to fly. The weather did not improve, and, as a result, C.K. was stuck in fly camp overnight without his gear and without a sleeping bag or cold-weather garments. Understandably, C.K. was more than a little upset when Frank did not return until the next day. Had the weather turned colder that night, Frank's miscalculation might have ended in a fatal disaster. Alaska weather can be ruthless and is often the most dangerous part of a trip.

By the time Dad and I got there, C.K. had cooled down somewhat, and he had his gear out to go fishing. What bothered him most was that Frank had treated the incident as a joke, saying, *"Ha, ha, you had to rough it overnight without your gear."*

It was not funny. It was careless planning on Frank's part, the result of a muddled brain, soaked in whiskey.

In hindsight, once we realized the shameful state of Frank's hunting operation, we probably should have called it quits and left for home. But, despite the lousy conditions and the inherent risks, there was the captivating pull of the wilderness: the sweet fresh air that fills your lungs, the endless stretch of tundra that begs to be trodden, the invigorating sting of brisk wind on cheeks stashed behind a desk too long. We were here to hunt, and that's exactly what we were going to do, Frank and his knucklehead crew be damned!

The next morning our guide quickly disappeared to hunt caribou, leaving the three of us to fend for ourselves. In my view, you can hunt or you can guide, but you can't do both—especially if you are being paid to guide. Although Frank wasn't paying these fellows, he had failed to secure experienced, licensed guides. Real guides aren't there to shoot a caribou out from under you; they do their own hunting before or after your stay, and preferably in a different area. There should never be a question whether your guide is competing against you for the same game you are hunting. You should feel like you are on the same team. It's a real downer to arrive in camp, only to be shown "the biggest trophy in the country," recently collected by your guide.

Yes, indeed, Frank's operation was in shambles. Gone were the first-rate guides—Alaska residents who knew the weather, the terrain, the animals pursued. Frank needed professionals who earned their living at the craft and knew what they were talking about—clearheaded fellows whose life-and-death decisions you could trust. Such a guide was Jeff

The author's dad took this monster barren ground caribou while making the best of a bad situation.

Welch. Instead, we had a couple of twerps from Missouri who could not figure out how to set up the pup tents in fly camp!

While C.K. fished in a nearby river, Dad and I hiked the hills and scouted for caribou. We didn't see much. We mostly made large loops, not allowing camp to get too far from sight. Having once experienced the work involved in getting a downed caribou back to camp, I recalled Jeff Welch's wise words from three years before: "We don't kill caribou far from camp."

There was another reason why we didn't go too far. In all honesty, I wasn't keen on getting lost. The Alaskan tundra is not as featureless as, say, the Great Plains of North Dakota, where one rolling patch of land looks identical to another, making it nearly impossible to keep your bearings. But, as in the desert, judging distance in Alaska is tricky, and the rolling tundra can hide a whole herd of caribou, your camp, or even a river. You are likely to stumble upon one of them as if it had appeared out of nowhere. (A GPS unit would have come in quite handy back then.)

I spent most of the next day perched on a high ridge overlooking a river bottom. Hunting caribou on the open tundra with a bow, I decided, was about as productive as throwing a handful of pebbles at a flying duck. With a personal range of only thirty yards (I know, I should have practiced more), the best plan for me was to scout for caribou below. I glassed for caribou headed toward either the thin grove of aspen trees along the river's edge or the clumps of alders that covered the higher, sloping banks. These could be used as cover to make an ambush.

Deciding that a hunt with a friend was better than fishing alone, C.K. had elected to guide my dad. They hiked for miles across the tundra, thinking more about finding a trophy bull and less about what it would take to carry it back. As they crested a hill, they glimpsed what looked like a lone bush in the middle of the tundra. On second take, the bush turned out to be a set of huge, chestnut-colored antlers sprouting up into the gray sky. Dropping to the ground, the hunters checked the wind and carefully planned their approach. They proceeded, crouching forward to hide their forms, and discovered that the horns belonged to a giant bull and its sizable harem. The caribou, still unaware of the hunters' presence, were lying on the tundra but clearly out of range.

With no cover whatsoever between them and the herd, the men would be forced to crawl within shooting distance. Now on their bellies, they took their time, advancing inch by inch. When they were as close as they figured they could get without spooking the herd, Dad slid his pack forward and eased the rifle on top. When he looked through the scope, he couldn't see the bull above the curve in the tundra. He glanced back at C. K.

"Can I shoot off your shoulder?"

"What?"

"That's how they do it in Africa," Dad explained, "if you can't find a good rest."

"OK," C.K. whispered, grudgingly, "but you'd better not miss!"

C.K. obliged, the regal bull stood, and Dad took it with one well-placed shot.

Only when they reached the downed trophy did they realize their tremendous accomplishment. The dark antlers glistened like polished wood above a beautiful white cape. The tops and bottoms were broadly palmated, and points and beams sprouted everywhere. Quite simply, the rack was a thing of beauty.

Next came the hard part: butchering the big animal and carting the meat and horns back to camp. I should tell you that Dad was quite fit. He ran three miles a day, played handball four to five times a week, and lifted weights. He had run several marathons. He was in better shape than fellows half his age, me included. But when he arrived in camp that night, hunched under the weight of the hide and horns carried on his shoulders, you could see he was done in. Both men, in fact, were spent. Drawing on the last of his reserves, Dad managed a proud smile, staggered the last few yards, and laid the stupendous trophy at my feet.

"What a fantastic caribou!" I said.

Dad was too tired to respond. He simply stretched his stiff back and stared at the antlered wonder lying on the ground.

"Don't forget," C.K. gasped, straggling in and dropping both backpacks with a thud, "I was your guide!"

The packs were filled to bursting with untold pounds of caribou meat. Both hunters plopped down, not caring if their seats got soaked in the tundra mush. They were not planning to get up anytime soon. Eventually, they recounted their exciting tale from where they were sprawled. I sure was proud of them. They had showed up the young knucklehead and, despite difficulties with the outfitter and guides, had pulled off a successful hunt. They were an inspiration to the hunting world.

When Frank arrived a couple of days later to fly us back to main camp, he was truly impressed with Dad's bull.

"That's the biggest damn bull we've killed in a long time," he said.

I felt he placed a little more emphasis on "we" than his role merited. The antlers, in fact, barely missed Boone and Crockett requirements.

On the short flight, Frank and I almost became one of the crash statistics that he and copilot Robert were so fond of discussing. On approach to the landing, Frank steered the nose of the plane into a quartering wind, which had picked up considerably. An instant before touchdown, the wind shifted or gusted—anyway, it slapped us broadside with enough force to toss the plane onto its side. We were now literally flying sideways, the ground only an arm's length below the left wing. Clearly, either the wing was going to catch and we would cartwheel into oblivion, or we would flip completely and land upside down. One was no better than the other in terms of our odds for survival. The surprising thing was how suddenly our predicament had come about. One instant we were flying along fine; the next, we were dangerously out of control.

Then, just as suddenly, the plane righted itself, and we bounced hard on the tundra strip. When we climbed out, Frank was ghostly white.

"That's the closest I've ever come to a real crash. The kind you don't walk away from."

He marched straight to the supply tent for a bottle, and we didn't see him till dinner. By then, his eyes were red and beady. Still he managed—fueled by adrenaline—to get the story out without a slur.

My good friend Dale Bilhartz, who was on the trip, was depressed over the whole situation. Apparently, nothing had improved during our absence. The only happy member of the hunting party was Dodi Speece, who had been too cold to venture from the dining tent and shot her bull when it wandered into camp. Dale had ventured out alone, but he didn't see much. He told me Frank finally had taken him hunting late one afternoon. When they spotted a band of caribou, Dale got set up in shooting position and waited as the caribou approached. There was a good bull in the herd, at least to Dale's eye. The bull came within seventy yards and stopped and stared at them. Dale had the bull in the cross hairs. His gun rest was perfect. The caribou's head was as good as hung on his wall back home. All he needed was the OK from Frank.

"He looks good to me, Frank."

Frank looked the bull over in his binocular.

"No, Dale, I don't think you'd be happy with that bull."

"All I want is a representative head. I don't need a record one."

"Dale, I think we can find you a better bull."

"This is our fifth day, Frank. And it's the best bull I've seen. I'd really like to take him."

"No, I don't think you'd be happy with him. We can do better."

Frank stood and strode off, and Dale watched the biggest bull he had seen turn and trot away. As you can probably guess, Dale didn't see another shootable bull on the trip.

As for me, I had nearly given up trying to shoot a caribou with a bow. There just wasn't enough cover, and the piddly migration was not sufficient to bring caribou past a randomly selected hiding spot. I suggested to Dale that we head out together on foot. Even if we didn't find a caribou, we would have a grand time marching across open country, solving the world's problems and reliving past adventures.

I was quite comfortable in the wet weather this time around. I had a new coat and pants and boots that did not leak. Because my body was comfortably warm, the cold drizzle in my face felt refreshing. All in all, it was rather mild weather for Alaska. Absent were the raging storms I had faced on my trip three years before, when the wind ripped at you from every angle, trying to knock you off your feet. This was pleasant bad weather (if there is such a thing), the kind of weather my British ancestors surely faced in the English countryside. Damp weather was in my genes. I could march in it all day. And, though you don't seem to see as much wildlife when hunting in drizzly weather, the animals you do see seem to hold better, as if reluctant to move about and make themselves any wetter. On a bright, sunny day animals are friskier and more apt to run at the first sight of you.

We marched over hills, through valleys, along creekbeds, and across lengthy beaver dams. The beaver dams, we discovered, were the most practical way to traverse the deeper creeks and streams. The risk in negotiating the precarious wooden structures was that the dams formed frigid ponds, and a fall into one of them would make for a cold walk back. The still water in the ponds was deep and clear to the dark sediment at the bottom, and the gurgling rush over the top of the dams was calming.

Sometimes we can forget how important something as unpretentious as a beaver is to nature's plan. Why, the benefits of the paddle-tailed rodents' handiwork to the ecosystem and other wildlife are numerous. The beaver's work is a reminder that every species has its place in the world order.

In the end, Dale and I had a great outing. We were truly at peace and had not a care in the world. To me, an important aspect of hunting is getting away from it all—turning off thoughts of work, family, responsibilities, undone chores, and the intimidating pile that was in your in-box when you left home. I am the first to admit that hunting is an escape. Hunting, you see, is my drug of choice. Hunting is medicine for the soul. It soothes and calms the nerves better than any high blood pressure pill invented. Hunting leaves you feeling refreshed, alive, and ready to tackle a world that just a few days ago you were ready to walk out on.

We are a part of nature, yet we try so hard to distance ourselves from it. If more urban folks in this world hunted, we would have less stress, less illness, and a much better understanding of nature. Productivity would soar. There should be a bumper sticker that says: "Go hunting. It's good for your health." Doctors should prescribe hunting trips for their patients. Employers should require every employee to go hunting for one week per year. Believe me, everyone would be the better for it.

In our wanderings we spotted a few caribou, but they were merely dots on the distant horizon. We got in that night tired in the body and legs from the full day's trek, and more than ready to satisfy the hunger we had worked up. We felt a sense of accomplishment, despite the fact that neither a bullet nor an arrow had been fired.

Except for Kathy Speece, who would collect a nice bull for her unfailing efforts and determination, the hunt was over for the rest of us.

Back in town, we met hunters who had been covered in caribou— endless herds that plodded indifferently through the middle of their camps! They claimed all you had to do was take a stand, wait a minute or two, and pick out the biggest bull to shoot. They practically sprained their faces grinning as they relayed stories of easy caribou for the picking.

That is how it goes when you hunt an animal whose presence depends upon its migration. It is either feast or famine. If you happen to be in the right place at the right time, it is like picking an apple off a tree. If, on the other hand, you aren't—well, you might as well be hunting caribou in West Texas because you will see about as many.

After our troubles on this hunt, I decided to add a necessary piece of gear to my kit: a Breathalyzer for the bush pilot.

South Texas Adventures

Chapter 23

I am one lucky fellow when it comes to hunting, having hunted many critters and in many places around the globe. But if I had to choose one animal to hunt for the rest of my life, there is no question that animal would be the white-tailed deer.

The white-tailed deer is an amazing creature. It is half psychic. It knows what you are going to do before you do. Just when you think you have it figured out, you haven't. A mature buck, where it is hunted, is one of the wariest, wiliest animals you will ever match wits against. If it weren't for that brief period known as the rut, when a buck grows insanely lovesick, why, you would never get a shot at one. Because I was blessed with a family ranch where I could regularly hunt whitetail, I made a lifelong study of the gray ghost of Texas.

Based on my first whitetail hunt, it's surprising I cared to repeat the experience. What I remember most is freezing my tail off. I was all of seven years old, out with my dad and his older cousin Jane, who had taught him to hunt as a kid. Driving to the hunting spot in the predawn dark in a topless Jeep guaranteed chattering teeth long before we arrived. My next memory is of sitting Indian-style on the ground, back against a knobby cedar post, feet so frozen I couldn't feel them, and Dad telling me every few seconds to keep quiet.

I don't think we saw a single deer. At least I don't remember seeing any.

Not surprisingly, I lost interest in deer hunting for a few years, preferring to hunt turtles, rabbits, snakes, frogs, and birds. They provided a lot more action and kept my short attention span from becoming overloaded. I would sneak to the edge of the ponds and take whatever unsuspecting small game happened to be in range. With a total disregard for conservation at that age, I took as many as I could shoot. My arsenal was limited to a .22 rifle and a .410 shotgun, both single-shot boyhood guns of Dad's. Eventually, Dad rationed my shells, limiting me to three boxes of ammo per day. I put this down on paper because it is better not to bottle up that kind of child abuse inside. Fortunately, I have long since forgiven him.

There was a time in the seventies when Doug Gary and his brother Wiley pulled up in a truck with a beautiful 14-point buck in the bed. This was the kind of South Texas buck that people dream about today, with a rack that was tall, wide, and heavy and horns the color of polished walnut. It was the kind of buck only South Texas can produce, the kind of buck that locals wouldn't think to mount. Back then, horns like that got tossed on a shelf in the tool shed and were never given another thought.

Soon family and friends had gathered around the bed of the truck to admire the magnificent buck.

"Wow, where did you find him?" my father asked.

Pushing up the brim of a worn felt cowboy hat, Doug smiled his quick smile and pointed.

"Just down yonder, below the house!"

Doug, the caretaker's son, was one of three brothers who had grown up on the ranch. It was a source of constant amusement to Doug that our family and friends felt we had to venture to the farthest limits of our land for a chance at a big mossback, while he often found the biggest buck of the year less than a quarter-mile from the headquarters. I guess that was our way of reproducing the experience of being out in the woods. You just couldn't get that sensation wandering behind the house with a gun, hearing pots and pans rattle in the kitchen, the cattle mooing from the corral, and kids' motorcycles zooming in and out of the compound.

Then came the really interesting part.

"Try to find where I shot him."

The result of a weekend's hunt for management bucks on the author's ranch.

(From left) The author with sons Levi and J.P. and daughter Lauren on one of their frequent rabbit hunts.

Doug let down the tailgate and dragged the heavy deer close so we could inspect it. We examined one side but found no bullet hole. With a helping hand, Doug flipped the deer over, and darned if we didn't strike out again! Exchanging quizzical looks, we repeated the process, this time more thoroughly. We even brushed back the fur around the shoulders and neck, sure to find evidence of a bullet hole. Again, we could not find where the buck had been shot. There simply was no sign that the deer had been taken by a gun. It looked as if the old buck had keeled over from natural causes.

With a grin, Doug pointed to the buck's left eye. Even then, the bullet hole wasn't noticeable until he moved the eye to reveal a tiny hole in the corner.

"You gotta be kidding!" we exclaimed. "Where were you aiming?"

"At the eye!" he said. "The buck was two hundred yards away, looking at me through the cactus. The eye was the only shot I had!"

Wiley nodded in agreement. Had it been anyone other than Doug Gary, I wouldn't have believed it. But, having grown up with the man and having witnessed his legendary shooting skills, I knew it was absolutely true. Interestingly, the .22-250 bullet did not exit the skull, nor did a single drop of blood.

Doug's choice of weapon, in fact, was a point of contention with my dad. Dad was a proponent of the Elmer Keith school of ballistics, where the bigger-caliber, bigger-bullet philosophy ruled. Doug preferred a smaller but deadly accurate, fast-moving bullet. They would go around and around about which was the better option, but the fact was, both men were exceptionally lethal with their weapons of choice. I saw Doug wound a deer only once. It happened on a frontal neck shot at close range. The buck thrashed about in the brush as if it had a cougar on its back. When all went silent and we went to retrieve it, we found no buck and no sign of it after an hour of searching.

Doug stood six feet, six inches, in stocking feet and carried two hundred and twenty-five pounds of ranch-hardened muscle. Ten years my senior, he was quite my hero when I was a kid. I felt privileged to accompany him then, as I did later in life, when our careers and time permitted. It was like having Daniel Boone as a guide. He could just look at a piece of cover and know whether it contained game.

Growing up on our ranch, Doug had the opportunity to hunt and spend more time afield in South Texas than anyone I know. Consequently, he acquired skills that most of us can only dream about. He was like an Apache in the woods. He never used a blind or a stand of any sort. He preferred to hunt on foot in the brush. He would sneak along a ridge, moving slow as molasses, testing each foot before he set it down, stopping every couple of steps to listen, paying attention to the direction of the wind as if his life depended on it. His goal was to see deer before they saw him, which is quite an accomplishment on foot—especially for a man of his size. That was precisely the method he used to come by most of the big bucks he shot.

Later, as the foreman of the neighboring Callaghan ranch, which comprised a whopping 180,000 acres, Doug spent his spare time in pursuit of coyote and bobcat pelts and the few dollars they fetched. Using a cheap Montgomery Ward cassette player and the tape of a wounded jack rabbit, he would call the predators to him. With his truck parked in a patch of camouflaging shade, he would place the cassette player on the ground fifty yards away or on top of the cab. He would get set in shooting position so no movement was required beyond a trigger pull once his quarry arrived. It was nothing for him to shoot 150 coyotes and 60 or 70 bobcats in a season. As I said, Doug Gary spent more time hunting in South Texas than anyone I know.

My Absolute Most Frightening Hunt

As a young kid I was fairly petrified of javelina. Old Man Gary, our ranch caretaker, had filled my head with horror stories of hunters,

J.P. with a javelina, also known as a peccary.

Levi took this South Texas bobcat at the age of seven!

cowboys, and dogs who were massacred by the vicious beasts. For those of you who aren't familiar with the javelina, it is a native, piglike animal with black, bristly hair and incredibly sharp teeth. When angered or threatened, javelina snap their jaws to make a fast *pop-pop-pop* sound—an alarming sound that instantly grabs your attention. A bizarre anatomical feature is a scent gland on its back that resembles a miniature human breast. My guess is that the gland has something to do with compensating for poor eyesight. Most likely, the malodorous scent—which is similar to that of a skunk—is used to locate and keep the pack together in dense brush.

The fact that javelinas often approach quite close, as if challenging your presence, only confirmed that these wickedly tusked animals were anxious to do me harm. Of course, that wasn't really the case. The nearsighted critters are mostly just trying to figure out if you really are something or simply a fencepost. Javelinas are generally harmless—unless you make the mistake of messing with them. Then, like any threatened or wounded animal, they will do whatever it takes to protect their own.

I was all of eight years old when Dad and I were out hunting and encountered a sizable pack of javelinas. With Mr. Gary's stories firmly in mind, I decided it would be healthier to remain in the Jeep while Dad went after them on foot. However, as I watched my dad recede into the distance, my imagination ran away with me. I had thoughts of killer javelinas circling to attack me in the topless Jeep. I even pictured the creatures climbing into the vehicle to get at me. I quickly stepped onto the hood, but that did not appear high enough to keep me out of harm's way. Despite the .22 single-shot rifle in my hands, I felt completely outgunned.

I jumped down and ran after Dad.

Together we approached the milling pack, now in the brush, and we got close—much closer than I cared to be. I could smell their musky scent, see their dark shapes moving around us. Right then, Dad cut loose with a semiautomatic AR-180, at which point all hell broke loose. Javelinas were dashing every which way, some right by us, and Dad was laying them down, one after the other. Dust flew everywhere at once. Earsplitting squeals and grunts filled the air. Dad's gun continued to explode in my ears. Then came the threatening sound of jaws popping all around us. It was more stimuli than my young mind could take in.

I figured this was Custer's last stand, and soon we would be no more than a memory. Amazingly, the battlefield cleared of the opposing army.

I was glued to Dad's side as he explored the brush to assess the damage. Three javelinas lay sprawled and out for the count, invisible behind bushes or clumps of cactus until we were right up on them. A fourth was wounded in the hindquarters. It abruptly rose up on front legs, hair bristling along its back, jaws snapping like steel traps and making about as much noise. By the time Dad got me situated to finish it off, not five paces away, my hands were shaking so badly I could hardly aim the little rifle. I would like to attribute the shaking to buck fever, but this was a case of sheer terror. That javelina boar looked bigger and more menacing than a grizzly, more ferocious than a growling tiger.

It looked like death ready to snatch my soul.

In all honesty, that pint-size javelina was more frightening than any buffalo, lion, or bear I have met since.

The Rifleman

One of my favorite activities as a twelve-year-old was to wander off in the brush with my new gun—a Browning .22 lever-action rifle. As a hard-core fan of the TV series *The Rifleman,* I was in heaven with this high-capacity weapon. Not only could I picture myself as Lucas McCain patrolling the grounds, but my hunting productivity took a big leap from the days of my single-shot weapons.

Often I would take the caretaker's dogs with me, looking for rabbits or other small game to shoot. Sheba was a big, tough-looking German shepherd, capable of striking instant fear into any illegal alien trespassing on the ranch. Sheba was a real sweetheart, however, once she knew you were on the A list. Sissy, a smaller shepherd mix, was a combination of extremes, depending upon whom she was encountering. Around us kids she was subservient as a newborn pup, displaying the submissive behavior of rolling her head or body onto its side. But let an illegal alien, javelina, coyote, or other threat approach the house or us kids, and she transformed into a guard dog of the first order, willing to risk life and limb to protect her pack.

Although the dogs' presence probably served to chase off more rabbits than not, there was something about having a dog or two in on the hunt with you, even if it was a tad counterproductive. I never was much of a quail hunter, at least not in a group. There are simply too many guns in too confined an area. Since I shied from hunting quail with my dad's friends, rabbit hunting was the closest I got to the companionship of hunting with our four-legged friends.

The ranch dogs and I would roam for miles, exploring new country and finding all kinds of adventures together. We would return thoroughly exhausted from the heat of an average South Texas winter day. I even

The author's father with a nice, wide buck.

got a rabbit now and then, usually one that the dogs ranging ahead of me had missed.

Once, without them, I shoed up a huge buck near the house pond. I took a couple of quick steps to one side to better watch it bound off into the brush. I wasn't allowed to shoot at a deer with a .22, but I sure could admire one as it darted off. I lifted a foot to take one more step to see around intervening brush. Fortunately, I glanced down in mid-stride. Coiled on the ground was a three-foot rattler.

I immediately froze, then retreated a few steps. If you must have poisonous snakes, I guess the one positive thing about a rattler is that it at least has the courtesy to warn you. In this case the surprise was that the snake had failed to rattle a warning. Maybe it was asleep; maybe it was in a daze from the warm sun. Whatever the case, I promptly did my Rifleman best to end its biting career.

Game Management

In my late teens, I mastered the punishing kick of the .30-06, and a string of mediocre bucks fell to the big gun. There was no such thing as game management back then, at least not for us. Ours was a sizable ranch, and no one hunted on it but family and friends. It was a two-buck county (now it's a three-buck county), and we shot the first average buck that showed for meat, then concentrated on getting a trophy with the second tag. Most of these first bucks were immature, two- or three-year-old bucks that should have been left to mature and reach their true potential. We should have been shooting does for meat because we had loads of them. Too many, in fact.

But the old-timers' mantra "never shoot a doe" had been hammered into our heads. Such an adage made sense in the twenties and thirties, when the deer herd was underpopulated as a whole. That changed, however, when the blowfly was eradicated in Texas. The deer population exploded, and the herd expanded beyond the carrying capacity of the land, eventually taxing the limited resources of this desert country. An area that previously had a density of one adult deer to fifty acres now had a density of one adult deer to ten or twelve acres. The result was less food to eat and smaller bodies and antlers. The deer were literally shrinking before our eyes.

The second problem came when trophy deer hunting increased in popularity in the seventies and eighties and hunters continued to remove primarily bucks. Soon the buck/doe ratio was skewed—one buck to five or six does.

In the late nineties we hired whitetail guru Al Brothers and adopted a trophy management program to address these problems. We removed four hundred and fifty does in the first three years, which is no easy feat. You really have to work at it to remove that many deer. As to bucks, we put antler and age restrictions in place. We began removing mature bucks with eight points or less as well as all spikes.*

The results? Our ratio dropped to one buck to 1.25 does, and our density dropped in half to one adult deer to twenty-five acres. The average field-dressed weight of a mature doe soared from sixty to ninety pounds. The average field-dressed weight of a mature buck grew from

---

*One benefit was that we provided a lot of food for needy folks through the wonderful program Hunters for the Hungry. We also provided hunting opportunities to underprivileged teens through the Texas Youth Hunting Program, sponsored by the Texas Wildlife Association. This win-win program offered free hunting to kids who had the desire but not the means to hunt. It also helped land owners remove excess deer. Further, our lease hunters embraced trophy management in full. In recognition of these efforts, our ranch won the 2001 Wildlife Conservationist of the Year award for South Texas.

125 to 175 pounds. A good set of antlers went from 140 to 160 Boone and Crockett points.

The Bulletproof Buck

A couple of the bigger deer that people took on our ranch were deer we had seen and mentioned to someone else. For instance, there was the wide-horned buck below the house that turned out to be darn near "bulletproof." This hardy buck soaked up lead from three different guns before giving up the ghost!

Alexandra and I made a quick hunting trip to the ranch one weekend in the eighties. When our hunting vehicle—a VW Thing—wouldn't start, we had to resort to hunting on foot. We headed below the house, which was where Doug Gary always said the big bucks were, anyway. A mile or so from the house we found several does foraging in an old root-plow strip. Just then, a magnificent buck appeared at the opposite end. Its heavy, dark horns had my attention. The most noticeable feature, however, was their width. They spread several inches past each ear.

But the buck was over two hundred yards away, and I was shooting offhand. Before we could plan an approach, the buck whirled and bounded for the brush. I placed the sights on the vanishing tail but decided it was not worth the risk of wounding the buck.

"We'll come back tomorrow," I told Alexandra. "Let's leave so we don't disturb him further."

We went back the next morning, our last day to hunt, but Mr. Wide did not put in an appearance. Which explains why his antlers were as wide as they were. He didn't get that way by being foolish.

I told my dad about the incident, and the following week he tried his hand at locating the buck. Mr. Wide had fooled me, but he did not fool Dad.

At least not at first.

In practice for an upcoming safari, Dad was using a .375 H&H Magnum—about twice as much gun as needed for a South Texas buck. Or so one would think.

Sure enough, Mr. Wide appeared in the field, sniffing the ground for a willing doe. When he turned broadside at one hundred yards, Dad let him have a Winchester Silvertip in the shoulder. That was when the unthinkable happened. The buck did not jump. The buck did not fall like a ton of bricks. The buck did not stagger under the impact. The buck simply ran off.

Dad waited, then began a thorough search of the area. He expected to find the buck crumpled up no more than thirty yards away. To his amazement, he found no sign of the buck. Nor did he find any sign that the buck had been hit. He returned to hunt that evening, hoping the buck might revisit the doe-favored strip, but the big deer had vanished without a trace.

The next morning Dad's friend C.K. Lawson tried his luck at the same spot. Shortly after daybreak, he saw a buck hobbling at the edge of the brush. Putting his scope on it, he clearly saw the wound Dad's bullet had made in the shoulder. The buck then turned and headed into the brush, and the only shot offered was what we call a Texas heart shot. C.K. quickly sent a .30-06 bullet up his rear, and the buck disappeared.

C.K. happily went to claim his prize, but, as in my dad's experience, there was no buck to be found. C.K. searched the whole area but came up empty-handed. He finally returned to the ranch house with a tale of equal disbelief.

The next morning it was young Brian Anding's turn at that pasture and the now-famous buck that refused to die. It was a still, foggy morning when Brian climbed into the portable tripod he had set up in the dark. It overlooked the root-plowed strip. Some time after daybreak, the fog slowly lifted, and a shadowy, reclining form appeared in the adjacent *sendero*. It was the same buck, lying in the open, not fifty yards away, struggling to lift his head. Quickly finishing him off, Brian was the one to take the Bulletproof Buck home for his wall.

So what was up with a .375 failing on a broadside, shoulder shot? Dad found out the hard way what several PHs in Africa later confirmed. The Silvertip, according to them, is a poorly designed bullet that often shatters on impact and provides little in the way of penetration. Which is exactly what happened in this case.

Regardless, that was one tough buck!

A Sticky Incident

A wildlife biologist will tell you that prickly pear cactus is an important source of quick food energy for deer. But anyone who has met with the business end of its needle-sharp thorns will openly cuss this green villain's existence. Prickly pear is covered in two types of thorns: large, yellow, toothpick-sized thorns on the face of the pads and smaller, dark-golden thorns that grow in clusters on the outer edge like the bristles from a brush.

As kids, we got the golden thorns in our hands when we chopped at the inviting pads with hunting knives. Anyone who has stepped a single foot into the South Texas brush has felt the sting of these thorns in his legs or other parts of his anatomy and has had to pause to pluck them out. Working a summer job as a teen on the neighboring Callaghan ranch, I

Lauren takes her first deer.

often winced at the thought of falling off a horse into a table-sized cluster of the wicked cactus.

I delayed that fate until I was nearly forty, though it didn't involve a horse.

I was out hunting javelina with a bow, and I had just stalked through a maze of waist-high cactus. When I was within twenty yards of a solitary boar, it turned broadside, and I launched a futile arrow over its back. The porker chuffed off, and I never saw it again. Hunt over.

I needed to retrieve my wayward arrow, but I found my path blocked by a solid hedge of cactus. Hesitant to backtrack through the maze and circle the entire area to look for it, I decided to jump over the prickly barrier instead.

Bad idea.

The reason I shouldn't have attempted that maneuver probably had something to do with the reason I never played sports in school. Dreadful coordination. Consequently, I misjudged the distance and failed to account for all cactus pads in the vicinity. My right fist connected with a pad of sharp thorns. The reflex was to jerk backward in the middle of the jump, suddenly halting my forward momentum. That was not good.

J.P.'s first deer.

One foot swept back to keep my balance, and most likely would have, had it not met clumsily with the shin of the other leg.

That's when I started the slow, horrifying, and irretrievable journey backward into the hedge of cactus behind me.

This can't be happening! my mind screeched.

Both hands went rearward to stop my fall, palms landing painfully in the thick pads. It was about like landing on a family of porcupines!

When I tell you that I had a thousand thorns in me from top to bottom, I am not exaggerating. The worst off were my hands, which took the weight of my fall. Thorns were jammed deep into the meat of the palms and fingers, right to the bone in places. I had over a hundred cactus thorns in each hand! What saved the rest of me was that my jeans, belt, and shirt took many of the thorns. I staggered up, somewhat in shock, adrenaline pumping. The thorns carry a small amount of poison. Five or six were no big deal, but what about several hundred? Was it enough to hurt me beyond the physical pain I was in?

I had to get as many out as I could. I started with my hands. I clutched at the thorns, pulling them out one, three, even ten at a time. I should have slowed down, for many of the smaller ones broke off below the surface, but I was in a slightly panicked state. Besides, pulling them one at a time would have taken all day.

How would I get home? My clothes were stapled to my form, and when I glanced over my backside, I was appalled. I looked like a human cactus with all the golden thorns protruding, a perfect transfer from the cactus I had squashed.

Slipping off my boots, I carefully unbuttoned my shirt and pants and peeled them off. Thankfully, a good number of thorns remained in the cast-off fabric. I must have looked a sight, shuffling to the truck in boots and boxers! Even as I went, I was pulling thorns from my swollen hands, back, legs, rump, and arms. I couldn't get in the truck, however, until I got all the thorns out of my rear end—at least the ones that had not broken off. It was growing difficult to feel for them with the ends of my fingers, which were swollen and stinging from their own wounds. Driving back to the ranch house, I had to sit on the edge of the seat, holding my thorny back off the seat. To steer, I could use only the tips of my index fingers and thumbs; the rest of my hands were sprouting broken spines.

Alexandra had just arrived from Dallas with the kids and was talking to Bill Hollon, the border patrol officer whose family lived on the ranch. Bill had just driven in from work. I couldn't blame them for laughing when I got out in my underwear.

"Whatever happened to you?" Bill asked.

It took a couple of days with tweezers and a safety pin to get the majority of the thorns out. The rest were left to fester and work their way to the surface over the next few months.

I will leave the wildlife biologists to their own opinions on cactus, but, as for me, I would just as soon banish it from our lands.

Gun Accidents

Sometimes the most dangerous threat to a hunter is the hunter himself—like the time as a teen I was out hunting javelina with Doug and Wiley Gary.

It was a beautiful winter afternoon, the skies clear and the temperature mild. We had been driving around the ranch in a pickup when we spotted a large pack of porkers rooting in the open of a root-plowed strip. I was particularly happy because Wiley was with us. This was the first time he had set foot in the field with a gun since his return from Vietnam. For several years we had tried to get him to go hunting with us, but he always had some excuse why he couldn't make it.

One day he confided that when he stepped in the brush, he wasn't looking for deer or javelina. He was looking for tripwires and Viet Cong with guns. It made me tear up to hear it.

This was a special day for the three of us as we stalked up on the rooting porkers, still oblivious of our approach. As we neared, we fanned out abreast of each other, rifles at the ready, waiting for Doug to give the nod. I was shooting a .30 carbine and carried a Colt Model 1911 loaded on my hip. Wanting the pistol out of the way, I had slid the holster behind my hip, over my right cheek.

As one, we dropped the hammer on the unsuspecting pack, and the field came instantly alive. There was motion in every direction. When the pack finally regrouped and ran for the brush, we gave chase, stopping now and then to shoot at the fleeing pigs.

It was during one of our mad dashes, while I was sprinting to keep up with the long-legged Gary boys, that the pistol on my hip went off.

My immediate fear, even though I felt nothing, was that I had shot myself in the lower leg, the pistol being pointed down at my calf. Fresh in my mind was the story of the World War II veteran at the health club who had showed me the scar from a German bullet in the middle of his thigh. He said he didn't feel a thing; he just fell to the ground with the leg bone blown in two.

I was lucky. It was a complete miss. But it sure woke me up to being more vigilant in the area of gun safety while afield.

Some twenty years later, my ranch neighbor wasn't so lucky. Carl Young, with a .454 Casull revolver in hand, was searching in thick brush for a wounded deer. When the brush grew so thick that he had to bend over to push his way through, he holstered the gun at his side. Just after that, a branch caught on the hammer of the gun, letting it fall back with enough force to fire the shell. The bullet struck Carl below the calf, destroying the bone and tissue in its path.

His cell phone was out of range, so he had no way to call for help. His biggest worry was that he would bleed to death before someone found him. He crawled on hands and knees to the road so he would be easier to find. Luckily, his family knew where to look for him when he was late to return. Unfortunately, the injury resulted in the loss of his leg from mid-shin down.

Karl Kinsel, our friend and the son of our long-term cattleman at the time, took a .38 special slug in the belly. He was in the back of a pickup when a friend holding the pistol either tripped or fell, causing the gun to go off. The bullet passed through a Texas-size belt buckle Karl was wearing and came to rest against his spine. He spent the next six months in the hospital recuperating from the tragic accident.

The doctors informed him that had he not been wearing that thick buckle or had the gun been loaded with .357 magnum cartridges, the bullet most likely would have continued on through the spine, paralyzing him below the waist.

The good news was that both men survived their accidents and were able to get on with their lives.

I ran into both of them at the same time at a Texas Wildlife Association convention, and when it hit me that they were the only two Texans I knew who had suffered gunshots, I quickly introduced them.

******

Even at the age of nine, I prided myself on safe gun handling. So I was mindful of the direction of the house when I strolled some distance away to shoot at songbirds in the brush with a single-shot .22. What I forgot to take into account was the caretaker's house a couple of hundred yards to one side. It was concealed by the brush I was now shooting into, and it just never crossed my young mind to consider bullets traveling that far through brush.

Some time later, I heard my name yelled out, and I returned to the house. My dad was standing on the front porch, and he did not look happy.

It turned out Doug Gary had been working underneath his car when he heard bullets whizzing past him. He called my dad to ask if someone was shooting a gun near the house.

I felt absolutely horrible. I broke down in tears, afraid to face my hero, Doug, convinced he would hate me forever for this treacherous act. Later that evening, I finally gathered the courage to meet him face to face and make my apology. The big man literally towered above me as I tried to get the words out.

Big-hearted Doug was already smiling and making light of it, but I didn't pick up another gun for some time after.

Short Takes

My good friend Jim Lewis had his hands full one afternoon when he allowed his two young sons, ages nine and seven, to accompany him on a bowhunt in South Texas. It was typical South Texas hunting

The author's wife, Alexandra, and the ranch patrol.

weather: 95 degrees. Once in the blind, the commotion of two youngsters exceeded his naïve expectations. He saw his prospects for success dwindling quickly. After several failed attempts to quiet his sons, the last hour of daylight finally arrived, and Jim said, "OK, boys. That's it! No more talking."

Not a minute later, a small hand poked him three times in the ribs.

He turned and glared at the seven-year-old. Then Jim went back to studying the landscape out the blind window, hoping to glimpse a thick-horned South Texas buck sneaking its way through the prickly pear and mesquite toward the corn feeder placed at bow range below.

Another minute passed, then *poke, poke, poke.*

He glared again, but this time the seven-year-old looked truly distraught.

"Dad," the boy whispered, "it's real important."

Jim sighed.

"OK, what is it?"

"Dad, what do we do if a polar bear comes?"

******

Paco was a ranch dog, a short-haired collie mutt who took a liking to us kids. Seeing there was mutual affection, Doug Gary let us take him to Dallas, where he promptly turned into a heavyset city dog.

Once, when we returned to the ranch with Paco in the car, a funny incident took place.

The Garys were raising an orphaned white-tailed fawn. They had named her Baby and fed her milk from a bottle. As our family unloaded the car, Paco caught sight of the tiny fawn and made a beeline straight for her. Worried that our dog would kill her, Dad ran after Paco, yelling at him to come back.

Mr. Gary saw what was happening and pulled my dad aside.

"Don't worry. Your dog can't catch that deer."

Paco continued to chase the fawn around the houses of the compound. Pretty soon Paco came running by with his tongue hanging out, while the young fawn leisurely pronked ahead of him. After another lap or two, Paco collapsed in the shade. The fawn stopped and returned to browsing. This chase operation went on repeatedly throughout our stay.

Fast-forward a year.

The family arrives at Thanksgiving break. Paco sees the fawn and remembers how much fun that little game of chase was. Only now the fawn is a mature doe.

Paco takes off at a dead run for the doe. The doe lifts her head and watches Paco approach. She does not run. She simply watches as he nears. When Paco is nearly upon her, she raises up on her hind legs and lashes out at him with her front hoofs, striking a couple of solid blows. Paco yips, turns tail, and runs for his life. Baby chases him off, delivering one or two more blows to his backside.

Poor Paco had to spend the rest of that trip cowering on the front porch, lest the ruthless doe hunt him down and exact her vengeance.

******

One afternoon, as a young teen, I was out hunting with Dad's friend C.K. Lawson. We were driving a VW Thing with the top and windshield down when two bucks suddenly jumped up in a brushy field and dashed off into the bright afternoon sun.

"Big buck!" C.K. hollered. "Big buck!"

I had them in the scope before C.K. had even brought the vehicle to a stop. The sun glinted off their antlers like the shower of sparks from a welding torch, blinding me. It was a running shot, but how could I let such a big buck get away? Clearly, the deer had no plans to stop.

I fired at the lead buck, and they both instantly disappeared, as deer can do when they want to.

"Did you hit him?" C.K. asked.

"I think so."

"How big was he?"

"Pretty big, I think."

We got out and stalked through the low brush, looking for blood or hair as we went. Before we found any, we stumbled upon the buck, lying stone dead in the short scrub. Or perhaps I should say "a buck." This sure wasn't the buck I had pulled the trigger on. Why, this was a peewee five-pointer!

It was a yearling with spindly, light-colored horns. The beams were no bigger around than my index finger.

"Oops," C.K. said, with a laugh. "I guess he isn't so big."

I had to laugh, too. I felt a little better that a hunting veteran like C.K. had been fooled as well.

That's what happens in hunting when you let excitement win over patience.

To this day, we still joke about my "Big Buck."

******

There was the time C.K. was halfway up a ladder to a tower blind when his rifle swung around and hit the metal structure with a loud clang. A trophy buck in a *sendero* stuck its head out to see what all the noise was about. Of course, C.K. wasted no time in taking advantage of that *faux pas.*

Another time, while he was noisily field-dressing a buck, a trophy buck appeared to see what he was up to. That, too, was a mistake on the buck's part.

******

A good friend of mine, who was attending the University of Texas at Austin, returned from a hunt late one night with a field-dressed deer in tow. Because no deer-processing facility was open that late, he was

Levi with the heavy-horned whitetail he took with his friend Ben Halliday.

left with a dilemma. He carted the carcass into the dorm and up the elevator to his room. He then proceeded to butcher it in the shower! That is definitely one you don't write home to mom about.

******

Our friends the Leyendeckers in Laredo claimed javelina made great pets. We figured they should have known, having made pets of coyotes, bobcats, hawks, and other sundry creatures. Over the years they'd had several of the little pigs as pets. With their sharp canine teeth and musk gland removed, the javelina were apparently pleasant and social and a great delight. They would run to the door with the dogs to meet the kids when they got home from school and jump into bed with them at night.

One day a pet javelina got out of the yard. When it encountered the neighborhood dogs, it began to chase them. The javelina was used to playing with the Leyendecker dogs, but the neighborhood dogs sure

The author's biggest South Texas boar.

weren't used to playing with a javelina. Unfortunately, a dog owner mistook the playful javelina for a wild one and called the police. The police came out and shot the javelina, thinking it was attacking the dog. In the fray, no one noticed the collar around its neck.

******

Two of the worst drought years in South Texas, in my lifetime, were 1996 and 1998. In the first, rain stopped in November and did not return until May. The 1998 drought was shorter but more intense, with no rain recorded from April through the end of August. Combine that with blistering temperatures—above average for even a desert area like South Texas—and you have the makings of disaster. More than fifty illegal aliens died that year from heatstroke while on their journey to find work on this side of the border.

On this particular August afternoon, when the thermometer registered 113 degrees in the shade, lease hunter Nash Brown and I were driving around the ranch to check on the work that had been done by the grader to smooth several roads and *senderos* used by hunters. With the air conditioner on high in the truck, we didn't think much about the heat. Then we dropped over a steep creekbank and found ourselves looking at mud.

Mud! What in the heck is mud doing here in the middle of a drought? I thought.

Even stranger, the mud wasn't at the bottom of the creek; it was on the side of the steep bank.

It turned out the motor grader had broken an underground pipe that pumped water to various water troughs around the ranch. With the pipe broken underground, the escaping water had nowhere to run, so it soaked a patch of ground the size of a bed mattress and three times as thick. Before my foot could react and hit the brake, the front end of the crew cab had sunk in to the axle. Even with a shovel and jack, there was no budging the truck. We worked on it for an hour or so, but our only accomplishment was to work ourselves into a lather. There was nothing left but to walk back to the house, exactly three miles away.

It didn't sound like much. But if it was 113 in the shade, it was 130 degrees in the sun. Soon into our trek we felt the sweat being squeezed out of us like an orange in a press. We looked as if we had taken a shower with our clothes on. It was surprising, too, how quickly the heat sapped our strength. For half the trek we were walking due west and facing the relentless ball of fire in the sky. It felt as if we were walking inside an oven, with red-hot elements all around us. The ground beneath our feet was griddle hot. I was twenty years younger than Nash, and I won't mention how many fewer pounds, so I knew he felt even worse than I did.

Of course, we were kicking ourselves for having brought no water with us in the truck.

We made it back without serious consequence, but I guarantee you I never leave the ranch house without a cooler full of water.

******

As an older teen, I was out trying to rattle up a buck on a new *sendero* in a pasture that was so overgrown it was hardly hunted. It was a cold December morning, and I was wearing a goose-down parka that was good for keeping me warm, but its nylon shell was noisy in the still air. There was a deep drainage at the side of the *sendero.* I settled down into it on my knees for cover.

Rattling the horns in my hands a few times, a big-bodied buck stepped out in the *sendero* a few hundred yards distant. It was looking my way, clearly interested in finding the "other buck" that was rattling. When I clattered the horns again, it lowered its antlers and came running. Boy, my heart started in my chest. I couldn't tell how many points it had, but it looked like a bunch, and its horns were dark as molasses.

Then the buck veered, disappearing into the bordering brush. I remained as quiet as I could and hoped it was still headed my way. I cocked my head, listening to the morning still. I figured I would hear the buck when it got close.

Then, suddenly, a loud snort exploded to my left from the brush.

I turned my head to see the buck standing broadside, not ten yards away. Its head was raised, and steam gushed from its nostrils with each breath. The spectacle was even more fantastic from my low angle, as I kneeled in the drainage below the surface of the ground, looking up at this magnificent animal. There was no question it was a shooter. But I wasn't sure how to get the rifle up to my shoulder and pointed in its direction without it seeing or hearing me, especially in that noisy parka. At that close distance there was simply no way. Whatever I did would have to be in one swift motion.

I made the decision to throw the gun up and shoot the moment the cross hairs met the buck's shoulder. The only problem was that when I threw the rifle up, the butt of the stock landed on top of my shoulder instead of against it.

Young Chilton kids with a trophy-size rattler killed by ranch foreman Ervin Newman. Even without the head, it measured over six feet long.

There was no time to make a correction, and I knew there would be consequences. In any case, I yanked the trigger, the gun roared, and the scope punched me between the eyes with the force of a ball-peen hammer. The buck charged off.

I am not sure which of us was more stunned at this sudden turn of events. I staggered out of the drainage, a bit dazed, blood pouring down my face. Even from there I could see the red trail left by the buck. And I had no trouble finding the thirteen-point trophy a few yards away.

The scar has faded over time, but not the memory of a great hunt.

******

One time an armadillo appeared in the *sendero* where I was still-hunting for deer. The funny-looking creature was headed my way, so I stopped and stood there to see what it would do. It trotted right up to

The author's last buck, taken on his family's San Roman ranch in South Texas with his best friend, Scott Halliday. This old brute weighed 192 pounds field dressed.

me in its armor-plated shell, then froze less than three feet away when it suddenly realized something was there.

Still undecided as to my identity, the prehistoric animal raised up on its hind legs, balanced by an armored tail, with its front paws hanging like those of an upright kangaroo, and began to sniff loudly at the air for my scent. I moved not a muscle and tried not to blink.

The armadillo finally dropped to all fours, crept forward, and sniffed my foot. Its wet nostrils actually left a smudge mark on the leather toe of my boot! Eventually, the football-shaped animal decided I was nothing to be concerned about and went on its way.

******

About once in a decade the South Texas coyote population experiences a rabies outbreak, and you hear stories of mad yodel dogs attacking ranchers and their pets. To combat the outbreak, rabies vaccine, inserted in edible treats, is dropped from aircraft over "hot" areas. During one of those periods in the nineties, a rabid coyote came into our new caretaker's yard and attacked his dogs.

When Bill Hollon rushed onto his front porch to see what all the barking and growling was about, he found his two blue heelers in the midst of a deadly battle with a slobbering, psycho killer. The mad coyote was slashing and biting at his dogs in a wild, nonstop frenzy. When Bill yelled out to try and break them up, the crazed varmint turned and set its sights on our surprised foreman.

As a border patrol officer and helicopter pilot, Bill regularly carried a pistol on his belt or in a shoulder holster. Luckily, he did so that day. Quickly kneeling and placing his sights on the charging menace, he began unloading his weapon at the animal. The zombie mutant shrugged off the bullets like raindrops. Bill emptied the gun just as the rabid canine collapsed at his feet.

At that point both dogs arrived on the scene, determined to get in the last licks, and they plowed into the dying coyote with jaws drawn. This complicated the matter for Bill, who tried to separate his pets from the rabid animal and got scratched up in the process. As a result, he had to undertake the series of rabies vaccinations. Fortunately, the improved series of shots is now administered in the arm and not in the abdomen, as in days of old.

Bill's dogs required vaccinations of their own, plus a couple dozen metal stitches—metal to keep them from biting them out. Otherwise, they were back on patrol the next day. A ranch dog's work is never done.

✳✳✳✳✳✳

Late one night in the seventies, Mr. Gary was roused from bed by his dogs' barking and howling—distressful sounds that seemed to be coming from all directions at once. Grabbing a lever-action .22 magnum, he opened the porch door to find four javelina chasing Sheba and Sissy around and around the house. In the moonlight he began shooting at the black beasts as they streaked by in the front yard. He eventually killed three out of the four. Quite some shooting for a small-caliber gun. And at running targets. And in the dark of night.

No one can say South Texas boys don't know how to shoot.

Years later, another group of javelina returned for revenge. This time the story had a tragic ending. By that time, Sheba was showing the effects of age and the demands of ranch life on a dog. Blind in one eye and completely deaf after being kicked by a cow she had chased for fun, old Sheba was no longer the dog she once had been.

Waking one night to the sounds of a loud brawl, Mr. Gary stepped onto his front porch to find Sheba and Sissy trading vicious bites with several raging javelinas. The little tusker is a tough match for a dog. All head and body, javelinas are hard to get hold of, and they can swap ends in a heartbeat. Going in for a hind leg, a dog can suddenly find itself facing a mouthful of snapping teeth. The eyeteeth of the adult javelina are long and razor sharp, capable of delivering a fatal bite or ripping flesh like a scalpel. Stories about javelinas and their snapping teeth are legendary.

Mr. Gary got in a few shots at the intruders before they departed at a run. The dogs were hot on their heels, and all parties were quickly swallowed in the dark of night. Some time later, Sissy came back slashed and limping, but poor Sheba was never seen or heard from again.

******

Conrad Speece and Kramer McKinney, friends of mine and both doctors, were deer hunting in Mexico when Conrad shot a couple of javelinas late in the day. With night coming on, he didn't have time to field-dress them, but he didn't want to leave them on the ground for fear coyotes or other predators would make short work of them. In that part of Mexico, there were no trees to speak of, only runty bushes, so Conrad used the next-best thing: the blind.

Yes, he carried those musky critters up the ladder and stowed them inside the blind, planning to return early the next morning to finish the job. Well, as so often happens in hunting, the plan changed, and he didn't make it back to the blind until a couple of days later.

Weather conditions had not been ideal for his little storage operation. It was 105 degrees in the shade on the afternoon he climbed the ladder of the blind to determine the condition of his charges. Conrad opened the blind door, took one peek inside, closed the blind door, and descended the ladder.

"We need to burn it," he said to Kramer, waiting below. "Just burn the blind."

"What?" Kramer piped up. "Ya big sissy. Why, I've seen stuff in operating rooms that would make a billy goat puke. Can't believe you'd let a coupl'a javelinas bother you. What kinda doctor are you, anyway?"

"Be my guest," Conrad offered, stepping aside.

Big-bellied Kramer clamored up the ladder, all the while grumbling about medical school, sissies, and whatnot. At eye level with the floor of the blind, he pulled open the door, reached a hand inside, and grabbed a rear leg. With all his might, he jerked the tusker out and over him.

Did the tusker land on the ground as intended? Not quite.

The rotten, half-baked carcass pulled apart, emptying its putrid contents all over the good doctor. Kramer spent the next half-hour doubled over, emptying his own stomach.

A little late but the two doctors were finally in agreement: They burned the blind.

Dog Tales

Chapter 24

Snakes and Dogs

Benson came to us when he was three and one-half years old. My wife found him in the paper: "Large dog. 90 lbs. Lab mix." The "mix" turned out to be three-quarters yellow lab and one-quarter chow. I wasn't crazy about chow. I was even less optimistic when my wife suggested we go take a look.

"Nobody gives away a good dog," I groused. "Only problem ones."

As we drove up to the house, a big amber-colored dog got up from the shade and came out to bark at us. He was neither chained nor captive behind a fence, which was exceptional in itself in a Dallas neighborhood. Most dogs would have run off. I had to admit he was a handsome specimen, in his prime. He was well-muscled, with a proud tail, a sleek coat, and a powerful bark that reverberated all the way down to your toes. He assessed us correctly as no threat and made no further advance.

It turned out the mother of the young couple was terminally ill in England, and they had decided to return. The couple felt it cruel to lock the dog up for the six-month quarantine required by the British government, and they were simply looking for a good home.

We loaded Benson in the back of the Land Cruiser, and off we went. I was worried he might be homesick and mope about, but when we got home, he went straight to the den and flopped down on the floor, as if he had been our dog from day one.

✳✳✳✳✳

Rattlesnakes are a constant threat to ranch dogs. Dogs can't resist the slow-crawling reptiles, yet they lack reflexes quick enough to escape the lightning-fast strikes. South Texas rattlesnakes grow to immense sizes, with enough venom to kill quickly, depending on where one is bit. We managed a dozen or so trips to the ranch before Benson ran into one.

My wife and my sister Kay were out for a walk at the ranch when they noticed Benson confronting something in the road ahead. As they neared, they realized it was a rattlesnake, as thick around as a wrestler's arm. The snake was coiled, head raised, and ready to strike. Its rattling would wake the dead. Benson and the snake were going at each other, each trying to bite the other in the face. The two went back and forth for what seemed an eternity. Alexandra and Kay kept yelling for Benson to come, and Kay threw a water bottle at the snake, trying to distract it.

Finally, Benson broke off and trotted over, panting and happy as could be. Alexandra looked him over and saw no sign of snakebite.

On the return, Benson ran ahead of them, jumped in water troughs, and dashed from scent to scent, as always. When I later drove up to the house, Benson was lying in the yard, and the girls were chatting on the steps of the porch. Only there was something wrong with Benson's head. His left eye was swollen shut, and his right cheek was puffed out, as if he had a ball stuffed inside it. I wondered if a cow had kicked him.

"What happened to Benson?" I asked.

The girls jumped up.

"Oh, my gosh, the snake must have bit him!"

By the time we got Benson in the back of the Suburban, he wasn't doing well. His entire head was swelling, and his cheek had swollen to grotesque proportions. I got out a snakebite kit, hoping to suck some of the venom out, but, search as I might, I could not locate the snakebites. His hair was simply too thick.

A young fellow named James was working for me at that time. He jumped in the back and held Benson as I sped to town. I called Seymon Deutsch, the prominent Laredo businessman who was also our cattleman. I had also hunted with him in Africa.

"Seymon, who would you recommend for a snakebite?"

"Take him to Jane the vet," he said. "She'll know what to do."

Thirty minutes later, now an hour and a half after the bite, we pulled into Jane's Veterinary Clinic. Jane was a tough, wiry gal with an ever-present cigarette dangling from her lips. She gave it to you straight and didn't give a damn what you thought. The animal's best interest was all she had in mind.

Once we got Benson on the table, the first thing she did was to remove his collar. I hadn't even noticed how tight it had become. The swelling had spread into the neck, and his head was now the size of a basketball. Both eyes were swollen shut, and Benson's tongue was hanging out of his mouth. His panting was heavy and raspy. He was in trouble.

"His throat is swelling shut," Jane explained, bluntly.

"You've got a choice to make," she continued. "The choice is whether to give him the antivenin or not. There is a chance it will kill him. The antivenin is made from horse serum, and if your dog has eaten horsemeat in his diet, he may have developed a deadly allergy to the serum."

I looked at Benson lying there on the table. He was motionless except for the labored panting. He was also drooling profusely, not in a normal way.

"What would you do if he were your dog?" I asked.

"I'd give him the antivenin."

"Then let's do that."

She stabbed an IV in Benson's front leg and put him to sleep to slow his wildly beating heart and his labored breathing. Then she administered the antivenin in the same leg, this time administering it drop by slow drop. She cautioned again that it might kill him.

"We'll know pretty soon," she said, cigarette still clamped in her teeth.

Her demeanor and actions were not unlike a medic on the battlefield. She was fighting death. It wasn't pretty, and she was ready to get down in the trenches and kick the crap out of it. She took it personally. She was the kind of person you are glad to have on your side in the midst of a tragedy.

Benson lay asleep. As the last of the antivenin pressed into his vein, Jane and James discussed the health of his horses and other animals Jane had treated. She remembered them all.

A moment later, Dr. Jane sucked in a deep breath and pronounced, "He's going to be OK. He'll live."

She showed me the two bites. One was just above the left eyebrow. The other, incredibly, was inside the right cheek. The snake had bitten Benson while he was jerking back his head, lip flying up.

Then she proceeded to caution me on the possible lasting, devastating effects of snake venom, an evil concoction that is meant to destroy the tissue and organs of its prey. In effect, the snake's prey is digested from the inside before the snake even begins the process of swallowing it.

"There is a good chance that the tissue and muscle in his face will decompose. If so, it may slough off to the bone. Also, he may go blind in his left eye."

The next afternoon we returned to pick up Benson. He was a little unsteady on his feet, and his head was still enlarged. He looked like one of those wrinkled Sharpei dogs, his eyes thin slits in a puffy brow. He slept most of the next twenty-four hours and drank gallons of water, and by the next day, he was much better and ready to venture out. We were lucky.

No tissue damage. No sloughing of muscle down to the bone. The sight in his left eye was fine.

Two years went by before Benson crossed paths with another diamondback rattlesnake. In the interim I had searched for a dog "snakeproofing" class but had no luck finding one in our area. These classes, offered before hunting season, teach bird dogs to avoid snakes. The dog is trained to retreat on all senses—sight, smell, sound—and receives a shock each time it senses a snake and does not retreat.

You would think getting bitten would be enough motivation, but apparently it was not. One evening we were at a pond, planning to grill outside for dinner, and I was in the process of gathering firewood. The kids had been bouncing around with way too much energy, so I had sent them to run a lap around the pond. They had just returned and collapsed in the shade of a tree, where I was stacking wood in an open grill, when my son, Levi, asked, "What's wrong with Benson's face?"

One glance told the story. He was lying rigidly still on all fours. A trickle of blood oozed from a swollen cheek. He was breathing hard, thick drool hanging from his jaw. Damn!

Since we didn't see the snake, I was not sure where it happened or what size snake it was. Perhaps it was on the perimeter of the pond and Benson had flushed it up ahead of the kids. Maybe he found it somewhere else. In any event, I was thankful it had not bitten a kid. The only thing for certain was that we needed to get Benson to Laredo quickly.

After I got his collar off and started toward the highway, I phoned Jane. There was a problem, however. She didn't have any antivenin. There was a shortage, she explained, and what was available was being diverted to human use.

I called Seymon.

"Hang on," he said. "Let me call Dr. Spruiell."

Seymon phoned me back within the minute.

"He's got antivenin."

He gave me directions, then said, "I'll meet you there."

We pulled around back because the doctor's office was already closed for the day, and Dr. Spruiell came out to meet us. He was the old-timer war veteran—been there, done that—when it came to treating snakebite. He also informed me that he did not have antivenin.

"What? Seymon said you did!"

"Can't get it," he said. "Too many dogs dying from allergic reaction. Pulled it off the market."

Which story was I to believe? Human use or allergic reaction? The bottom line was, we couldn't get our hands on any antivenin.

George Alexander with Rusty (left) and Speck in a rare calm. Sitting still for a photo is the last thing on a good bird dog's mind.

Seymon came driving up from work in his suit.

"What do we do now?"

Dr. Spruiell led Benson and the whole family into the darkened facility, switching on lights as we went. By way of introduction, Seymon started talking to Dr. Spruiell about Africa—a common bond among the three of us—and asked him all about his latest safari. Dr. Spruiell relived his adventures as he prepped drugs and instruments. Benson was now on the table, with the kids surrounding their wonder pet, afraid he was going to die. As before, Benson's breathing was growing labored, and he looked sick. He was stone still and panting.

The vet put Benson to sleep, and Seymon jumped right in to help. He held my dog's head as Dr. Spruiell instructed, ignoring the blood and slobber that was getting on his suit, just as he ignored the dust and dirt when called out to our ranch during store hours to check his herd or a broken fence.

When the vet pulled out a scalpel, Alexandra took the kids to the other room.

Dr. Spruiell cut into the swollen fur of Benson's throat, where an Adam's apple would be if he had one. The incision was a good three inches long. The doctor spread the thick skin back from the wound with gloved fingers and pointed with the scalpel inside my dog's throat.

"Look at this. You can see where the poison is already working on the tissue. See how it's turning black."

And it was. It looked like black ink had been absorbed by the sinew and muscle.

"Will he be OK?"

Dr. Spruiell nodded his head.

"I think so. We've got to get that poison, let it drain. It will follow gravity to this spot. We won't even have to sew it up. It'll grow back when it's ready."

Then he administered a syringe full of steroids and wrote a prescription for oral antibiotics to ward off infection from the snake's nasty fangs. We left Benson asleep on the table.

We went home downhearted and glum, and the kids cried and prayed for Benson. None of us slept that night. When we got there the next day, Benson looked about the same as the last time he had been bitten: rather woozy on his feet, with a head the size of a pumpkin. Forty-eight hours later, he was outside chasing critters. The wound on his neck slowly sealed itself, just as the vet had said it would, leaving no visible scar.

So I would have to say both methods of treatment worked equally well.

George's Dog Speck

My friends George Alexander and Buck Foley were hunting in thick brush country north of Corpus Christi when they heard George's dog Speck raise a troubled howl. A short silence followed. Then came the familiar grunts and squeals of javelinas and, finally, the horrid, vicious snapping of numerous jaws. Suddenly, Speck really began to yelp and growl. There was another sudden silence, and George reckoned Speck had gotten away from the wicked creatures. Just then, the hair-raising ruckus began afresh, and soon Buck was shouting, "George, the javelinas got your dog!"

"Shoot 'em!" George shouted back, bashing his way through the brush toward the horrible sounds of his dog being ripped apart.

"I can't. I'll hit Speck!"

"Shoot 'em!" George hollered again, now running in the direction of Buck's voice and Speck's distressed howling. "They'll kill him if you don't."

Still running through brush, George heard Buck shoot repeatedly, and he soon saw a cloud of dust rising over the apparent battlefield in the brush. Once he broke into the clear, he saw that the javelinas had cornered Speck against a wire fence, and he later learned from Buck that the whole pack had been snapping, biting, and tugging at Speck from all sides before Buck's shooting drove them reluctantly into the brush. Speck, a bloody, crumpled mess at that point, was beyond barking.

Staggering up, Speck limped to George and collapsed at his feet. Blood oozed from deep gashes in his hindquarters, back, shoulders, neck, head, and chest. Worst of all, both bones of his lower jaw had been bitten clean through, and now his maw hung down grotesquely against his chest.

George had only a second to gape at the dreadful sight lying at his feet, for the javelinas soon changed their minds and came charging back out of the brush. They did not retreat until George and Buck had shot five or six in the face from a distance of some fifteen feet.

Once the javelinas had retreated into the brush for good, the men bundled up Speck and rushed him to the animal hospital in Corpus, where the vet sewed the awful gashes shut and hooked him to an IV.

The crucial problem of Speck's severed jaw had to wait until George could get him to a vet in Dallas. There, a vet pinned and wired Speck's jaw shut. He instructed George how to feed Speck with a feeding tube and gruel made from canned dog food and water mixed in a blender. He would use a large syringe attached to rubber tubing to pump the gruel into the dog's stomach. Three times a day, George had to insert the rubber tubing through the gap in Speck's front teeth—the javelinas had knocked out all the lower incisors—and slowly pump the gruel down into the stomach.

After a couple of weeks of this treatment, Speck was nearly wasted to bones. Something was wrong. His vet recommended the acclaimed animal clinic at Texas A&M University. There Dr. Crane replaced the steel pins with screws, and he unwired Speck's jaw, informing George that the emotional trauma from being unable to open his jaw was probably the cause of Speck's degeneration. (On one occasion, Speck had ripped the wires out on one side with his paws.) He also cautioned that there was a chance the jaw might not heal properly, being left unset.

Dr. Crane's first theory fortunately proved correct. Soon Speck started adding weight to his emaciated frame. Several operations and thousands of dollars later, Speck regained the full use of his jaw, except for a suspected numbness in the chin.

A Dog's Best Friend*

Most anyone would rappel the unexplored depths of an abandoned well to rescue a child. Now imagine, if you will, how few would do the same to rescue a dog. But George Alexander of Dallas, Texas, did just that.

The tale began one December afternoon while he was quail hunting on Jim Sedbury's West Texas ranch with several friends. George was hunting with one of his hardier pointers in the fringe of the brush, and it was nearing the end of a long, dusty but successful day bird shooting, when he heard Rusty suddenly yelp. Something about it didn't sound right, so George tried calling Rusty back. Nothing. He called once more and waited, but there was no sign of Rusty.

When dusk fell and Rusty still had not returned, George knew something was wrong. He'd had a dog run off before, but rarely at the end of the day, and never for this long. Waiting at the vehicles with his friends and drinking a scotch, George played over in his mind the yelp Rusty had made. Now he recalled a definite echo about it. As the thought struck him , he turned to Bill Hartman, a taxidermist friend who had hunted on the Sedbury ranch for over twenty years:

"Bill, you happen to know of any old wells on this place?"

"No," Bill said, after some thought, "not a one."

George waited. But, after a few minutes, he decided to have a look himself. Toddy in hand, he started into the brush where he had last heard Rusty. The brush was thick and the light was failing fast, but, after some searching, George discovered the unmistakable round of concrete marking a well. The date imprinted in the mortar curbing at the top was July 20, 1919. And then, in the sand at its base, George saw what he was afraid of—a set of Rusty's paw prints.

Most ranches on which George hunted had cattle watering troughs, and, because his dogs were accustomed to jumping into them for a drink and a quick cooling off, he deduced at once what Rusty had had in mind. This looked to be a hand-dug well, which meant there was a good chance that it was no more than ten or fifteen feet deep. George called down the dark hole, but there followed only silence.

*First published in DSC *Hunters Quest,* November 1988.

After returning to his Suburban for a flashlight, George shone the powerful light down into the endless dark, down to the bottom of the well, and at the faint end of the beam he could just make out the crumpled form of Rusty. It wasn't the shallow well he had hoped for. George called down the well again, but Rusty did not answer. He was either dead or in deep shock. Unsure what else to do, George now tipped his scotch and dribbled a small amount below. A second later, he glimpsed some movement. Rusty was still alive.

Upon his return to the vehicles, his buddies' advice was unanimous.

"Too bad, but you gotta shoot him, George. An' a good dog, at that."

"Yep," another agreed. "Best send some lead down there right now before he suffers any more."

"That's a real shame, George," added his good friend Buck Foley. "Rusty was a darn good dog, too. It's almost like losin' one of my own."

"I'll do it for you, George," another consoled him. Don't you worry. Just let me fetch my rifle."

But George didn't see it their way. He took a deep breath and stared back at his buddies in the dark.

"Nope," he said, sighing. "Come mornin'—if Rusty's alive, I'm goin' down there and get him out."

His friends gaped at him as if he'd lost his head. They quickly tried to talk him out of it.

"George, that's crazy talk. No use gettin' yourself killed on account of a dog."

"That's right, George. He ain't a gonna make it anyhow. What's the use in riskin' your own life just so's he can die up here?"

"I'm gettin' my gun, George," another persisted. "It's the best way."

But there are few hunters like George Alexander, fewer still as dedicated to the sport as he. Hunting had preoccupied more than three-quarters of his forty-four years. He got his first shotgun at the age of eight, though it wasn't until he got a driver's license some six years later that the world of hunting truly opened up to him. From that day forward he never saw another weekend home during dove or quail season. Every Friday after school, he would load his dogs into the family Suburban, head into faraway game country, and hunt the whole weekend through, not returning till late Sunday night (a habit his wife, Linda, has yet to break him of). Being without money for lodging, George spent the nights in the Suburban with his dogs, no matter how much fresh cow dung they had rolled themselves in, no matter how many ticks and fleas they might have collected in the course of the day.

The next morning the men huddled around the well and listened as George called down the dark hole. Even in the light of day, the well was just as dark. The flashlight now proved useless. At once, a whimper drifted up from below. They all heard it. With a mirror he had brought from the ranch house, George reflected sunlight down the deep shaft, and he soon saw Rusty sitting at the bottom, looking up.

Now came the task of figuring a way to descend the well, the depth of which was still only a guess.

Using a ranch tractor, they tried lowering George with a length of cable, which made an awful screech against the concrete rim of the well. Because the tractor was geared so low, the descent was dangerously jerky, and about ten feet into the well George called it off. He worried the weight of the cable might topple the brick rim of the well and shower Rusty and himself with a cascade of bricks.

Back at the ranch house, they phoned the nearest town of Aspermont, but the only help they could find was a retired fellow who ran a wrecking service in his spare time. An hour later, the man showed up with a '56 Dodge one-ton wrecker that ran even worse than it looked. The sight alone left George feeling more than a little uncomfortable. His concern was soon justified when, on their way out to the well, the transmission on the wrecker went out in the deep sand.

It was almost noon, and George was growing doubtful that Rusty had much time left. But, since the old wrecker was now his only hope, George set quickly to fixing the rickety transmission. Two hours later, he got the wrecker running again, and they made their way slowly across the deep sand toward the well.

Once there, the old man let a measuring wire down into the well. The wire dropped down, down, down—seemingly forever. Watching it, George began to wonder if perhaps this was a bigger task than he could handle. Most of all, he marveled at the fact Rusty was still alive after such a great fall. Eventually, the wire stopped.

Fifty-six feet! Nearly six stories of descent into an unexplored hole little wider than the length of his arm.

"That truck of mine's only got some forty feet of cable on the spool," the old man told them.

They had to attach a twelve-foot length of chain, fastening an old tire at the end as a seat for George.

It was now close to 2 P.M., and Rusty had been in the well for nearly twenty hours without water, possibly bleeding (inside or out).

Luck turned against them again. As they started to wind the spool out, the release rod on the winch snapped in two. Cursing,

George now wondered if maybe someone higher up was sending him a message. Nevertheless, they returned to the ranch house to weld the release rod, then hurried back to the well and refastened it to the shaky old winch.

George went to the well and peered once more into the untold darkness. He whistled, and at once Rusty whimpered back.

"OK," he said, as he slipped the tire up to his back end. While George checked the knot in the chain with the eye of a hawk, his friends continued to counsel him against what he was about to do.

"Best let me finish him, George," one friend pleaded, gun in hand.

But George stubbornly shook his head, unable to cast that fate upon his dog. You see, George himself had been shot thirty years before. All of thirteen years old, he was out quail hunting with an inexperienced friend when it happened. His dog went on point, the covey burst, and his friend carelessly pulled on a close stray and shot off the elbow on George's right arm. Today, though he can manage little more than thirty degrees of movement in that arm, his friends readily boast they have yet to see the man who can outshoot George Alexander on quail.

"Better think it through again, George," Buck Foley cautioned.

But George was already swinging his legs over the side of the well. Buck probably knew George best, and he also knew it was a waste of breath.

With his right hand clutching the chain to his chest, the other firmly against the inside wall of the well, George began the painstaking descent into nothingness. The wall was brick for a few feet before it hit limestone. Then the wall turned to rock and sand, with strange, dank growths of vegetation poking out from between the layers. George thought of the tarantulas and scorpions and spiders that surely lived in the well as he felt his way down the wall with the fingers of his left hand. The air soon grew clammy and cool.

"You're about a third of the way," Buck called down to him.

It was dark inside the well, and the mouth above nothing more than a full moon overhead. After a minute or two, his eyes adjusted, and the dark turned to an encasing cylinder of dimness. In spots he saw where Rusty's toenails had scraped against the shaft wall in blind desperation.

Peering between his legs as he dropped lower and lower, he prayed that the winch would not lose its hold nor the chain slip its knot. Soon George glimpsed Rusty sitting at the bottom.

When he finally reached the bottom of chiseled rock, George had never had a dog so happy to see him. Rusty wagged and licked and panted in elation, despite the cramped quarters and a marked difficulty in his ability to stand on all fours. George, now straddling Rusty's hind end, ran his hands carefully over Rusty's trembling coat to check for obvious injuries or broken bones. Having noted none, George took off his belt, punched a new hole in it, and buckled it snugly around Rusty's flank. His friends sent down another belt at the end of a rope, and George secured it around Rusty's chest. Next, he secured the two belts with the length of rope, creating a makeshift harness. He double-checked the rope and harness, then called to his friends to take him up. They winched George out of the well first, for if Rusty should happen to slip from the harness, his fall could likely hurt or even kill George.

The cable now squeaked with strain as it started its ascent. "Hang on, Boy," George reassured his dog with a pat. "We'll have you out in a second."

The trip up didn't seem nearly as bad, perhaps because it was out of, instead of into, the unknown.

Once George was out of the well, he and his friends, in tug-of-war fashion, hoisted Rusty slowly up out of the well. They lifted him carefully over the rim, then set him gently on the ground and removed the belt harness. Later x-rays and surgery revealed that Rusty's pelvis was cracked in three places, his right hip joint broken in two, but at that moment Rusty was so glad to be out of the well that after lapping up a half gallon of water and relieving himself on a nearby bush, the indestructible dog set out on three legs trying to hunt up quail.

In fact, George had to chase him down and put him in the kennel to keep him still.

That was five years ago. You will be happy to know that Rusty is now ten and still hunting as hard as ever.

Part IV

Tales of Fiction

Ernest Hemingway believed that a piece of nonfiction could not compete with a work of fiction. I could not agree more. Fiction has always intrigued me. It is ironic that I would rather read about something that never happened than about something that did.

It is unfortunate that fiction seems to have disappeared entirely from the hunting genre. Where are the Ruarks and Hemingways and Fords to continue the craft of hunting literature? Sadly, the art seems to have died with these masters. Perhaps the demand for their work has ceased. Nowadays every hunting article is "how to" or "where to," and I feel that we in the hunting community are the worse for it. We have lost a great opportunity to spread our message to the nonhunting community through the lure of a good story. How many nonhunters would actually read an article about how to pack for a mule-deer hunt or where to find a trophy moose? Now, compare that to a short story like Hemingway's "The Short Happy Life of Francis Macomber," which can reach millions of people who do not hunt.

I hope that one day soon a new set of literary masters will arise to restore the craft of hunting fiction and, in so doing, carry our prohunting message beyond the choir. For now, however, I present you with four short stories of my own, in the hope that you will find them equally, if not more, entertaining and fulfilling than the nonfiction portion of this book.

A Mamba by Any Other Name*

Chapter 25

I t was toward the last of his safari that it happened.

One afternoon, having successfully collected nearly every big-game animal he had come for, Jackson Taylor set out on foot from camp with Shabani, the tracker, looking for guinea fowl. They had stumbled across one or two coveys of the crested variety, and Jackson was having a grand time shooting at them and missing as they dodged between the dry tufts of grass and scrub, while Shabani, trotting along behind, shouted in Swahili for him to shoot again and again.

But the flocks of hustling guineas wisely stayed ahead, just out of range. When he slowed, they slowed. When, upon recovering his strength, he pushed forth with a sudden burst of speed, so did they. Only when he happened upon an unsuspecting flock did he manage to get one before they took to the air. Thundering up from the ground with the commotion of a flock of wild turkeys, they would eventually return to the ground some hundred yards away. With their surprisingly capable and seemingly inexhaustible legs, they would continue to try to elude their hunter. The chasing was as much fun as the shooting, and so he had kept after them, even when he knew the effort was futile.

In-between flocks, he and Shabani would stop to catch their breath and wipe the beading sweat from their brows. Inevitably, Shabani would commence trying to get some point across, often resorting to hand signals, which were of little help.

The sun was still high above the tops of the trees, which were mostly acacia and *miombo*. Here the ground was black from the charred remains of a sizable burn. Only the parched, head-high grass, the runty bits of scrub, and the fallen trees and limbs littering the ground had been burned. The healthy trees were left untouched. New green shoots of grass poked up here and there like cat whiskers all across

*Published in *Sporting Classics* magazine, March 1990.

the burn. It was this new growth that had brought the game flooding into the area.

"*Kanga upesi!*" Shabani said in gasps, as they came to a stop after another unproductive but invigorating chase. Understanding only the first word, Jackson knew it had to do with the guinea fowl they were chasing.

"*Upesi?*" Jackson asked, huffing.

"*N'dio. Upesi mingi sana,*" Shabani told him, with a grin that showed his big yellow teeth.

Jackson shrugged. He had no idea what Shabani was saying.

"*Upesi. UPESI!*" Shabani insisted, as though repetition and volume would make the meaning clear.

Finally, Shabani gave up, resorting to the tried and true.

"*Jua kali,*" (sharp sun) he said.

Jackson had learned on his first day that meant it was very hot.

"*Jua kali!*" Jackson agreed, wiping his forehead once more.

His shirt was soaked through at the neck and under the arms, and he could feel the beads of sweat now running down his back. But it was a pleasant, exhilarating feeling. And his head was swimming with the slight euphoria that comes from pushing oneself to exhaustion. He could not have named a happier, more exciting time in his life than that moment.

After a minute's rest, they started on. Soon they came to the river—the same narrow, smooth-flowing river that ran beside camp. The murky water wound its way around large, flat-topped acacias and clumps of wait-a-bit brush that eventually grew quite thick as the river approached the rocky hills beyond. It was at the base of these hills that they had collected a large male leopard—he and professional hunter Robin Smith. . . .

******

The cat had come at dusk to feed on the impala bait hung from the high, well-silhouetted branch of an acacia, the two hunters concealed inside a grass-thatched blind. Jackson's heart had charged into his throat when he heard the leopard's claws bite into the bark of the tree. At a nudge from his professional hunter, Jackson eased the barrel of his rifle through the tiny peephole in the thatch and put his eye to the scope. Any distance between him and his quarry shrank abruptly to nothing when the spotted cat, crouched bigger than life on the limb above the bait, turned its head in his direction and cast its cold green eyes on the blind.

It was like coming face to face with a killer in a dark alley. It didn't matter that the killer did not have a gun. The killer had claws that could disembowel you as handily as a surgeon's scalpel and jaws that could crush the vertebrae at the back of your neck with one powerful *snap!*

Jackson had been quite ecstatic about killing it with one shot, for he had read numerous accounts of how easy it is to wound the spotted cats and what a menace they are to follow up once they've been injured. That was three days ago. . . .

******

He and Shabani were now working their way quietly along the riverbank. The brown, muddy water of the river was slipping silently past, opaque and with the consistency of molten milk chocolate. A loud splash came from somewhere downriver as an unseen hippo went crashing into the water. The uproar sent a family of baboons on the opposite bank scampering for the trees, hooting and hollering as they went. The male of the tribe, sauntering slowly after them, glanced over its shoulder now and then and flashed its teeth. Just then, a grassy patch burst to life with the rusty-red forms of a leaping herd of impalas. The agile antelopes sprang into the air one after another, while the males, in a separate herd, stuck their necks out long and low so that the tips of their lyrelike horns scratched at their bucking backs.

The river was slipping quietly along on their left. To their right, a lofty, flat-topped acacia towered up from the sandy soil, casting its shade in patches about them. They were searching the banks of both shores for sign of the fleet-footed guineas when Jackson suddenly became aware of a thin, fast-wriggling movement on the shady ground beside him. It happened so fast that before he could think to run or to jump, the snake had raised its ugly head and bitten him on the calf through his pants.

Shabani jumped aside, exclaiming, as the blackish snake whipped past him and slithered over the riverbank and into the muddy water.

"Christ!" Jackson blurted out, as the realization hit. And it hit him as solidly as a bat hits a home-run ball.

Dropping hastily to one knee, he jerked his pants leg up over the calf. And he at once saw two puncture marks each oozing a droplet of fresh blood—terrifying proof that the snake had indeed bitten him.

He looked hopefully to Shabani, who had squatted beside him and was now probing the wound with his black fingers.

"What kind of snake?" Jackson demanded.

After a blank stare, Shabani began rattling away in Swahili, not one word of which did Jackson understand.

"What kind of snake? Snake. SNAKE . . . what kind?" Jackson cried.

Shabani presently rattled on again, and he said something about camp and something about Robin and something about the river, but nothing Jackson could understand about a snake.

Jackson searched his memory for any knowledge that would help him. He knew there were probably five hundred species of snake, 80 percent of them deadly. He also knew that poisonous snakes typically come with one of two types of venom: that which poisons the blood and tissues, and that which attacks the nerves, causing paralysis and finally death from either suffocation or heart failure. The former category is comprised of the puff adder and the boomslang; the latter is comprised of the cobra and the mamba, both the green and black varieties.

Jackson felt certain it wasn't a puff adder. His tent boy had killed one in camp on the third day of safari, and he had studied it quite closely. It is a fat, sluggish snake, with a spade-shaped head and reticulated markings. Nor, fortunately, was it a gaboon viper, another extremely deadly snake. He had seen one inside a glass cage in the museum in Nairobi, so he knew "his snake" wasn't a gaboon viper. He had read on the small plaque beneath the glass that a gaboon viper is maliciously gifted with both types of venom and the ability to inject one or the other, or both. The snake that had bitten him had had no fan to its head, so that ruled out a cobra. And it was too big for a boomslang. Which left only one other snake that he could think of—that he did not want to think of because it was possibly the most deadly of all. He pushed the thought quickly aside.

Shabani was still rattling away, though Jackson could understand nothing.

Well aware that to slow the venom's spread he should move as little as possible, Jackson now pointed back toward camp and issued the following instructions: "Camp! Robin! Get Robin!" and as the thought struck him, he stripped off his belt and tied it snugly about his lower thigh. Then he limped to the acacia and slumped down against its base.

"Camp! Robin!" he cried again, realizing Shabani had made no move to go.

Shabani began waving a hand at him and shaking his head, his face showing true concern.

"Happana, Bwana," he said. *"Mamba mto. Mamba hapa!"*

The tracker's words could not have hit Jackson more forcefully. Instantly, he felt chilled all over, as if the temperature had fallen fifty degrees. The feeling intensified until it felt as if there were a thousand bugs beneath his skin, all crawling and scratching and trying to get out at once.

"*Mamba,*" Shabani insisted, pointing to the river where the snake had disappeared.

And then it hit him why Shabani would not leave. He recalled Robin's account of the fatalist mind-set of Africans. Shabani realized there was nothing he could do, and was telling him so. Jackson should simply sit back and accept his fate.

"No!" Jackson roared. "Get Robin! Robin! Now!"

Shabani hesitated, a rather puzzled look on his face. He then motioned with his hand for Jackson to follow.

"No! Camp now!" Jackson pleaded, angrily.

By now, he was about ready to point his gun at the stubborn tracker to get him going. But, after another minute's stare, Shabani reluctantly whirled and started at a fast trot in the direction of camp.

Now alone, Jackson laid his head back against the tree, briefly wincing. So that was it. His worst fear realized. A mamba. It was over. With a terrifying shudder, he registered that he had somewhere between two and twenty-four hours left to live.

This overwhelming thought numbed him from head to toe. Soon he felt a great, suffocating pressure bearing down on his chest, as though he were pinned beneath the crashing spill of a giant waterfall. Seconds later, a wave of nausea wracked his entire body. What surprised him, when the nausea finally ceased, was what popped into his mind first. He suddenly realized he would never again see certain things. These thoughts came piling painfully into the station of his mind like the cars of a runaway train.

His first thought wasn't of his wife or his kids or his mother or work. Strangely, it was the family golden retriever, Max. Then came his wife and his kids and his mother and work, and the desperate, compelling notion that somehow he must speak to his wife before he went. He must. But, God, what would he say? What could he say? Perhaps the safari company could place a call to his home in Houston from Arusha and broadcast it over the radio back to camp. If he made it back to camp.

He knew he was going to die.

The startling thought numbed him again. Then a ripple of tingles shot through his entire body. These odd sensations left him feeling as if he had just woken from a dream. Suddenly, it seemed that his entire life—everything he had ever said or done or experienced up to this point—had been merely a hazy dream, and that he was just now waking, these last few hours before he died. It was as though he had been snapped strangely awake by a sense of total, horrifying awareness.

Everything appeared altogether different as he glanced around—everything in this new world seemed to be so startlingly in focus and in color. He felt as if he had been suddenly, but ironically, blessed with a badly needed pair of eyeglasses, now, in his last hours. The leaves of the acacias were green as he had never seen that color, their branches surprisingly intricate structures, their bark a complex fascination. The blue sky budding above the tree's canopy and the few puffy whites pushing slowly overhead appeared alarmingly and strikingly real, as if all the thousands of skies and sunsets and panoramas he had witnessed in his lifetime, as he now recalled them, were nothing more than a collection of lackluster imitations painted by second-rate artists.

All around him the trees and the bushes and the tufts of grass seemed curiously alive; they fairly swelled with life and previously unnoticed movements. He guessed he had been too closely and intimately involved with them before to notice. Or, perhaps, it took his looking at them from a standpoint of near death to see this. The occasional bits of breeze made sounds in his ears the likes of which he had never heard. When he glanced down, his hands—how many times in his life had he seen his hands?—were a wonder to him. He discovered freckles he hadn't known were there, and creases in the palms, and the exact shape and color and texture of his fingernails, as though they had all along belonged to someone else and were just now his. At the base of his thumb he noticed a faint scar he'd picked up in the third grade while play-wrestling one of his classmates—and had all but forgotten. A callus on his right middle finger from pushing a pencil at work. And the small veins and capillaries that wormed their way beneath his skin like—like miniature snakes.

Jesus!

Just then, he felt a distinct shortness of breath. Was the poison taking effect already? It seemed so quick. He attempted a deep breath, briefly shutting his eyes. It definitely was becoming much harder to breathe than normal. He could feel the beads of sweat breaking out on his face and neck, his heart knocking to get out of his chest, and he glanced down at the shotgun across his lap, which brought a haunting thought to mind.

Now we'll see if you put your money where your mouth is, he said to himself.

Five years ago, Jackson had watched his father wither and die from cancer. Toward the end, when the medications failed to dent the pain, Jackson had promised himself that should he fall prey to some similarly debilitating disease, he would, without question, opt for some quicker way out.

With this in mind, Jackson pulled the shotgun around and laid it lengthwise between his legs so that the end of the barrel was now pointed at his chest. He would wait, he told himself, until the pain became unbearable. Then he would do it. He found himself pondering, with a startling rush of fear, whether between the eyes or in the roof of the mouth would be better. If he were lucky, maybe he would simply slip unconscious—before the pain got bad.

A second later, however, he was struck by an encouraging thought. The idea came into his head that he might beat it, that somehow he just might live. But this wishful fancy was quickly struck down by the recollection of something he had once read in a book. It was the story of a mamba angered by villagers hoeing in a field. Running amok, the mamba had savagely struck a total of thirteen. Before the sun had set the following day, all thirteen had died.

A few had made it into town for antivenin. But antivenin, administered in even the slightest amount too little or too much, can be equally deadly.

There was also the amazing story, which might have brought a glimmer of hope if he had only recalled it a little sooner, about a mamba victim who had actually survived a bite, the only person known to have done so. A game biologist, bitten on the thumb while milking a mamba for its venom, saved his own life by sawing off the digit with the blade of a pocketknife, a feat he claimed took less than fifteen seconds.

Christ, Jackson thought angrily, *you just slit your own throat. If you'd been thinking clearly instead of chasing him back to camp, Shabani could have cut your leg off at the knee.*

He cursed himself, recalling how quickly and skillfully the tracker had dropped the hindquarters off the buffalo. A human leg would have been a piece of cake.

If he'd had a knife, he might have tried it himself. But, as he thought it through, he doubted he could finish the job without passing out first. And, besides, it was probably too late.

Jackson drew another deep breath. It felt extremely shallow, with even a touch of pain as he breathed in deeply. He glanced at the shotgun in his lap. It looked as new to him as the hands that now held it. *God, let them hurry!*

It was perhaps half an hour, though to Jackson it seemed a good bit longer than eternity, before he heard the Land Rover approaching from upriver. Finally, he caught glimpses of it as Robin came driving at top speed, weaving around the brush and trees and raising a large cloud of dust in his wake. He could see Shabani hanging on in the back.

As the vehicle skidded to a stop in front of him, Robin displayed a rather nonchalant expression and a jubilant indifference that took Jackson by surprise.

After a sigh and a grin, Robin said, "Why, my good friend, you look as if you've just done battle with a buffalo—and lost."

Which stunned Jackson for a moment. But then he blurted out in a rush: "Have I a chance with the antivenin?"

"Antivenin?"

"Yes—for God's sake, let's try it."

But Robin just sat there. He wasn't looking at him with the expression of someone facing a man who was about to die. In fact, Robin was looking at him with the interest of someone about to step down from the cab and join him for a cup of tea.

"You shan't be needing any of that, I'm afraid."

"Jesus! It won't work on mambas?"

The rather queer expression returned to his face.

"That wasn't a mamba," he said.

"It wasn't?"

"Good heavens, no. If it had been, I'd be out a bloody bundle in trophy fees. Although I dare say I wouldn't mind keeping that handsome kudu of yours for myself. It would hang quite nicely on my porch at home."

"It wasn't a mamba?" Jackson repeated in disbelief.

"Not at all."

Still perplexed, Jackson glanced questioningly at Shabani and said, "Well, then, why the hell was he crying, 'Mamba! Mamba!'"

Turning his head to make a quick exchange in Swahili, Robin grinned widely from behind the wheel, then fell at once to laughing. He carried on again in Swahili, and now Shabani too was laughing.

"What? What's so funny?" Jackson demanded. "What is it?"

"I—I'm sorry, Jackson," Robin said, trying to compose himself. "You poor, poor bugger—"at which point he broke into another laugh. "You misunderstood him completely. Shabani wasn't telling you that you were bitten by a mamba. Christ, he was trying to tell you not to sit so close to the river because of the crocs. You poor chap, *mamba* in Swahili means 'crocodile.' You aren't going to die! That was just some rubbish water snake that got you. Shabani had quite a good look at it. They're completely harmless, I assure you."

It took a second for what Robin had said to sink in. But when it did, it settled over Jackson like a freshly heated blanket on a blustery cold day.

"Jesus!" Jackson exclaimed with a loud sigh. "Jesus f-ing Christ!" he said, snapping onto his feet, a new man.

As he stripped the belt from his throbbing thigh, he could feel the life flooding back into him. He hobbled over to the car and rested against the side and pounded the sun-heated hood with his fist. Then he sucked in a deep, painless breath of air and sighed again.

And all the short drive back to camp, and throughout most of the rest of his trip, Jackson Taylor found himself studying his hands.

World-Record Ram

Chapter 26

Corey Apperson could hardly contain his excitement as he swung into the saddle on his first morning in fly camp. He gazed above the dark green of the pines and wondered which of the surrounding slate-gray peaks held the new world-record Stone sheep. He knew it was there. It was simply a matter of finding it.

"Which bowl you reckon?" he asked, impatiently, anxious to be on the trail before the day dawned any brighter. Harry, his guide, seemed to be moving at a snail's pace, fussing over his saddlebags like an old lady fussing over the contents of her purse. This bothered Corey considerably. He was paying top dollar, and he expected top service.

"So what's the plan?" he repeated, irritably.

Harry didn't respond at once. For one, his client's demanding tone of voice didn't sit well with him.

"Like I told you, we're gonna ride out across this creek bottom flat, then up the ridge to see what we see," Harry mumbled over a shoulder as he secured the saddlebags to his horse's rump. The big bay stamped a front hoof and blew a cloud of steam from its muzzle into the frigid air.

Harry was used to being boss on the hunt, and he didn't give a flip how much money this "dude" had, or how many companies he was president of, or what the outfitter might have promised him—while they were in Harry's camp, they would do things his way. Period.

Like a couple of old rams, the two strangers had butted heads the day before within minutes of meeting in camp.

"I know, but . . ."

Harry didn't answer. Perhaps he was dragging his feet a little, knowing how much it irked the city slicker. Regardless, he didn't like to blab it up, not right before a hunt, anyway. Afterward, if a ram was taken, you couldn't shut him up. But before a hunt, Harry felt it was bad luck to say too much. The bottom line was this: He had a job to do and he would do it, and he didn't need some spoiled city yahoo trying to second-guess his every move. His job, quite simply—in exchange for a large sum of money—was to put this fellow on the stupendous ram Harry had spotted last season with a client who had already filled his tag.

The same ram he had photographed with the wildlife biologist hired by Corey to verify Harry's claim, the ram he had spotted a third time while scouting solo last week for this very hunt. *But sheep don't stay put like a mountaintop, buddy. They move. So the big ram could be anywhere in these mountains. But that ain't a problem because I can find it. Don't you worry about that. I can find it!*

So far he had kept these thoughts to himself. And if he hadn't, it wouldn't be the first time he'd had to tell a client to cool his jets. Too many hunters arrived in Harry's camp with unrealistic expectations or, worse, a sense of business urgency. *This isn't a fast-food shop where you place your order, then drive around to the second window to pick it up. This is sheep hunting.* And Harry knew sheep hunting. If he hadn't learned a thing or two about trophy sheep hunting in twelve seasons, with thirty-two rams to his clients' credit, then who the hell had? If Mr. Texas would just chill and let him do his thing, Harry would put his ass on the blankety-blank ram. That much he knew.

Harry settled a gray felt cowboy hat on his head, the grease-stained brim crimped and bent into that one-of-a-kind look that makes a favorite hunting hat, and checked his gear once more. Up on top of the mountain was no time to remember whatever it was you forgot.

Once mounted, they marched in single file along a worn game trail that wound through damp forest, the horses dropping their heads now and then to nibble dew-soaked grasses growing in the openings. It wasn't long before they left the trees altogether. The trail continued beside the slick, mossy banks of a chuckling creek, across an open muskeg bottom that sucked at the horses' sinking hoofs, then climbed the rolling foothills of the Muskwa Mountains beyond. These hills were covered in a quilted patchwork of color, displaying swaths of green and gold, rust and gray, yellow and red, and the dark green teepee of an occasional spruce. Topping one foothill, they paused to take in a magnificent sight below: a beaver dam shaped like an igloo and the small lake it had made beside it. The tranquil mirrored surface reflected back a nearby stand of rich blue-green firs and the pale blue sky and the one or two cotton-ball clouds that hung above it.

An hour later, the spectacular Muskwa Mountains, which had disappeared from view as they negotiated the lower foothills, now reappeared ahead of them, even more resplendent than before. The slate-gray bowls and sheer rugged peaks soon towered into view on three sides as they left the creek momentarily and crested a bald knob in the enormous basin. It was tremendous country. Big. Daunting. Humbling country. It produced the effect of looking at a million stars on a dark night: The rugged terrain shrank a man's ego and put him in his place. That's what Harry liked most about it.

Corey, however, was too full of excitement over the potential accomplishment ahead of him to register such feelings. It would take tackling the steep slopes on foot, traversing sheer cliffs, and hanging on by all fours to generate those feelings in him—all of which were in his future. Right now he was fantasizing about the world-record ram within his grasp. Though such ambitious thoughts might be typical—what hunter steps into the woods without visions of tagging a world-record trophy?—in truth, your average hunter has better odds of being struck by lightning than he does of taking a world-record head! But Corey Apperson wasn't your average hunter, and this wasn't your average big-game hunt. The ram in question had been spotted, pictures taken, biologists consulted, the horns "measured" to within an inch of actual size, and plans to collect it laid months in advance. Furthermore, not only was he far from average when it came to hunting, he was exceptional when it came to tackling any quest.

By the age of three, Corey Apperson had memorized every U.S. president. At five he could tell you the batting average of each major league baseball player of the past decade. At nine he was selling some of the products he had invented door to door. To state that Corey was a goal-oriented fellow would be a vast understatement, for he was a man entirely dedicated to his quests and passionate in his goals—obsessed would be a better word. The man lived for achievement. Once he got hold of an idea, got that target in his cross hairs, he was absolutely unwavering in his persistence to have it. It was no surprise, then, that upon graduation from Princeton, Corey had marched through the business world with the same zeal, making business deals and targeting acquisitions like so many properties in a monopoly game. The business world facilitated his passion to collect, to acquire, to trade. He had made his fortune early.

But there was a price to be paid for driving himself so hard: Corey's health had suffered. Had his doctor not informed him, at age forty, that he was in good shape for a man aged sixty, hunting might never have entered the picture for Corey Apperson. The doctor had warned his wife that her husband had better find a hobby if he wanted to see his fiftieth birthday. The stress of work was killing him. So she bought him an African safari and sent him on the first real vacation he had had in twenty years. He returned with a smile, a boatload of trophies, and a new mission in life.

Over the next two years, he returned to Africa five times, adding various trophies to his collection. He applied his passion for the business world to his newly acquired hobby, quickly turning hunting into an all-absorbing activity. He mapped out all the great big-game collections of the hunting world and set dates by which to match those achievements. The cats of the world by next year; the buffalo of the world by Year Two; the spiral-horned antelope of Africa by Year Three.

His trips were planned with these goals in mind so that he could collect the animals in the most efficient manner possible, for time—not money—was Corey's most precious commodity. If a flight to Africa connected through Europe, for instance, he would take advantage of that to book a three-day wisent (European bison) hunt in Austria on the layover, thereby adding a buffalo to his collection on his way to hunt Lord Derby eland in the C.A.R. There, he had made prior arrangements with the outfitter to travel to a remote section of country to harvest the rare Harris bushbuck, a subspecies of this spiral-horned antelope.

In this manner Corey had secured every major (and minor) collection in the big-game community by the age of forty-eight. He was a member of every hunting club of any size in the country and was well known in the big-game hunting community. A call to an outfitter from Corey Apperson was returned immediately because, first, Corey was no tire kicker—he had made up his mind to hunt a certain animal with a certain outfitter long before he ever dialed the phone—and, second, a call from Corey most likely meant he would book dates and send not a deposit but payment in full in order to guarantee his slot.

Now fifty-two, with all the great collections behind him, Corey's goal had shifted to taking world-record trophies of whatever species he could find. To succeed, he relied upon outfitters, other hunters, wildlife departments, and contacts from around the world who knew of his interest and the generosity bestowed on those helping to locate such an animal. Regrettably, the size of his pocketbook often proved a detriment, bringing out droves of charlatans and con men promising all kinds of world-record sightings. Sometimes the hardest part of the hunt for a world record was the hunt for an honest lead. To his credit, Corey was now the number-one world-record holder for common reedbuck, red forest duiker, woodlands caribou, and saiga antelope. But what he wanted—what he needed—was a world-record animal that inspired awe in the hunting world. And that animal, if there ever was one, was one of the four recognized bighorn sheep of North America. The Chadwick ram, the current world-record Stone sheep, had been taken by L. S. Chadwick in 1936 in this same area of the Muskwa Mountain Range of British Columbia.

Corey had studied the famous ram on display at one of the national hunting conventions. It was like coming face to face with something out of a Greek myth. The horns were that unreal. All you could do was stand there and shake your head at the horns that came up and out and back and down, then curled in to the cheeks and forward and up and out and back down at the tips, so symmetrical and so long that they didn't seem real. He simply had to reach out and touch them with his fingers, even with the security guard looking at him. They were perfect: the pecan-colored sweep of bony sheath gnarled at the bases and the darker age rings showing each year of age with the gaps between them shrinking as they neared the skull, and the absolute perfect tips—unheard of in wild sheep, which regularly broom one or the other or both.

Yes, the Chadwick ram was quite a sight. It dwarfed the Stone sheep Corey had taken years ago—a barely legal ram found on the first day of hunting in the bottom of a ravine and taken without the normal taxing efforts required of a bighorn sheep hunt. The fact that he was now hunting a ram larger than the Chadwick—larger if the measurements from the photographs were correct, and he had every reason to believe they were—filled him with intense satisfaction as he mimicked his guide and secured his horse to a runty spruce on the alder-choked banks of the creek. Soon came an adrenaline rush to match the grade at the foot of the mountain they now began to climb. Somewhere around here were the famous Muskwa and Prophet Rivers, though he had yet to see them.

Looking up, all Harry could see was the convex curve of the slope shielding the higher peaks and bowls from view. His feet were making the motions, but, in all honesty, his heart just wasn't in it. Personally, he would rather have seen the ram go to another client. One who could appreciate the ram beyond just wanting another notch on his belt. But he wasn't the outfitter, and he didn't own the hunting company; he was merely the guide. He didn't have a say past whether he would or wouldn't guide the fellow, which was to say whether he wanted to keep his job or not. And keeping his guiding job was now a priority, what with the logging accident he had suffered last year.

Sheep hunting had never paid the bills, but trying to overlap it with vacation from lumberjack work made it easier to justify—at least financially—to his wife, Sarah. Privately, she hated to see him gone for ten weeks straight, but she knew how much Harry loved sheep hunting. He was a different man when he returned from the sheep mountains. He came home daily from the logging mountains fatigued and edgy, but he returned from the sheep mountains full of himself, with a hundred stories about the clients he'd had and their adventures together.

But the logging accident had changed everything. It was one of those careless accidents that should never have happened, but when it did, it happened in the blink of an eye. He had said, "No!" and the operator at the switch thought he said, "Go!" and turned the big log loose too soon. The giant timber bounced off the trailer of orderly stacked trunks, hitting Harry across the back and shoulders as he tried to dodge the plunging threat. In truth, he was lucky to be alive. The doctors had told him so. A little one way or the other and the falling log would have crushed him dead. Or left him paralyzed. What he got was a broken shoulder and a pinched nerve in his back, and the doctors wouldn't clear him to return to work—at least not logging work.

But what other work was there in Fort St. John that didn't involve taxing your back? Certainly not any work he knew. There was cattle wrangling and logging and construction—if and when the local economy was on the go—and there was a mason's job always open from his high school Indian buddy Dan Proudfoot. But every one of those jobs threatened his back and disqualified him for worker's comp, which disqualified him for the job. So he was on disability, making sixty percent of his regular salary. Guiding sheep hunters didn't come with any disability insurance to hamper the process. As always, you worked at your own peril. If you fell off the mountain and broke your back, you were simply let go, and another able body was hired to take your place. It was purely a labor of love.

That labor was about to start. As the terrain steepened and the soil thinned to reveal the gray rock underneath, they began making switchbacks up the slope with Harry pausing now and then to let the huffing hunter catch his breath. They were in Harry's country now. Pinched nerve or not, he could out-hike, out-climb any city boy alive. But the pace they were now making was not encouraging. Corey had to keep stopping, and he was already sweating—not a good sign because the terrain only increased in difficulty and altitude from here. But Harry had guided worse, and he knew he would make do.

Just then, Harry himself stopped and pointed.

"Ewes," he said.

Bathed in sweat, Corey fished out his binocular to view the curious, staring animals. Though the miniature, upright horns differed considerably from their male counterparts, the females shared the same white head and neck and the salt-and-pepper gray torso of the breed, a cross in color between the snow-white Dall and the dun-colored bighorn.

"Beautiful," Corey huffed. "Now, where's their big boyfriend?"

After a moment, the ewes trotted out of sight. Harry just turned and started up the slope.

Soon they mounted a ridge that allowed a limited view of the land ahead. A great, bald, slick dome of rock towered up on their left, surrounded by taller bowls and peaks in the distance, and Harry gestured toward the odd structure.

"Folks say that's where the Chadwick ram was taken. Chadwick wounded it and his guide carried on to finish it."

Corey handed over his camera, saying, "Here, take my picture with it."

The top of the ridge offered relatively flat terrain, but the relief was short-lived. The slope increased in grade as they continued, and the soil gave way to rocks and boulders that matched the dark gray of the bodies of the sheep, making their quarry that much harder to detect. The late morning sun, having crested the peaks, warmed them considerably. August weather was unpredictable in the northern clime: It could be sunny and eighty degrees, or snowing and twenty, and you had better be prepared for either extreme. All the same, Corey was soon streaming in sweat. As they rounded a shoulder in the mountain, a barreling wind set his teeth to chattering while they stopped to glass ahead.

By the time they topped the next rise, Corey was already sweating again from exertion. Following Harry's lead, he dropped on all fours and crawled over the crown to prevent "skylining" themselves. They crawled until the next valley came into view. A breathtaking panorama was split horizontally by sharp contrasts in color. A verdant green saturated the lower valley, while a prison gray painted the rocky bowls and summits, which pierced a sky of the most intense and infinite blue. Harry dug a spotting scope from his pack. After peering squint-eyed through the smaller end for some time, he simply said, "Yep. That's him."

"Where?"

"Tucked in the shade of that far bowl. The youngsters are the ones out in the sun. That's how I saw 'em."

It took some glassing before Corey locked on the white specks of heads a mile or more away. Then he stared through his own spotting scope, fiddling with the zoom and focus until a shaded white head came into view. It took his breath away. This was his ram! The ram he had dreamed about for six months. It was a living clone of the Chadwick ram—only bigger! The horns were unspeakable. Beyond belief! Corey had to chuckle to himself. He was looking at what would become known around the world as the Apperson ram. His name would be immortalized in the hunting community. He was experiencing history in the making. There was no question this was the most incredible accomplishment of his life, worth every penny he had promised the outfitter if a world-record head was taken.

But Harry brought Corey quickly back to earth. Seeing the ram and reaching the ram were two different things, he explained, his head ticking to one side, a consequence of the pinched nerve. Harry then led a quick retreat, circling to lower country and out of sight of the rams. Corey hated to give up altitude, for every step given up was one that had to be re-fought later. But that was sheep hunting.

Soon they began the backside ascent of the neighboring mountains. Here they were faced with a rocky gorge that flowed with a jumble of toaster-sized rocks and water running beneath them. They began the taxing climb, working their way from one wobbly rock to the next as if on randomly built steps, except, if you weren't careful, this staircase could shift and pitch you off. They had to pause now and then for Corey to catch his breath in the increasing altitude. The temperature felt a good thirty degrees warmer in the relatively still air of the gorge, and now he carried a bandanna in one hand to mop the flowing sweat.

Though reaching the top of the gorge was an accomplishment to Corey, it was only the first of several escalating challenges ahead. Keeping out of sight of the sheep required a trek across some dangerously steep terrain. Corey slipped twice while traversing a shale slide, painfully banging an elbow on his second fall. Then came a stretch of sheer rock cliff that meant hugging the mountain with all fours. You had to grope your way from handhold to handhold, while searching for equally firm toeholds in the crumbly outcrops of stone. In places, a fall would be fatal. It was a slow, tedious business, and a couple of times Corey called ahead to Harry to call it off—he couldn't do it. But each time Harry talked him through it, and as they conquered the last stretch, Corey breathed a sigh. Continuing up the backside of the mountain, they reached a sheep trail, which made for easy going. But then the jumbled shale slides and rocky cliffs began anew.

Four hours had never passed so slowly—the time it took for Corey and his guide to reach the summit to peek below on their quarry.

"Damn!" Harry said. "They're gone, eh! Moved off."

Hearing those words was beyond a letdown to Corey. He felt utterly crushed. It was like having a business deal fall apart in the eleventh hour after months spent putting it together. There were no words to express his dismay. He just shook his head. He had felt so close to success he could taste it. He had shot the ram several times in his mind. This wasn't the ending he had expected, wasn't the deal he had signed up for. Having witnessed the ram with his own eyes only made the disappointment that much greater.

"We took too long getting up the backside of the mountain," Corey finally stated.

You took too long, Harry thought. *I could'a been up here in half the time.*

They spent the rest of that afternoon above timberline, traversing bowls and glassing from mountain peaks, but they never saw a sign of the record ram. On the return to camp, Corey's horse spooked when its hoofs got stuck in a muskeg bog, and it began to buck, throwing Corey off in the process. The spongy muskeg made for a soft, albeit rather wet, landing. Corey was tired, wet, and sore by the time they reached camp at dark.

The hunt continued in this manner for the next four days, with Corey only getting more tired, wet, and sore at the end of each day. His feet had blistered badly, and both big toenails were purple from pummeling the ends of his boots on the downhill slopes. During those four days, they sighted numerous rams, but none was the monster he had glimpsed the morning of his first day. It had either moved off or found a hiding spot. Anyhow, they had searched the surrounding bowls and peaks until much of the terrain was recognizable even to Corey.

On the sixth day, the climbing was worse. Not because the terrain was any more difficult, but because Corey was wearing out, and his feet were causing him endless grief. The men had reached the point of covering so little ground that Harry wondered whether taking the big ram was even a possibility. Opting for a change in strategy, Harry had taken to leaving Corey on the lower saddles, then scampering up the slopes on either side to glass for the big ram. What they needed right now was a big dose of luck—to be in the right place at the right time.

Except for a few passing showers, the sunny weather had mostly held. Today's blue skies were marked by striations of high, faint, frosty clouds, and the wind had grown fierce in the last hour, whipping at their flesh every chance it got and promising changes to come.

Mounting yet another saddle, Corey collapsed on his rear and removed his left boot. Blood had soaked the sock around his big toe and he worked to replace the bandages.

"Wait here," Harry said, "while I climb this peak to the right and have a look."

Then he pointed to the dark clouds swelling over the horizon like a battleship. Corey had been too busy with his feet to notice them.

"I don't like the looks of those clouds. Snow, most likely. If they continue our way, we'll head for camp, eh? But don't move from here until I get back. Got it?"

Corey nodded, pulling on the sock and boot gingerly. He flopped back against the tundralike turf, resting his head and catching his breath. This hunt was much, much harder than he had anticipated—harder than prior sheep hunts on which he had merely collected a representative head. But luck had been with him before on other hunts, and luck would be with him again. As he lay there, the relentless wind began to seep into his clothing and chill the sweat that had accumulated on the climb. Soon he had the shivers. He got up and moved to the lee side of the saddle, not entirely out of the wind but not directly in it as before. There he had a better view of the lower slopes of the mountain that rose to the left, and he settled into the spongy turf to watch below while he awaited Harry's return from its twin to the right.

An eagle of some sort sailed out over the valley. Propelled by rising thermals, it required no more than an occasional flap of its wings to remain aloft. Corey watched it cut back and forth until it floated out of view. Then he pulled out the peanut butter sandwich that he had been too fatigued at lunch to eat. He took a bite and looked up, and there in front of him, not a hundred yards down the slope, was the sheep of his dreams! The dream ram was trotting from left to right across the incline beneath him, toward the backside of the mountain he was watching, now directly away from him, the tips of its great horns flaring out to the sides. It had happened so fast, Corey didn't think to grab his rifle until the ram was at a bad angle for a shot. Moving quickly out of range, the ram soon disappeared around the shoulder of the mountain.

The good news was that the ram did not appear to be spooked. In fact, Corey was certain the ram had not seen him. Corey jumped up and spun around to glance up the mountain, but there was no sign of Harry. He couldn't yell for him—that would alarm the ram. He couldn't wait for his guide to return, either; the ram could be miles away by then. There was only one thing left to do. He had to go after it himself.

Feeling flush with the sight of the big ram and forgetting for a moment the pitiful state of his feet, Corey started at a brisk walk toward the spot where he had last seen the ram. As he neared, he slowed, his gun at the ready, and he crept cautiously forward, looking both up and down in case the ram had changed direction while out of sight. Here several ravines rumpled the shoulder of the mountain like oversized corrugated tin, but, thankfully, they were shallow and not too difficult to negotiate. On his third ascent, Corey caught sight of the bright white of the ram's head rising out of a ravine ahead. The big ram suddenly came to a stop, facing up the mountain, and turned its enormous head his way, the two curling horns the color of petrified wood sweeping out unendingly.

Their eyes locked.

At that point, instinct took over, and the .300 Winchester exploded in Corey's hands before he even realized he had the cross hairs on the dark shoulder. But he knew the shot was good. There was no doubting that. The big ram bucked, lunged over a hump in the ground, and then disappeared around the mountain. Then all was silent except the ringing in Corey's ears as he shook his head in disbelief. He smiled to himself and laughed the laugh of triumph that one makes even in solitude at a sensational accomplishment.

Now his battered feet, momentarily quieted by adrenaline, cried out in pain as he hobbled to where the ram had been. There in the sparse grass he found the encouraging sign of frothy lung blood, which brought another smile. He studied the terrain ahead, but a sharp bend in the mountain offered no sign of the ram. Its trail, however, was easy to follow. The steady blood spoor contrasted highly against the dull tans and pale blonds of the short-cropped turf. He knew he would find the ram. At one point, Corey considered returning for Harry—which would also allow the ram time to stiffen and die. But Corey was too anxious to touch the ram he had fantasized about for months. So he pressed on.

As he rounded the shoulder, the slope to his right rose impossibly steep. He figured the ram had either continued around the curve or dropped down to the left, and he now looked there. Just then, the giant horns appeared at an angle below him, and then the whole ram staggered into view. Corey placed another bullet in the shoulder, and the ram collapsed and rolled down the incline, knocking loose clods of turf and snapping a couple of dwarf spruces on the fall, rolling ever faster, next cascading down a shale slide and finally hanging up on a boulder wedged in a narrow chute below. A cloud of dust hung in the air around the still body.

Descending was not particularly quick or easy, but with his gun slung across his back and adrenaline fueling his progress, Corey used all fours to lower himself within fifty yards of the precious treasure. Then he basically slid on his butt down the crumbled shale, never pausing to think how he would return up the slick slide or noticing the sheer cliffs on either side of the chute, effectively cutting off the top of the mountain from the bottom.

He had more immediate concerns. The first thing he did upon reaching his trophy was to finger the incredible, one-of-a-kind horns. Fortunately, they had not been damaged in the tumble. Scrunched there on the boulder with the ram, he hastily pulled a tape from a pocket and began measuring the curl of each side. The right horn went over 54¼ inches, so, even after the expected shrinkage of the "drying period," it was far longer than the Chadwick's 51⅝ inches. The left went 54 inches. There was no doubt this ram was the new world-record Stone sheep! He was looking at the Apperson ram. It was a tremendous, magnificent feeling.

But now he had to find his guide. Balancing on the cramped quarters of the boulder with the sheep, he stood stiffly and looked for a route back. As he did, he noticed the threatening clouds rolling overhead. He would have to hurry.

Corey took a step in the loose shale and slipped. His legs shot out from under him, and he landed with a thud on the boulder plugging the chute. The boulder stopped his fall, but his weight was enough to knock the boulder loose—and instantly both he and the ram went tumbling down the chute. As he fell, Corey grabbed the only thing available to grab, which was the protruding end of one horn. He clung to the horn with his right hand, trying to keep the heavy animal from plowing into him, but then he turned loose to face the bigger problem of how to stop his fall. He had no more than turned his attention ahead when he reached the end of the chute, which, to his complete surprise, ended at a vertical face.

The next thing he knew, he was flying through the air, flailing helplessly at the sky. Looking below, he was faced with a sight that nearly stopped his heart: a jutting rock shelf rushing up at him at dizzying speed. Corey and the ram smashed into the shelf only a few feet apart, a shower of shale cascading around them, and he heard more than felt the crunch of bones in his legs, hips, chest, right arm, and left cheek. There was no breath left in him, and none would come. That was the most immediately frightening thing. Eventually, his lungs allowed some air in. He tipped his aching head to survey the wreckage of his body. The lower halves of both legs were at odd angles, and the jagged, bloody end of a shinbone poked through a pant leg. His broken right arm was of no use and the broken ribs grated as he sucked for breath. Worst of all, his nightmare was just beginning. The canopy of dark clouds overhead was soon complete, and the first flakes of snow began to swirl onto this hidden shelf on the side of the mountain.

******

Harry was late getting back to the saddle. He had spotted a group of rams bedded beneath a rock face but could not get a good look at them. So he got comfortable and waited with his spotting scope trained on them. But when the snow started, Harry gave up and hustled down the slope to where his client was waiting. Only his client wasn't there. He thought he had heard a couple of shots, but had chalked them up to another of the outfitter's camps. Harry searched either side of the saddle in the building snow flurries that blurred his vision beyond a short distance. *Now, where the devil did he go?* Harry tried to put himself in his client's place, tried to think what he would do if he were Corey Apperson. He called out his name repeatedly but heard no reply—not surprising in the dampening hush of the snow and the brisk wind that brought it. He made another search of the saddle and the slopes leading below, and finally decided the American had headed for lower country and camp when the snow started. But there was no sign of him, and a three-day blizzard continued to blanket the country in snow.

Years later, a newlywed couple was hiking in the Muskwa Mountains on a backpack trip arranged by the bride's father. The June weather was perfect, the blue sky beautiful as they tested their young legs against the rigors of the lower slopes, taking pictures of whatever wildlife they came into contact with.

"Look at this," said the young man, stooping in the clutter of rocks at the base of a rock shelf. He lifted up a worn hiking boot to show his bride.

"Who would leave a boot out here?" she said, with a laugh.

"No telling."

He dropped the boot and walked on.

"Oh, look at that."

The young woman pointed up at the shelf and the weathered sheep skull resting on the edge, and the horns that curled up and out and down, in and up and out and back down.

"Cool," was all he said.

She started to take a picture, but decided it rather grotesque, and they continued down the rocky slope to their campsite below.

The Coin Toss

Chapter 27

The day had been miserable. From morning on, nothing had gone right—nothing at all. Sometimes when a day starts badly, it gets better as it goes along. This one went from bad to worse. And now the evening promised to be the worst of all, unless, of course, the snow stopped so we could find our way down the mountain to camp. If not, the night would be even colder than it was right now—but I didn't want to think about that.

Spending the night in a blizzard in the High Altai Mountains of Mongolia was not an option—my guide and I weren't prepared for it. My heavy winter coat and gear, which cost me dearly in airline overweight charges, were uselessly stowed in camp. And here we sat, hunkered against a heartless mountain, colder than I have ever been in my life. The roar of the wind was deafening. The hurtling snow blinded our eyes, stung our hides. My frozen hands ached. Our options were quickly running out.

It was the vodka, I reflected, that had started our troubles. Bringing vodka to camp had been a mistake. When our Mongolian guides stumbled from their yurt at dawn, fighting over the last swig in the bottle, I knew the morning hunt was a write-off. I had hoped, however, the evening hunt might be salvaged so that we could take advantage of the unseasonably mild weather we had been experiencing. I should have realized this morning that the day couldn't be salvaged.

✳✳✳✳✳

"What's all the yelling?" my friend David asked, still bundled in his sleeping bag, as I stooped to enter through the squat, square wooden door of our yurt.

For him the hunt was over. He had taken his ibex the day before, so there was little incentive to leave the comfort of a warm bag for the morning chill. His ibex, in fact, had been the cause for the previous night's celebration with the vodka.

"The guides are still drunk," I told him. "Cook must be drunk, too."

I stared at the lifeless stove in the center of the round yurt. The old woman, stout as an Eskimo, had not appeared to start the morning fire. The tin box beside the stove remained piled with dried dung—camel, yak, and goat. I sorted through the clumps of dung, unsure which was which, though I suspected the light-colored pancake patties were yak.

"Use the dark, rounded ones," David said. "They've got a higher BTU content."

"Only an engineer would know that. Or an Aggie."

The next trouble came when our driver, Tulga, could not get the Russian 4x4 started. Because he didn't drink, he was the only sober staff member in camp, and we could hear the mournful *ruh-ruh-ruh* as he cranked the stubborn engine time and again. Next came the *clink-clink* of metal on metal as he tinkered under the hood.

Then, at lunch, I got the runs. The first pangs of intestinal gas had hit upon waking, and I had hoped it would pass. It didn't. It was the yak cheese or the yak yogurt or the steaming bowls of yak milk (each terrible-tasting in its own right, though the yak cheese was the clear winner in the gag contest). The vicious yak products had fermented in my bowels and finally had gotten the best of me, further proving why no one raises these noxious animals in the States. The latrine, an open pit in the ground, had been embarrassing enough to use once a day; now I was hovered over it every few minutes, my privates exposed to the world. Granted, the world was comprised of only three or four nomadic Mongolian families camped in the valley around us.

"You'd better take your Cipro," David cautioned.

"I'd rather fight it off," I said, wanting to save the antibiotics as a last resort.

I would endure the symptoms until either a fever developed or dehydration became a concern. Having battled several lower-intestine disruptions in East Africa in my younger days, I found it best to wait them out. But there was a downside. The only thing worse than going several days without a shower and a change of clothes was adding diarrhea to the equation, with the inevitable chafing that ensues when hiking and sweating and climbing in the mountains.

As a result, it was late when we drove out from camp that afternoon. It was later still when we parked the 4x4 at the foot of the ancient mountain range and started the climb up, huffing. It was really late when my guide Bataar spotted the giant ibex descending the peak of the same mountain we were ascending. Even my untrained eye could see that this animal was special—the way the magnificent ribbed horns swept back to its rump, like a rainbow arched above its muscled trunk.

My first impression, even amid the excitement of a trophy in sight, was that we should turn back, since only an hour of daylight remained. It would take an hour of climbing to get in position to take the ibex, leaving us in the dark of night to cape, skin, and cart the animal down the mountain. Bataar, hung over as he was, was in no shape to negotiate the steep slopes in the dark, much less cart seventy pounds of cape and horn on his shoulders. I knew I wasn't—even sober. There are smarter things to do in life than to hike in mountains in the dark.

Sukh, our young, sumo-size interpreter, had remained behind, sick with the runs as well, so it was just the two of us. But you can do amazing things with hand signals, and the language barrier had not been a problem—at least not until the snow hit an hour later, while we were still making our ascent. To say the snowstorm hit us suddenly would be an understatement. One minute it was mild and sunny and we were picking our way up a sparse rocky slope. The next instant the wind hit like a freight train, the dark clouds boiled over us, and the whirring snow swallowed our world. It was as though we had fallen through the ice into the depths of a murky winter pond.

Then the fever hit.

So here we are, four hours later and in the dark, and things don't look good. What I am feeling is mostly anger—anger at myself. I should have insisted that we head down when Bataar motioned with a hand to sit tight at the start of the storm. Normally, you must place an abundance of trust in your hunting guide and his judgment. That is why you are paying him, after all. So that's what I did. But deep down I knew that we were making a mistake not to take action against the storm, not to take cover in the lower ravines, choosing instead to sit tight, exposed on this open outcrop of rock. Sitting tight was like—like giving up.

A fire is what we need. I could remove the powder from the shells in the case on my belt, sacrificing my teeth to twist out the bullets if I have to, but there is nothing to burn. There is not a single tree in this land, not a single bush up here on the mountain. The snacks in my backpack are covered in unburnable foil. The gale-force wind would snuff out any flicker of my lighter.

So now I curse the little bastard, and I curse myself for obliging him. To his credit, I know it would have been difficult to see our way down in the dark and in the snow. I know that we could easily have stumbled off an unseen cliff or the ripping wind might have knocked us off our feet or if we had started to tumble, there would have been no stopping in the slick snowfall. Staying here, where we did, however, was suicide. It is the final poor judgment of my worthless, hung-over guide. But it is too late to do anything about that.

My left hand aches. The fingers are mercifully numb, as are my feet and right hand, but the rest of the hand is throbbing like someone just whacked it with a baseball bat.

The snow isn't going to stop—I realize that now. This isn't just a passing storm. This is a "socked-in" blizzard. The kind that can rage for days. The kind that hit my friend Dr. Bob Speegle thirty years ago in these same unforgiving mountains—a fifty-year blizzard, they called it. He was in a 4x4 on the return to Khovd when it hit. When he didn't show for the next couple of days, the outfitter called his wife to tell her that he was dead. It was impossible to survive a storm with such low temperatures. The town was in awe when he showed up alive five days later, suffering only mild hypothermia and having lost no body parts to frostbite. But Bob was in a truck in the valley, and I am on the exposed slope of a mountain.

I think of the coin toss David won yesterday. That decided his fate—to remain in camp today. Had I called "heads" instead of "tails," I would have been the one to hunt ibex yesterday. I would be the one in camp today. I would be the one having to call his wife when David didn't make it back.

I think of my wife and three kids, and it's like a knife twisting in my gut.

Five-year old Amanda, who blocked the door on the morning of my departure and said, "No, I don't want you to go!" The tears on her small cheeks. How I promised her I would be home in two weeks. . . .

And then the boys.

Who will tell them how to handle the bullies that bloody their noses? How to behave on their first dates? Show them how to hunt and fish and handle themselves in a man's world? Who will walk Amanda down the aisle at her wedding?

Who will replace me at work? That sneaky, brown-nosing weasel, Paul?

Then, hardest of all: Who will be the "next" luckiest man in the world to capture Samantha's heart? Will he treat her as well as I did? Will he be as kind? Then the unthinkable: Will he be better?

My guide is staring at me. Whenever I lift my head, hoping to see a lull in the whirling snow, I see him staring at me through the eerie blur of white against the darkness of night. He wants to see how I do. How this city boy, this American with a raging fever, will do in a Mongolian blizzard.

I'm right here with you, Flat Face. I'm every bit as tough as you are. You hear that? You vodka-guzzling son of a b----! Why'd you have to go and do that, huh? Why'd you have to get drunk and lose your judgment? Get us stuck in this storm? Why the hell didn't you see it coming? You'd think a thousand generations of living in these godforsaken mountains would produce at least a little weather savvy. Didn't you see the signs? Like the ram heading downhill, something like that?

If my hands didn't hurt so much, if I could make a fist, I'd punch you right in the nose—right in the middle of your ugly face—for what you have taken from me. For what you have robbed from me. What is the penalty for robbing a man of his life?

My bowels are acting up again. I need to get up, undo my pants. But it is too cold. Fingers won't work. Legs won't move. Finally, I must resign myself to remaining huddled in a ball, my ass and legs too numb to take comfort from the temporary warm liquid running down them. For the first time in this whole ordeal I want to cry—rail at the indignity inflicted by a foe that doesn't fight fair, that makes a grown man crap his pants.

It's getting hard to lift my head now, but I want to see the squint-eyed bastard. He is still looking at me, only now his face has filled with snow. His eyes, too. They are open. Staring. I reach out to shove him, and he doesn't budge. He is frozen. Frozen solid.

I guess I won, Flat Face. I guess I won.

Deserted Islands

Chapter 28

Had I known then what I know now, none of this would have happened. I would have stayed home, Jinxy would be alive, and I wouldn't be missing my left ear. All hindsight, I tell myself—yet I continue to torture myself with "what if's," replaying the events in my head and racking my brain to reshape them into a less horrific outcome.

Lying awake at night, I see Jinxy (his real name was Henry Harrison, but no one called him Henry, not even his parents) and his sly smile and that twinkle that came into his eye when an adventure had taken hold in his mind and he was trying to figure how to talk me into it. I think what an unlikely pair of friends we were—best friends, actually, since junior high. He was a jock and a good-looking sort who brought girls around like—like a worm on a hook brings fish (that's Jinxy talking; I could never have come up with an analogy like that), while I tend to be the cautious, introverted type who can't throw a baseball or shoot hoops or score a soccer goal in the face of skilled opponents, the kind of things Jinxy did with ease. Not surprisingly, my friend brought the same skill and grace to the outdoor sports, reading bass and tracking deer like rivals read the opposing school's team. A passion for hunting was one thing we shared, and my family had a South Texas ranch, so naturally Jinxy spent as much time there with us as he could. It was frustrating because I had been hunting all my young life, and this city kid who has never set foot in the woods shows up, and he instantly spots more game than anyone and handles himself afield like Daniel Boone.

Eventually, I resigned myself to the fact that hunting was simply one more thing he was better at. I decided not to let it bother me, and our friendship was the better for it. Jinxy dragged me on the coattails of his athletic success to all the high-school parties that I would not have been invited to or was too shy to attend. We drifted apart in college; then came weddings and work, his divorce and my kids. Occasionally, we found time for one of Jinxy's big-game hunts or fishing adventures to some exotic land or a trip to the family ranch after whitetail.

So it was that we fell into our typical roles when he called from Boston in June of last year.

"New Guinea," he said. "This August. They have the most amazing fishing in the world. Incredible! They—"

"I'm sorry, Jinxy, I can't. I—"

"No, listen. This is a once-in-a-lifetime! I spoke with some fellows who just went. You hire an offshore fishing boat for a week, cruise the coast and islands, and land the goddamn biggest groupers you've ever seen. Two-hundred-pounders! There's some sort of tropical phenomenon going on that's bringing fish from all over. Just throw in a lure and reel them in, one after the other. What do you say? It'll be fun."

I had tried to explain the heap of extended tax returns piled for review about my office and the kids' activities and the little vacation time I had left, but in the end Jinxy won out, and before I knew it, I had an airplane ticket in hand, and the trip had arrived.

My first apprehensions came when we arrived at the pier. The boat we had hired was a dirty, run-down vessel, and our guide spoke maybe three words of English. As usual, neither obstacle fazed Jinxy, and in no time—the grogginess of jet lag be damned—we were out in the soft chop, throttle wide open, heading for several islands, invisible on the horizon, that our guide pointed out on a map. An hour and a half later, we slowed to a stop in the bluest water you have ever seen—calm, deep water that turned aqua in the shallows, then clear and frothy on the gentle surf of the white sand beaches of the islands. Rods and reels were broken out, and on his first cast Jinxy jerked alive with a hit, set the hook, and bent his rod in half fighting something big on the end of the line. After a twenty-minute fight, he brought the behemoth fish near enough to the surface to see the reticulated black markings and the football-size mouth of his prey. Sighting us, the grouper got a second wind and dove.

"It's goddamn Moby Dick!" Jinxy yelled, and I dropped my rod to watch.

Our smiling, toothless guide readied a gaff, and after its next rise, we had our first fish landed.

For the first two days the fishing was spectacular, as promised, from dawn till dusk. Our arms were sore by day's end from pulling in fish that weighed as much as we did, and in the evenings we grilled slabs of white grouper meat over a wood fire on the desolate beaches of the islands—islands we had completely to ourselves. There was not another human in sight—not even a sign that another human being had previously touched them.

On the evening of the second day, the sharks arrived, looking for easy prey. Cruising dorsal fins announced their malicious presence, and you could see their dark shapes in the shallows, their torpedo outlines as they passed beneath the boat, searching for the same fish we were. It bothered me that they were poaching on our turf. It was like having another hunter suddenly appear beneath your hunting stand, or a fisherman cast into the same patch of water where you had just settled a lure. There was no etiquette on their part. Now and then they took a fish on the line before we could land it, or they took part of the fish, and we landed what was left. But after a while, we got used to them, and, except on those occasions when the scoundrels stole our catch, we ignored them, and the sharks became no more conspicuous than the odd-looking seabirds overhead that pestered us for scraps.

The trip was everything Jinxy had claimed it would be until bad weather struck on the third day. In every hunting or fishing trip there is an element of the unexpected—which I guess is what makes it an adventure. But in this case, we were clearly unprepared for and outmatched by the weather that arrived. We were drifting in the shallows, pulling in even bigger fish than we had during the first two days (perhaps it was the weather that was driving them into the shallows), when the sky to the east loomed up black and stormy over the island we were fishing.

"Monsoohn," our guide stammered, clearly frightened by it, and he made quick preparations to get under way.

Whatever the case—whether the storm was partially blocked from sight by the island or was moving unusually fast—it was on us before we had time to respond. The smartest thing would have been to beach the boat and to wait it out in the protection of the thick jungle of palms and fronds. But our guide had a different idea. He turned the boat for the mainland and gunned the engine, hoping to outrun the storm. It seemed a senseless act, even at the time, but he was the guide, and, in the hunting and fishing world, it generally pays to listen to your guide.

So, with a shrug, Jinxy and I settled into the stern of the boat, setting our teeth against the pounding of the boat in the suddenly rough sea. The dark clouds quickly overtook us, bringing strong winds and pouring rain. Once in open water, the waves grew from a choppy nuisance to giant, white-capped swells, and our guide's boating skills proved less than seaworthy. He raced the prop when the engine lifted in the air and dangerously stuffed the bow into the foot of oncoming waves.

It wasn't until this moment that I thought about life jackets. None of us had one. I felt suddenly vulnerable, exposed, like you do in a naked dream. I crawled my way into the grimy cruddy and searched under scattered blankets and gear, but found nothing like a life jacket. I did find two moldy seat-cushion-type floats and brought them back, handing one to Jinxy.

"THIS FELLOW HAS NO CLUE WHAT—" Jinxy started to roar above the wind, but he never got to finish.

After cresting a steep wave, the boat plunged down the backside like a runaway roller coaster. At the bottom, the bow stuffed into a fifteen-foot swell and went under. We were instantly covered in water, as if we had jumped off the high dive—except the water was pounding us from above. It felt like I would never stop sinking, like the water was trying to push me to the bottom of the sea, but then the plunging sensation stopped, and the cushion clasped in my arms did its job and pulled me to the surface just when my lungs were about to burst and I thought I could hold my breath no longer. Jinxy popped up a moment later. A few floatables appeared around us, soon scattered by the force of the storm.

We never saw sign of the boat or our guide again.

Fortunately, the water was warm, or our story would have ended there. We remained adrift for a night and a day, while the monsoon continued to rage and the waves threatened to drown us in spray. There was nothing to do but hang onto our square floats, shut our eyes against the burning salt, and gulp at air when we got the chance. At first I worried the sharks would take us, but then I realized they were probably the least of our worries, and I thought little more about them. The thunder and waves and wind made talking impossible. I thought of my wife and kids, and I prayed—something I had not done since grade school. I prayed that I would see them again. I prayed that we would make it. I prayed because there was nothing else to do, except gasp and spit and blink the never-ending salt from your eyes and mouth and choke it back when it tried to force its way into your throat and lungs.

Then my foot bumped something hard in the water, and I thought shark until I pushed back with both feet, and I stood up in the water (until the next wave hit) and realized it was land. LAND!

My eyes opened, and amidst the waves and wind and dark clouds there was the unmistakable rise of trees ahead, and we paddled and kicked and used up every bit of strength to reach it. We pulled ourselves onto the beach, and Jinxy rolled onto his back and laughed in triumph and relief, and I just tried to catch my breath. We were alive! After a brief rest, we staggered up to take refuge in the green growth. The rain came in torrents that stung our hides. Once we were tucked away in the undergrowth, our sudden elation turned to more practical thoughts. Where were we? Was this island inhabited? How could we signal a passing ship?

"Water!" Jinxy said, with a look that read "Eureka!"

He had apparently dredged up a piece of survival info from the numerous outdoor magazines he subscribed to. "What if we are stuck here for a week or more and there is no fresh water? We've got to save this rainwater. Look for something to store it."

We gathered some halves of coconut shells and lay them at the edge of the growth to collect the falling rain.

"Matches?"

"Nope."

"Crap," he said. "Everything in the daypacks! Knives, rope, flashlights. Hell of a lot of good that does us now."

I dumbly shook my head. Our next order of business, when the storm let up, was to explore the island—was it even an island at all? Maybe we were on the mainland. We might push a hundred yards through the bush to find a village or an abandoned settlement of the many Western oil companies that worked in the area before the New Guinea government chased them all out. But what we found we did not expect. And it didn't take long.

Jinxy led the way. The green growth was thick and wet, but it parted easily enough, so we pushed through it instead of trekking the thick sand of the beach perimeter. Then we stumbled upon a well-used trail in the jungle. Jinxy guessed wild boar until he found a track in the mud. A bare human footprint! And it was fresh. It brought an instant feeling of relief, a sensation of well being. We were saved! It was just a matter of following the trail until we met up with our mystery traveler or ran into others who could help us.

We picked up the pace until I had to run to keep up with Jinxy. Soon we came to a small clearing, a clearing that had been made by man, for the bush had been chopped down. Jinxy paused for a moment to look for human tracks, and I bent over to help. Before we could find any tracks, however, we found the track makers themselves. When I looked up, there were several natives standing at the opposite end of the clearing. They were naked except for crude leather loincloths. One fellow wore a stubby grass skirt. Bones and pig tusks and other odds and ends adorned necklaces and ankle bracelets, and one or two of the natives had a bone through his nose or ears. Their hair was straight and black and caked with some sort of white chalk. The fellow in the skirt, apparently a chief or leader of some sort, gestured forth with a short spear and uttered something.

"We are lost," Jinxy said. "Our boat sank."

The natives started toward us, and, suddenly, more of their kind appeared around us. They motioned and grunted for us to follow and led us down another well-used path to their village. Grass huts sprung up here and there under the heavy green canopy of jungle, and the women and children came out to greet us. The kids were smiling, and I thought, OK, we are going to be all right. It may take a while to signal a ship, get home, but we have made it.

Shortly after thinking those happy thoughts, I would realize how wrong I was, realize exactly why the kids were glad to see us. Just then, the men all fell on us, wrestled us to the ground, and tied our hands and feet with vine ropes. They then carried us to the center of the village, where the women began tending to a large pit and the wet charcoal remains of what, before the monsoon, had been a fire. The giggling children scattered into the jungle, returning with dead wood and brown grass to toss in the pit, while the men shared drink from a gourd and grew giddy. Soon the fire was started, and the eager villagers continued to return with more wood, which they piled anxiously onto the blaze. Jinxy and I looked at each other in speechless awe.

"Jesus," was all he said.

From behind, I felt a sudden tug at my head, and, with one swipe of his blade, the chief had removed my left ear before I had any idea what was happening. I watched in horror as he walked off, my bloody ear jiggling in his fingers. I heard the tribe sound off in jubilation, but it took a minute for the horrible reality to sink in. The pain I felt was more psychological than physical. The look on Jinxy's face was infinitely more horrifying to my soul than the actual pain from the wound. We had come face to face with evil. The feeling was overwhelming. It was unreal. This couldn't be happening. But it was.

I felt the blood run warm and wet on my neck, then fill my ear hole (like hot water in a Jacuzzi), and I shook my head against the ghastly sensation.

The chief handed my ear to a young child, who began to gnaw the morsel like a chew toy. When the chief returned and approached Jinxy, Jinxy began to curse and shake his head vigorously so the chief could not do the same to him. After several failed attempts at his ears, the chief grabbed up a rock by the fire and bashed my friend in the head. That is really all you need to know. I will tell you that I believe the blow killed him instantly. I will not tell you what happened the rest of that night, nor what they did to Jinxy, what little I saw between periods of panic and tightly closed eyes—though I heard it, every damn bit of it!

Out of respect for my friend I will let it go at that.

When I awoke late in the night, I began screaming my head off when I realized that what had happened had not been a dream. But no one came out to silence me. The villagers were all asleep in their huts. I believe my movements were automatic at that point, for there was not much going on upstairs. My conscious mind had checked out. I was numb. I was out of my head. The horror of what had been done to my friend and what was in store for me was simply too much for my mind to process. When I finally quieted down, I rolled over to the rock that the chief had used to kill Jinxy, clutched it in my hands, placed the sharpest edge against the rope binding my ankles, and began to saw back and forth as best I could while bound by the ropes. It did not take long. The primitive ropes gave way to the steady friction. I tried to stand, but the cramping in my hamstrings prevented it. After some rubbing and stretching, I made it to my feet, and I left as quietly as I could, trying to find the path we had arrived on and follow it in the light of a half moon that showed low in the sky.

When I got to the beach, I wasn't sure what to do. There was nowhere to swim to, and I knew I couldn't stay there. Finally I decided to hike the boundary of the beach but stay down in the water so that any footprints would be erased in the surf. I hiked until dawn, but I cannot tell you whether it was one hour or four. I had reached a sharp bend in the island when a sound caught my ear. I glanced out past the surf, my eyes roving the now calm horizon. It was a motorboat, not half a mile away. I took off my shirt and began to wave it overhead while I ran crazily back and forth on the beach. Unbelievably, the boat turned and made in my direction.

The blond-haired skipper of the small craft shook his young head as he beached the boat.

"Good thing I caym along here when I did," he said, in an Aussie accent.

All I could do was nod my head.

"These islands are deserted."